WOMEN AND MUSEUMS, 1850-1914

MODERNITY AND THE GENDERING OF KNOWLEDGE

⇥ Kate Hill ⇤

Manchester University Press

Published by Manchester University Press
Altrincham Street, Manchester M1 7JA, UK
www.manchesteruniversitypress.co.uk

British Library Cataloguing-in-Publication Data is available

ISBN 978 0 7190 8115 6 hardback
ISBN 978 1 5261 3667 1 paperback

First published by Manchester University Press in hardback 2016

This edition first published 2018

Typeset by Out of House Publishing

GENDER IN HISTORY

Series editors:
Lynn Abrams, Cordelia Beattie, Pam Sharpe and Penny Summerfield

The expansion of research into the history of women and gender since the 1970s has changed the face of history. Using the insights of feminist theory and of historians of women, gender historians have explored the configuration in the past of gender identities and relations between the sexes. They have also investigated the history of sexuality and family relations, and analysed ideas and ideals of masculinity and femininity. Yet gender history has not abandoned the original, inspirational project of women's history: to recover and reveal the lived experience of women in the past and the present.

The series Gender in History provides a forum for these developments. Its historical coverage extends from the medieval to the modern periods, and its geographical scope encompasses not only Europe and North America but all corners of the globe. The series aims to investigate the social and cultural constructions of gender in historical sources, as well as the gendering of historical discourse itself. It embraces both detailed case studies of specific regions or periods, and broader treatments of major themes. Gender in History titles are designed to meet the needs of both scholars and students working in this dynamic area of historical research.

Women and museums, 1850–1914

MANCHESTER
1824

Manchester University Press

OTHER RECENT BOOKS
IN THE SERIES

+⟫━◆━⟪+

For my mother and in memory of my father

Contents

Figures

Acknowledgements

I would like to thank many individuals and institutions who have helped throughout the gestation and birth of this book. First of all, I am grateful to the British Academy for funding the initial research project; and would like to record the very generous support of the University of Lincoln whose Lincoln School of Humanities research leave scheme gave me invaluable time for writing the book.

Bridget Yates made many helpful suggestions and made me aware of Sussex Archaeological Society Museum and of Gertrude Jekyll's Surrey collections. Sally Ackroyd, Alex Woodall and the Manchester Art Gallery transcribed and let me see the correspondence of Mary Greg.

I am grateful to the museums who gave me access to their records: Birmingham Museum and Art Gallery, Brighton Museum and Art Gallery, Bristol Museum and Art Gallery, the British Museum, Cheltenham Museum and Art Gallery, the Egypt Exploration Society, the Horniman Museum, Ipswich Museum, Leicester New Walk Museum, Manchester Museum, Museums Sheffield, Norwich Castle Museum, the Petrie Museum at University College London, Sunderland Museum and Art Gallery, Warrington Museum and Art Gallery, and Whitby Museum. In particular, the following individuals helpfully guided me through the records and documents of their respective institutions: Sam Alberti at Manchester; Joan Lyall at Ipswich Museum; Tony Irwin at Norwich Castle Museum; Mark Edwards at Whitby Museum; Helen Brown and Ann-Rachael Harwood at Cheltenham Museum; Stella Beddoe and Helen Mears at Brighton Museum and Art Gallery; Alex Corney at the Geffrye Museum; Fiona Kerlogue at the Horniman Museum; Gareth Salway at Bristol Museum; Tessa Sidey at Birmingham Museum and Art Gallery; Mary Hider at Leicester Museum; Craig Sherwood at Warrington Museum; Helen Poole at Sussex Archaeological Society; Martin Routledge at Sunderland Museum; Alistair Maclean and Louise Pullen at Museums Sheffield, Alice Stephenson at the Petrie Museum, Joanna Kyffin at the Egypt Exploration Society, Bryony Millan at the National Portrait Gallery, and Wendy Brown and Imogen Gunn at the Museum of Archaeology and Anthropology, University of Cambridge.

I am hugely indebted to colleagues who generously read and commented on chapters and drafts: Sam Alberti, Jim Cheshire, Arthur MacGregor. Many colleagues from the School of Humanities and then the School of History and Heritage at the University of Lincoln gave coffee, moral support and encouragement; particular thanks go to Krista Cowman who helped enormously with the formulation of the initial research project and shared her expertise on the women's movement with me.

Versions of some of the material included here appeared in other publications: 'Collecting authenticity: domestic, familial, and everyday "old things" in English museums, 1850–1939', *Museum History Journal* 4 (2), 2011; '"He knows me ... but not at the Museum"': Women, natural history collecting and museums, 1880–1914', in S. Dudley *et al.* (eds), *Narrating Objects, Collecting Stories* (London: Routledge 2012); 'Collecting and the body in late Victorian and Edwardian museums', in K. Boehm (ed.), *Bodies and Things in Nineteenth-Century Writing and Culture* (London: Palgrave Macmillan 2012).

Finally, thanks to my family which has cheerfully put up with the ever-increasing piles of books and papers around the house and all over the dining room table, and with my increasing distraction. Especially and above all thanks to David, who provided calmness and a solution in the face of a last-minute image panic.

Abbreviations

AAM	American Association of Museums
BM	British Museum
BM(NH)	British Museum (Natural History)
BSA	British School at Athens
EEF	Egypt Exploration Fund
LCC	London County Council
MA	Museums Association
MWPA	Married Women's Property Acts
NACF	National Art Collections Fund
SKM	South Kensington Museum
SPAB	Society for the Protection of Ancient Buildings
UCL	University College London
V&A	Victoria and Albert Museum

Introduction

In 1896, Beatrix Potter visited the British Museum (Natural History) and wrote afterwards in her diary, 'To museum, studying labels on insects, being in want of advice, and not in a good temper, I worked into indignation about that august Institution'.[1] A year later, *Temple Bar* magazine reviewed the exhibition of Mrs Delany's paper flowers at the British Museum (BM) (these had been bequeathed a couple of years previously by Lady Llanover, a descendant of Mrs Delany, apparently in fulfilment of George III's own wish that they should be held by this institution). The review described the bequest as 'a singular and pathetic monument of feminine ingenuity'. It went on to say that it had 'been placed under the protection of Mr Sidney Colvin [Keeper of Prints], probably because there was nowhere else to put it, but it must be confessed that it seems a little below the dignity of high art'.[2] These two sets of comments, confessing dissatisfaction with an important museum, and outlining generally understood limits to the value of women's contributions to another museum, suggest both the enabling and the constraining roles which museums offered women; it indicates that women used museums, but were subject to limits and sought to expand their field of action within them. This book, examining a range of ways in which women interacted with museums in the period 1850–1914, suggests that women sought to make museums more inclusive by reorienting them towards feminine concerns, while at the same time using them to try to enter a 'man's world' of scholarship and public disinterestedness. It argues that the examination of women and museums allows us to understand more fully the ways in which modernity produced ideas about gender, tradition, knowledge and community.

Remaking gender relations, remaking the museum

This is a study of how women and museums were remade, or remade each other, between roughly 1850 and 1914, mostly in English museums, but with occasional examples from Scotland, Wales and Ireland. It investigates a variety of women and women's roles in connection with museums: women working in museums, women donating to museums, women visiting museums; as well as women's involvement in trends that significantly impacted on museums, such as the growth of archaeology and anthropology, and the influence of Ruskinian thought on museums. It interrogates museums as unique cultural institutions which straddled the public and the private – or the domestic and the scholarly – to show how such borderlands opened to women (and were opened by women) during the period, but also tended to segregate women in specifically gendered enclaves which institutionalised feminine expertise as real and separate, but less important than masculine expertise.

It uncovers the ways in which women brought distinctive concerns into museums, focusing on education and what might now be called 'outreach', as well as on memory and emotional objects of various sorts; women's involvement in museums often came out of and reinforced family relationships and domestic practices. Moreover, such feminine engagement with museums can also often be read as an attempt to dissolve binary oppositions and hierarchies which were often reinforced by the dislocations and tensions produced by a modernising society and culture. Masculine privilege was defended through the process of professionalisation, the denigration of the domestic, the assertion of the ability to act and create as male, the exaltation of disinterest and atomic individuality, and the idea of the nation as a masculine community.[3] Women, framed as amateur, domestic, local, relationally oriented and as helpers rather than creators, both used these ascriptions to make space for themselves in the museum, and tried to breach the underlying dichotomising which tended to devalue those spaces which they had made. A feminine vision of modern culture did not distinguish between or ascribe differential values to knowledge and affect, research and engagement, old and new, seeing them all as ways of negotiating a new, modern world. As part of this vision of how their involvement with museums could be modernised, women sought to enter the professionalising world of museums, asserting identities as expert scholars and curators; but in this attempt they were only partly successful.

During a time of considerable change for middle-class women in Britain, why examine their relationships with museums? It is those very changes in women's lives, juxtaposed with the changes in museums at the same time, which make the conjunction so fruitful to study. Many of these changes could be glossed as 'modernity': museums were becoming widely diffused centres of popular education and entertainment, while women were becoming better educated, with greater legal rights over their own property, and more able to earn their own living in particular fields; they were becoming 'public' figures in new ways, most visibly through the campaign for women's suffrage, waged with increasing militancy from the end of the 1890s. By examining the relationships between two such areas of change, we can see that women made museums modern, while museums made women modern. During the period studied here, it was not clear what women would be, or what museums would be, merely that both were changing; some of the answers about the possible directions of change which were formulated are traced in this book.

Women emerge as following two major strategies or images of a new femininity; many of them highlighted 'essential' features of womanhood to justify roles as new professionals with a distinctive approach to museum work; as donors and patrons giving value to domestic memorial practices and creating a new form of collective memory for modern society; staging the museum as a space for liberatory experience and for political protest; and driving a deeper engagement of museums with their community. On the other hand, many of them strove to emulate male norms of collecting, donating and curating. This latter strategy might be better conceptualised as an attempt to de-gender the museum, eliminating the idea of gender competences of any sort. Neither approach was in itself totally successful, but the maintenance of both integration and separation in women's approach to museums was important for women's ability to take advantage of all opportunities that arose; it also, I suggest, sheds some light on women's wider strategies and aims during this period. Hoberman has recently suggested that for most of this period women tended to favour assimilation into male circles; whereas studies on US libraries and museums suggest women built on specifically feminine qualities alone to remake their involvement in these institutions.[4] In Britain, my study shows, women tried to be both feminine and masculine, in different ways and different places.

At the same time, museums were developing into institutions with increasingly diverse goals. Not only were they to be centres of knowledge creation and emblems of the nation, since the middle of the nineteenth century they had increasingly been seen as places to support governmental agendas of population improvement and 'governability'.[5] In the face of increasing concern not just about the behaviour of the poor, but of their deprivation and consequent disengagement from society, museums were also charged with 'outreach' and with attracting marginalised groups, including children, as well as the privileged. They increasingly acted not just as sacralised spaces of national myth making but also as everyday spaces embedded in the locality (though not at the same time; different institutions had different aims); and women were instrumental in imagining and achieving new sorts of museum.

This is, then, a story of mutual becoming, without, in many ways, a beginning or an end; certainly by the end of the period neither museums nor women had found a single way of being. Such a story, I think, is not only dictated by the findings of my research, but also avoids some familiar narratives which emerge particularly from women's history, and also from museum studies. Women are either seen, optimistically, as blazing a trail into new areas such as science, a story of 'progress' from oppression to liberation, or as victims of a modernity which devalued their contribution, looking back to a golden age before the formalisation of education.[6] Meanwhile museums suffer from amnesia and suppose that they are much more open, democratic and responsive than elitist nineteenth-century forebears.[7] I hope to complicate these narratives.

Although little work has been done on the history of women, or gender, and museums, that which does exist suggests that in the UK, the period between 1850 and 1914 was a crucial one both for perceptions of women within museums, and for their active engagement with these institutions. Previous work has mainly considered women as visitors, and as visitors specifically to art museums and galleries. Additionally, women have been considered as collectors of fine and decorative art.[8] It is important, however, to look beyond visitors, art and indeed national institutions. In the category 'museums', I include all institutions which collected things and displayed them to at least some of the public, from rocks and fossils to paintings and statuary. Not every museum can be studied, of course, but the small local branch museum and the amateur archaeology museum have as much to tell us as the BM and the National Gallery. This was a period of museological vitality; new types of museum, museum object and museum display were appearing, usually outside the 'universal survey' museums which embodied the nation.[9] Not only that, but we need to understand museums as much more than simply the buildings, or the people within those buildings. It has been suggested that museum have no edges – they are connected out around the world by complex linkages and networks. By exploring outwards into dispersed networks and less obvious or prominent actors, we can find a better, fuller picture of women and museums.[10]

Examining museums and women together, then, allows us to ask questions about how modernity, as a way of narrating or understanding the experience of change, figured gender as part of a professionalising, democratising and innovation-seeking society. As a topic it straddles the social and the cultural and requires careful analysis of the various forms of agency available to all the players in the game. Although I am primarily concerned with what women did, why, how and with what consequences, this involves also acknowledging what discourses did, what men did, what institutions and spaces did, and what objects themselves did. This in turn allows us to move beyond the issue of whether museums impose and maintain certain social patterns, or whether they allow excluded and marginal groups to challenge and reshape those social patterns. If theorists such as Bennett and Bourdieu have stressed the extent to which museums historically have been enlisted to produce governable populations, or to reproduce social prestige through cultural capital, commentators on contemporary museums have stressed their ability to empower excluded groups and offer arenas for the negotiation of the idea of the citizen, and of cultural significance.[11] Both the institutions and the users are, or can be, endowed with agency; agency is negotiated in a variety of sites and by a variety of means. A visit to a museum is an exercise in negotiating rules and norms, but so is donating to a museum: depending on wider discourses about object value, the curator's need for the objects, the respective social and cultural capital of donor and curator, and the nature of the object being donated.[12] Moreover, such a negotiation of agency continues as the object begins its museum life, making the investigation of museums a complex task; often, the way one investigates this issue depends on the sort of institution one considers museums to be.

The distributed museum

What kind of institution or organisation is a museum? There are many possible answers to this question, and the answers change significantly over time; museums have been described as temples, 'universities of the people', community centres and mausoleums; they have been compared to shops, exhibitions and fun fairs. When the history of museums was first investigated, it seemed that heroic curators and other individuals single-handedly drove forward the intellectual and pedagogical visions which shaped their museums.[13] In the late twentieth century, it increasingly seemed that individuals were unimportant, and the museum was an apparatus of sorts; a machine for creating knowledge, making citizens, disciplining populations and even shaping the Empire. A great deal of attention was focused on the impersonal ways in which power was inscribed in the institution, the spaces and the discourses of the museum; which importantly de-naturalised the workings of the apparently objective, disinterested individual-as-organisation.[14] However, such an analytical approach gave far too much weight to the power of the museum to propagate a unified, universal effect upon visitors. The most recent examinations of museums have recognised that they never functioned in a unified way, because they represented aggregations of different groups of people with different agendas. Curators were dependent on those who held the purse strings, whereas the committees in charge of museums might have to defer to the specialist knowledge of the curator. This led to compromises over, for example, the way in which the space of the museum was developed, which mitigated against any strong powerful effect emerging from that space.[15] Similarly, objects entered museums through a series of widely dispersed networks, of dealers, donors, fieldworkers and others with powerful agendas of their own; curators' abilities to control what their museum actually owned were limited.[16] Audiences participated in the project of making meaning from objects, however didactic the displays presented to them.[17]

The museum, then, needs to be seen as a *distributed* institution, as Gosden and Larson so compellingly argue.[18] It was the collective production of a wide range of people, some of whom were more conscious of this than others, but all of whom could have an effect. As a corollary of this, it needs to be seen not as a place where fixed meanings were produced and distributed, and clear roles acted out; but rather as a place where dialogue took place, about ideas, identities and valuations. This should not, of course, be seen as some sort of democratic paradise of openness; the museum defined the most important things, knowledge, and ideas in its culture, and therefore there was a huge amount at stake in the debate, and any means of loading the dice towards any particular group would be taken. The museum often tended to reproduce hierarchies already present in society; but it did also offer opportunities to new groups to remake social value. This makes it an incredibly rich institution to study; and as I argue in the book, by examining the museum as a distributed entity we can recover both the agency of a wide range of women, and the strategies which were deployed to try to contain that agency.

Public/private/domestic: gendered divisions in the late nineteenth century

Some extremely problematic concepts hover around both gender, and the museum, through the second half of the nineteenth century and into the early twentieth century. These are chiefly the ideas of home and domesticity, linked in complex ways to ideas about the 'public' and 'private'. Public and private might be seen as opposed, whereas the 'domestic' was associated with the private; though in fact, such ideas were under considerable pressure, especially around the *fin de siècle*. Commentators have traced the emergence of a largely middle-class ideal of gendered 'separate spheres' of public and private in the early nineteenth century, with the feminine associated with an increasingly privatised home, while men moved in the rational public world, basing their actions on intellectual, not emotional, motivations.[19] While such an ideal was clearly never in place, even the ideal came under pressure by 1900, by which point public and private, and the relationship between home and gender, were increasingly blurred and contested.[20] The home remained a heavily loaded concept but its relation to public, private, feminine and masculine became much more ambiguous. The home, therefore, the space of relationships, emotions, care and nurture, was no longer imagined as a blissful space of seclusion, and its links with public life were debated.

This could be seen in a number of ways. Women entered the public sphere in more assertive ways, colonising particular areas of public life, and were felt to be alarmingly immune to the 'feminine' attraction of home and family as they entered higher education and took on new occupations. They continued to assert, however, or even asserted more strongly, their domestic expertise, and ability to manage the relationships, emotions and material culture of the home and family. Women's identities were still very much rooted in the domestic, but this was increasingly a 'militant domesticity', asserting specifically feminine moral qualities which needed to be put to work in public.[21] In a number of ways, women brought the domestic into the public as a way of amplifying the female public voice. In higher education, new women's colleges replicated a domestic environment based on close, familial-type relationships to a greater extent than men's; women's charity work ideally took place in the homes of the poor even as it professionalised; and shops not only enabled proper, feminine consumption of items for the home, they took steps to ensure their spaces blurred the public/private divide.[22] Deborah Cohen and Jane Hamlett note the close association between suffrage campaigners and interior decoration, which was one of a number of ways in which women brought the home into public discourse.[23] Men also, however, claimed and created domestic spaces, both in actual family homes, and in alternative spaces such as universities; the material culture of the home was, as several commentators confirm, a key way in which ideas of the domestic, and the gendering of that domesticity, were asserted and contested. Men both rejected the domestic as effeminising, and claimed it 'back' from women.[24]

'Home', of course, was also a concept opposed to 'away', and the resonance of domesticity as both a national signifier, and a way of thinking about empire, was possibly at its height in the second half of the nine-teenth century.[25] Britain was seen by its own inhabitants and by foreign observers as a nation obsessed with houses and the idea of domesticity.[26] This made control of and the ability to speak for the home especially sig-nificant, as women's success in deploying domestic expertise in public realms indicated. The relationship between empire and home was more complex; the empire was spoken of as a family, and the export of British domestic practices seen as one of its most valuable effects or goals. Home and away could be seen as embodying gendered characteristics: as Hall and Rose suggest, 'symbolically, empire building and maintenance was a masculine task whereas the home-place was feminised'.[27] In the dis-tributed museum, it was often the case that men collected objects in 'the field' overseas, while women 'domesticated' those objects in a variety of ways which strongly affected the way Britons lived with and understood their empire; but this did not mean that women did not collect them-selves where possible, or that the meaning of objects 'at home' was not also heavily controlled by men.[28]

One effect of this is that because the home was so important a sym-bolic resource, and seemed in some ways so threatened by modernity (both by a commercialisation which reached deep into the home, and by women's perceived lack of commitment to domestic roles), inter-est in the historic home grew. Around 1900, domestic life in the past became a key cultural preoccupation. It had been of interest before this, of course; Macaulay had (briefly) described the 'dress, furniture, repasts' of past ages; while mid-century interest in history had fastened on the homes of the great, as well as the lives of more domesticated royals such as queens.[29] But around 1900, wide interest is apparent in the kind of historical home that might be relevant to a wider range of people than those who could aspire to the home life of aristocrats and monarchs; indeed, as Mandler has shown, interest in the aristocratic past waned after 1860. But interest in the domestic lives of those from a humbler station increased: Anne Hathaway's cottage and Shakespeare's birthplace became popular tourist attractions, partly because of their function as a shrine to a national hero, but partly also because they offered an attractive destination by making tangible a home not riven with the ambiguities of the 1900 home.[30] Even more notable were the series of 'Olde' streets at exhibitions such as Old London, Old Edinburgh, and Old Manchester and Salford, from 1884, 1886 and 1887 respectively.[31]

The domestic is also worth examining for the conceptual relation-ship it had with the museum. Although for most of our period they would have been understood as in opposition, the domestic aligned with the private, and the museum with the public, this was in many ways a temporary and incomplete separation.[32] Museums were rooted in elite homes, with their origins in the curiosity cabinets and picture galleries of the aristocracy.[33] Much nineteenth-century museum development was an attempt to align them away from the domestic and towards the public, 'official' realm: architectural models for museums started to follow the temple, cathedral, or department store; whereas objects' meanings were thought to be derived not from their family ownership, but from their objective characteristics, and the scientific context to which they belonged.[34] Yet my study suggests very strongly that the domestic and the museum were never as clearly opposed as some Victorian museums wished. Children, eminently domestic creatures, were repeatedly urged to form their own museum at home, which they should make as much like the real thing as possible. Meanwhile, urban elites in control of local museums tended to treat them as an extension of their own homes, holding social events there.[35] All these developments, importantly, also affected the gendering of museums, as girls as well as boys collected, and women were prominent at elite social events in museums.

The line between the domestic and the museum, then, was not clear, and it became even less clear as the period progressed. If the National Gallery was the 'nation's mantelpiece', provincial museums, Amy Woodson-Boulton suggests, were sometimes conceived as parlours for the working class to emulate the middle-class domestic Sunday (see also Figure 8 in Chapter 4).[36] As a corollary, 'private' and 'public' valuations of objects were not distinct either. Objects in museums could be valued for 'private' reasons such as the fact that they had lived in the home of someone in particular; while objects in the home could be valued for 'public' reasons such as their contribution to scholarship on art.[37] Thus, shifting meanings for public, private and domestic meant that women could draw both on persisting associations between their nature and key characteristics of the domestic – emotions, relationships, memory, craft, childcare – and public virtues such as scholarship and professionalism, which they were increasingly able to access.

In order to understand the role which gender played in the distributed museum, we also need to consider the relationship between gender and materiality. Studies of collecting and gender have not always paid sufficient attention to the ways in which apparently inherent gender characteristics were produced discursively, or simply by the different circumstances in which men and women could gather and value objects.[38] Nevertheless, I see the material as a key constituent of understandings of gender. It is increasingly clear that materiality could constitute gendered subjectivities, as well as reflecting them. In the very different work of Beverley Gordon, Dianne Sachko Macleod and Victoria Mills, the ways in which things opened up new interior worlds and new, more satisfying ways of being to women can be seen. Gordon examines a wide range of feminine collections, usually of things with little economic value; while Macleod examines the formation of large, important and valuable collections of objets d'art by wealthy, leisured women; but they both point to the kind of ludic relationship these women had with their possessions.[39] The intensity of their relationships with their things unlocked a kind of creative confidence for them. Mills, meanwhile, examines Victorian literary explorations of women and things, where again the objects helped the women to become someone else, to explore feminine identities, and to make new journeys into their psyches.[40] Thus there is evidence of what we might call 'women's things', and of distinctive feminine relationships with things which helped to constitute feminine subjectivities, as this book will show. However, it is also important to be aware of how women's relationships with particular objects were structured and produced by circumstances, and that when women had the opportunity they often sought out 'male' objects and used them in 'male' ways. Materiality was used to break down or remake, as well as to reinforce, gendered identities.

The book uses the ideas of the distributed museum, and the domestic or private/public divide, to understand the different ways in which women and museums interacted. It is important to capture the range and variety of women's involvement, and so these analytical ideas are drawn on in varying ways through the book. There are many nodes and relationships in the networks of the distributed museum, but they are all characterised by the active role that materiality – objects, spaces and material practices – play in them. Equally, domesticity could be invoked, and public and private could be blurred or made distinct, through the acceptance or rejection of objects from the home for museums; the valuing or devaluing of 'domestic' work like encouraging children, cleaning, or even arranging (an activity which was simultaneously the badge of 'proper' curating, and the mark of women's domestic genius); and male professionals' reliance on the unpaid and unacknowledged labour of their wives, daughters and sisters.

This study initially proceeds to examine the different roles which women might play within museums and to interrogate the idea of the museum as an entity with an inside and an outside. The first chapter looks at women working within museums as employees and volunteers. This is framed as 'inside' the museum, but in fact it recovers the contribution of women who while 'inside', have been largely hidden; traditionally, museum history engages with key figures such as curators, but in fact hardly any women had 'curator' in their job title, and their presence has been hidden from much museum history thus far, though they did work inside museums in surprising numbers. The chapter also considers women's relationship with the nascent professional body of curators, the Museums Association (MA), which shows some marked contrasts with the American Association of Museums (AAM) at the same time.

The second and third chapters are devoted to a consideration of women's donations to museums; such women donors were 'outside' museums but nevertheless acted as museum makers. The second chapter examines the donors themselves, their identities, relationships and strategies, while the third chapter looks at the objects donated, to see whether 'women's things' are identifiable, as well as to investigate what sort of journey women's donations made to the museum setting, and whether this was distinctive and affected their meaning. In these chapters, the ways in which 'ordinary' women used objects and museums to memorialise their families and to revalue objects which sat outside existing curatorial schemes of value are shown. Chapter 4 examines women as visitors to museums, in some ways the most distanced relationship which women had with museums, as they might visit only once, fleetingly. Nevertheless, in terms of numbers, this was the most important engagement which women had with museums, and the space of the museum, poised between the civic and the entertaining, was embraced by women as a space for imaginative travel, self-exploration and protest. These first four chapters, therefore, show that women were active both within and outside the museum, and recover the extent of their contribution and agency as museum makers.

Secondly, this book moves on to examine what might be termed different museum feminisms, or ways of framing a feminine input into museums. Women's museum patronage, understood as direct attempts to lead and shape museum policy which cut across several different roles, is examined in Chapter 5. Chapter 6 examines the ways in which the growth of the new human sciences, archaeology and anthropology, both within and without the museum context, offered new opportunities and new constraints to women. And in Chapter 7, women's development of a John Ruskin-inspired museology is considered.

These chapters show that women had various ways of marking their presence in museums. Women were drawn to archaeology and anthropology in substantial numbers, and fulfilled important roles in distributing objects to provincial museums, but their attempts to become archaeologists and anthropologists on the same terms as men were less successful. In archaeology, they were prominent in museums largely because they were kept out of fieldwork; while in anthropology conversely, their involvement in 'accidental' fieldwork allowed them to supply objects to 'proper' male anthropologists but they were rarely seen as having such status themselves. The point here is that their involvement in, for example, popular lecturing in museums, or fundraising, though it was significant, was not necessarily what they themselves wanted to do; they were segregated in particular roles.

Women patrons fared a little better, with their involvement in major donations, the creation of new museums, and involvement in the funding and management of museums and galleries. Here women strove both to follow the 'rules' of masculine museum making, and to develop alternatives which promoted the characteristics of the 'feminine' already established; for example, by prioritising aesthetically pleasing and emotionally charged objects, and encouraging the involvement of the working class and children. These alternatives were not always successful and sometimes served to confirm women as 'outsiders' in the museum world; they were not able to access 'mainstream' museum space and so created space outside that mainstream. Women's most successful attempt to remake museums was to be found in their enthusiastic espousal of Ruskinian ideas in a museum setting in the very late nineteenth and early twentieth centuries; in many ways this represents the culmination of trends in women's involvement in museums apparent earlier in the book. Although Ruskin's ideas about museums were often lukewarm and contradictory, and although men made the running in setting up the first Ruskinian museums in the 1880s, as the turn of the century approached women developed these ideas in more radical directions, turning museums into community hubs in deprived areas, and oases of traditional craft skills, where making was endowed with transformative and preservative qualities.

By adding in the idea of the distributed museum, and of the way that people and objects are linked in networks, to more traditional biographical and institutional approaches, along with attention to the discursive production of the museum by Ruskin, among others, I hope to recover a wider and deeper sense of women's involvement in museums – and in a range of different museums too. The research for the book was partly determined by the limits of the source material – there were fewer museums in existence before 1914, and some of those which were in existence have lost their nineteenth-century records. Moreover, the records which museums kept were not designed to foreground women's roles and contributions; indeed, their silencing of women's voices can even seem intentional. Museums were run by Boards of Trustees, scientific societies, university governing bodies and local government – all, until right at the end of the period, exclusively male. Yet by examining textual and material sources both with and against the grain we can find women in and around museums of different sorts.

Overall, the story of women and museums between 1850 and 1914 is a complex and varied one, not easily reducible to a single narrative. Engagement with museums produced new women (as well as more self-consciously New Women), who were museum professionals and workers, collectors and donors, visitors, patrons and scholars.[41] Women themselves created new museums which contained different objects, including more social history and domestic craft, displayed in more evocative and less classificatory ways, and which communicated much more fully with a wider range of people. And such engagements also produced new understandings of concepts like tradition, public and private, which formed part of the complex and contradictory patchwork of attitudes which was modernity. Women created new professional and public identities for themselves which were often rooted in the domestic; museums themselves took on new roles in collective memory, community engagement and popular education. However, such new female or feminine roles and identities also produced a renewed sense of the higher value of the 'masculine' museum.

Notes

1 Leslie Linder (ed. and transcr.), *The Journal of Beatrix Potter from 1881 to 1897* (London and New York: Frederick Warne & Co. 1966), p. 405.

2 *Temple Bar*, December 1897, p. 506.

3 Although this was never an absolute trend; see Catherine Hall, Keith McClelland and Jane Rendall, *Defining the Victorian Nation: Class, Race, Gender and the Reform Act of 1867* (Cambridge: Cambridge University Press 2000), p. 36.

4 Ruth Hoberman, 'Women in the British Museum Reading Room during the late-nineteenth and early-twentieth centuries: from quasi- to counterpublic', *Feminist Studies* 28: 3 (2002), pp. 489–512; Ezra Shales, *Made in Newark: Cultivating Industrial Arts and Civic Identity in the Progressive Era* (New Brunswick, NJ and London: Rivergate Books 2010).

5 The most important reference here is Tony Bennett, *The Birth of the Museum* (London and New York: Routledge 1995).

6 I have consciously tried to avoid the narratives often found in studies of women in a particular field, which can tend either to the Whiggish story of inevitable progress, or the opposite tale of descent from a golden age. For example, Ann B. Shteir, *Cultivating Women, Cultivating Science: Flora's Daughters and Botany in England 1760–1860* (Baltimore, MD: Johns Hopkins University Press 1999); P. N. Wyse Jackson

and M. E. Spencer Jones, 'The quiet workforce: the various roles of women in geological and natural history museums during the early to mid-1900s', in C. V. Burek and B. Higgs (eds), *The Role of Women in the History of Geology*, Geological Society, London, Special Publications 281 (2007).

7 As pointed out by Graham Black, *The Engaging Museum: Developing Museums for Audience Involvement* (Abingdon: Routledge 2005).

8 See, for example, Bennett, *Birth of the Museum*; Dianne Sachko Macleod, *Enchanted Lives, Enchanted Objects: American Women Collectors and the Making of Culture 1800–1940* (Berkeley, CA: University of California Press 2008).

9 Carol Duncan, *Civilising Rituals: Inside Public Art Museums* (London: Routledge 1995).

10 Chris Gosden and Frances Larson, *Knowing Things: Exploring the Collections at the Pitt Rivers Museum* (Oxford: Oxford University Press 2007); Rodney Harrison, 'Consuming colonialism: curio dealers' catalogues, souvenir objects, and indigenous agency in Oceania', in S. Byrne, A. Clarke, R. Harrison and R. Torrence (eds), *Unpacking the Collection: Networks of Material and Social Agency in the Museum* (New York: Springer 2011).

11 Bennett, *Birth of the Museum*; Pierre Bourdieu, *Distinction: A Social Critique of the Judgement of Taste*, trans. R. Nice (London: Routledge 1989); Lois H. Silverman, *The Social Work of Museums* (Abingdon: Routledge 2010); Richard Sandell and Eithne Nightingale, *Museums, Equality and Social Justice* (London: Routledge 2012).

12 Helen Rees Leahy, *Museum Bodies: The Politics and Practices of Visiting and Viewing* (Farnham: Ashgate 2012); Samuel J. M. M. Alberti, *Nature and Culture: Objects, Disciplines and the Manchester Museum* (Manchester: Manchester University Press 2009), pp. 95–101.

13 See, for example, Edward Miller, *That Noble Cabinet: A History of the British Museum* (London: Andre Deutsch 1973); William Stearn, *The Natural History Museum at South Kensington* (London: Heinemann 1981); Edward Alexander, *Museum Masters: Their Museums and Their Influence* (Nashville, TN: American Association for State and Local History 1983); L. W. Kemp, 'Biography and the museum', in M. S. Shapiro (ed.), *The Museum; A Reference Guide* (New York and Westport, CT: Greenwood Press 1990).

14 Most notably, Bennett, *Birth of the Museum*; Carol Duncan and A. Wallach, 'The universal survey museum', *Art History* 3: 4 (1980).

15 See Kate Hill, *Culture and Class in English Public Museums, 1850–1914* (Aldershot: Ashgate 2005), esp. chapter 4, and Suzanne MacLeod, 'Significant lives: telling stories of museum architecture', in Kate Hill (ed.), *Museums and Biographies* (Woodbridge: Boydell and Brewer 2012).

16 Alberti, *Nature and Culture*, esp. chapter 4; Gosden and Larson, *Knowing Things*.

17 Hill, *Culture and Class*, chapter 7; Samuel J. M. M. Alberti, 'The museum affect: visiting collections of anatomy and natural history', in A. Fyfe and B. Lightman (eds), *Science in the Marketplace: Nineteenth-Century Sites and Experiences* (Chicago, IL: University of Chicago Press 2007).

18 Gosden and Larson, *Knowing Things*, chapter 1.

19 The most extensive exploration of the nature and limits of the separate spheres ideal can still be found in Leonore Davidoff and Catherine Hall, *Family Fortunes: Men and Women of the English Middle Class 1780–1850*, rev. edn (London: Routledge 2002); note particularly the discussion in the Introduction to the revised edition.

20 Jane Hamlett, *Material Relations: Domestic Interiors and Middle-Class Families in England, 1850–1910* (Manchester: Manchester University Press 2010), esp. 'Introduction'.

21 Deborah Cohen, *Household Gods: The British and Their Possessions* (New Haven, CT and London: Yale University Press 2006), p. 105.

22 Erika D. Rappaport, *Shopping for Pleasure: Women in the Making of London's West End* (Princeton, NJ and Oxford: Princeton University Press 2000), p. 39.

23 Rappaport, *Shopping for Pleasure*, pp. 23, 29. See also Jane Rendall, 'Women and the public sphere', *Gender and History* 11: 3 (1999) and Judith Walkowitz, *City of Dreadful Delight: Narratives of Sexual Danger in Late Victorian London* (London: Virago 1992).

24 John Tosh, *A Man's Place: Masculinity and the Middle-Class Home in Victorian England* (New Haven, CT and London: Yale University Press 1999), pp. 179–183; Tosh, *Manliness and Masculinities in Nineteenth-Century Britain: Essays on Gender, Family and Empire* (Harlow: Pearson 2005), pp. 117–118; see also A. James Hammerton, 'The English weakness? Gender, satire and "moral manliness" in the lower middle class, 1870–1920', in A. Kidd and D. Nicholls (eds), *Gender, Civic Culture and Consumerism: Middle-Class Identity in Britain 1800–1940* (Manchester: Manchester University Press 1999).

25 This discussion is heavily indebted to Catherine Hall and Sonia Rose, 'Introduction: being at home with the Empire', in C. Hall and S. Rose (eds), *At Home with the Empire: Metropolitan Culture and the Imperial World* (Cambridge: Cambridge University Press 2006), pp. 25–29.

26 Cohen, *Household Gods*, p. x.

27 Hall and Rose, 'Introduction', p. 27.

28 See especially Chapters 3 and 6.

29 Thomas Babington Macaulay, *The History of England from the Accession of James II* (London: Longman 1856), p. 3; Peter Mandler, *The Fall and Rise of the Stately Home* (New Haven, CT: Yale University Press 1997); Rosemary Mitchell, *Picturing the Past: English History in Text and Image, 1830–1870* (Oxford: Clarendon Press 2000), esp. chapter 6.

30 Paul Readman, 'The place of the past in English culture c.1890–1914', *Past and Present* 186 (2005), pp. 147–199.

31 Wilson Smith, 'Old London, Old Edinburgh: constructing historic cities', in Marta Filipová (ed.), *Cultures of International Exhibitions, 1840–1940: Great Exhibitions in the Margins* (Farnham: Ashgate 2015).

32 Kate Hill, 'Collecting authenticity: domestic, familial and everyday "old things" in English museums, 1850–1939', *Museum History Journal* 4: 2 (2011), pp. 205–206.

33 Of course, such homes were not 'private' in the way Victorian homes were felt to be; but they were homes. The interplay between 'private' and 'public' collecting and

display are discussed by Ken Arnold in *Cabinets for the Curious: Looking Back at Early English Museums* (Aldershot: Ashgate 2006), esp. pp. 13–20.

34 Hill, 'Collecting authenticity'.

35 Diana Dixon, 'Children's magazines and science in the nineteenth century', *Victorian Periodicals Review* 34: 3 (2001), pp. 228–238; Hill, *Culture and Class*, p. 143.

36 Amy Woodson-Boulton, *Transformative Beauty: Art Museums in Industrial Britain* (Stanford, CA: Stanford University Press 2012), chapter 2.

37 Beatrix Potter's father enjoyed charitable art exhibitions in private homes because of the opportunity they gave him to inspect other people's houses: Leslie Linder (ed. and transcr.), *The Journal of Beatrix Potter from 1881–1897* (London: Frederick Warne & Co. 1966), p. 185.

38 See, for example, Macleod, *Enchanted Lives, Enchanted Objects*.

39 Beverley Gordon, *The Saturated World: Aesthetic Meaning, Intimate Objects, Women's Lives, 1890–1940* (Knoxville, TN: University of Tennessee Press 2006); Macleod, *Enchanted Lives*.

40 Victoria Mills, 'The museum as "dream space": psychology and aesthetic response in George Eliot's *Middlemarch*', *19: Interdisciplinary Studies in the Long Nineteenth Century* 12 (2011), online, available at http://19.bbk.ac.uk/index.php/19/article/viewFile/596/704, accessed 5 September 2011.

41 On the relationship between the label 'New Woman' (partly media driven, partly self-ascribed) and feminist or women's movements around the *fin de siècle*, see Sally Ledger, *The New Woman: Fiction and Feminism at the Fin de Siècle* (Manchester: Manchester University Press 1997), chapter 1.

Inside the museum: including or excluding women?

An examination of women working in museums between the middle of the nineteenth century and the First World War indicates that they were under-qualified, and regarded as unprofessional, but superlatively cheap or free labour, which in the cash-strapped world of smaller museums especially was a strong advantage.[1] They were recognised as good at tasks such as boring, mundane work, fine work with their hands, and traditionally female tasks involving cleaning, children and communication, especially with other women or the working classes, but were not seen as suitable for curatorial roles because of the leadership, research and commitment such positions required. It is not, therefore, that museums should be seen as either including or excluding women, as has sometimes been suggested; rather, we need to look at how their inclusion was managed, contained and negotiated by a range of actors in varying settings. There were, as I will show, surprising numbers of women working in museums during our period. However, uncovering their contribution is less easy than men's. Men's patterns of work and criteria of career success have structured the way in which women's work has been researched, leading to the persistent idea that women were invisible and inaudible in museums.[2] The norms of male career patterns and definitions of success have obscured the significant numbers of women working in museums, but if we pay attention instead to the distinctive strategies of women, we can see and hear them much more clearly, and can think about what they did, as well as what they did not do.[3]

Although museums were distributed organisations where a wide range of people and things formed networks of meaning production in a variety of locations, there is no doubt that the physical institution of the museum occupied a privileged position in these networks, and that curators tried hard to centralise the museum. Decision making power was increasingly, though never exclusively, vested in those with curatorial positions, over and above even those with financial power, such as local authority committees, universities, or major donors. Moreover, formal institutional roles were not amenable to informal access in the way that other aspects of the museum were, and therefore there were more often explicit barriers to women's involvement. While women were to figure relatively easily as donors and visitors to museums, as we shall see, they struggled more to access those roles which might be seen as most central to the museum as institution: paid curatorial work. Museums were the site of a determined, if not entirely successful, attempt at masculine professionalisation during the late nineteenth and early twentieth centuries, which built on earlier ideas about curation as a 'gentlemanly' occupation, and meant that while women could gain employment in museums, they could rarely become full curators.

Museum expansion, especially outside London, was driven by natural history in the nineteenth century, and also tended to enshrine a small number of men in paid or honorary positions with a great deal of authority over their museums.[4] However, museums underwent a fairly rapid development in their contents, organisational structure and personnel during the period, especially between 1870 and 1914, which changed the dynamics of the internal community of the museum in significant ways. It is important to recognise, however, that this development was not always linear and 'progressive', and its results did not necessarily impact on the roles of men and women in ways that might be predicted. As a result, this chapter argues that despite sometimes overt attempts to exclude women from museums, the institutions came to represent important opportunities for women to develop careers, and to influence the overall direction of development, which were not always present in other areas of intellectual work.

The development of museums was part of a trend towards a more professional career structure within science and culture which was particularly noticeable during the second half of the nineteenth century.[5] It has been noted that part of the process of professionalisation in the natural sciences was an attempt to purge women from the field, because the feminine had come to be associated with amateurism, frivolity and a tendency to replicate existing knowledge rather than to innovate.[6] Professionalisation, in other words, required the explicit exclusion of those who might damage the authority, as well as the earning power, of the emerging professional group.[7] Curators were a group who developed the apparatus of a profession later than some other groups, but nevertheless by 1914 had a professional body, and some elements of training were beginning to develop, so the effects of this professionalisation on women's opportunities in museums need to be examined.[8]

The development of the museum institution and profession cannot, however, be characterised simply as increasingly exclusionary. In the first place, this was because the process of professionalisation was so piecemeal and slow, and amateurs of various kinds continued to play an important part in museums throughout the entire period. Secondly, the expansion of the museum and the developments in science and knowledge production generally meant that there were a large number of new roles created, often supporting male professionals, which offered new opportunities to women. Thirdly, women were developing their own areas of gendered professional expertise which they could introduce into museums, such as educational activities and what might be termed, anachronistically, 'outreach', which male professionals were happy to leave to them.[9] This all meant that museums were, relatively speaking, a much more open field for women than areas such as laboratory work; they shared more characteristics with libraries, which rapidly feminised in the early twentieth century.[10] It should be noted, though, that in libraries, as in museums, women mostly worked as junior assistants on low wages and disproportionately did not have professional qualifications.[11]

By the point at which public museums were starting to expand in the second half of the nineteenth century, women had already colonised and become identified with the popular communication of science. Children's interest in natural history collecting was inculcated largely through books written by middle-class women introducing the techniques of collecting and preserving, the skills of close observation, and the basics of classification and Latin nomenclature. The view emerged, therefore, of feminine natural history expertise, and arguably of feminine knowledge in general, as associated with child rearing, domestically based, essentially 'hobbyist' in nature, centred on what we might call 'transferable skills' of observation, perseverance and self-discipline, and above all suited to popular communication.[12] While this could restrict the way women engaged with natural history, it also offered substantial opportunities in what has been characterised as a 'woman-centred scientific pedagogy' and could give women a platform to demonstrate new skills and competences.[13] Indeed, Lightman argues that women used illustration to highlight their detailed observation and accurate reproduction of specimens, which were widely acknowledged to be female strengths, but also increasingly to demonstrate their facility with advanced scientific equipment such as powerful microscopes, in order to bolster their own authority in the light of male assertions of the limitations of women naturalists.[14] Feminine gendering of natural history opened up opportunities for women as authors, illustrators, and mediators, and this was an important precedent for certain roles within museums which women went on to develop.

Museums, museum work and the Museums Association

Museum work developed during the late nineteenth and early twentieth centuries to include many different and new areas; it encompassed both 'hard' research science, field collecting, educational work, and increasingly complex collections management and conservation, and is thus potentially of enormous importance in understanding the ways in which women's employment changed during this period.[15] Moreover, museums varied in size, aims and constituency, from small, poorly funded local museums aiming to cover a wide subject range, to large, prestigious national museums and increasingly specialised university museums.[16] This goes some way to explain the different roles which women occupied; most significantly because the process of professionalisation reached different stages at different museums.

Jordanna Bailkin identifies the drive among curators to enhance their status, authority and remuneration by creating and enforcing professional standards and particular educational and training pathways as a key factor affecting attitudes towards women in museums.[17] It is certainly the case that the formation of the Museums Association (MA) in Britain reflected concern among curators about their professional status and salary levels in the field, leading to fears that poorly educated women workers could potentially undo any gains curators were making. Equally, though, the MA enshrined the contribution of amateurs with an early president, the Reverend Henry Higgins, who had worked on a voluntary basis at Liverpool Museums for some years, and amateurs continued to be part of the MA for some time.[18] Women were not absent from the MA in its early years but their contribution centred on 'feminine' museum practices, especially in children's education. They remained, however, somewhat marginal figures in comparison with the American Association of Museums (AAM), where women's emphasis on education and children brought them a more central role.[19]

The MA, of course, was dedicated to improving the professional career prospects of men. However, concepts derived from men's work patterns might not be applicable to women's.[20] The idea of a career path, a linear progression through time culminating in a series of ever more senior paid professional positions, is, I suggest, not helpful for thinking about women's work at this time. Women moved in and out of paid and unpaid employment in complex ways, and did not always measure success in terms of the achievement of a salaried position. Women might, for example, obtain a paid museum position, but then resign it upon marriage, and instead become a volunteer at the same museum. This stemmed from the external constraints upon women, and their creative responses to those constraints. Opportunities varied depending on class, expertise and marital status, among many factors; and they changed over a woman's life cycle. Moreover, this means that for women, professionalisation and amateur interventions were not always seen as in opposition: some women valued the position of amateur in its own right, while for others it might be a route into a professional position, or a way to continue working in museums after a paid position had been relinquished.[21]

A typology of women in museum research has been proposed by Wyse Jackson and Spencer Jones in their investigation of women in geological and natural history museums in the first half of the twentieth century. They propose five groups: the wife/sister/daughter; the museum assistant (whether paid or not); women who researched at museums but had no institutional affiliation; academics; and museum research scientists.[22] They go on to suggest that the first two categories were more prominent in the early part of the twentieth century, while the last three became more important after 1930. However, they also acknowledge that the boundaries between the categories are fuzzy at best, and that women frequently moved between groups or belonged to more than one at the same time. There are representatives of all Wyse Jackson and Spencer Jones's categories among the women I will examine here, and their analysis is particularly helpful when examining museums where specialisation, research and the advancement of knowledge were key aims. However, many of the museums which I have looked at were general museums covering all areas from zoology to decorative metalwork, and were generally less interested in the production of new knowledge than the museums studied by Wyse Jackson and Spencer Jones. For women, this opened up the possibility of utilising their assumed strength in popularising and communicating knowledge, in the museum context, and we thus see women who were neither researchers nor academics, but adapted the developing persona of the general curator, by giving popular public lectures and bringing their museum, as much as possible, to a popular audience.

Developing this idea further, historians of science such as Sally Gregory Kohlstedt and Leslie Madsen-Brooks have suggested that in museums in the USA, women used a gender-specific niche of education to reorient museums towards a popular audience, and away from their earlier function as specialist research institutions for scientists.[23] Kohlstedt examines three women who worked in museum education from a variety of backgrounds, and occupied increasingly important positions either in general museums, or in newly created children's museums; significantly, she shows their prominent role in the developing profession of museum work by examining their contribution to the AAM.[24] The argument that 'feminine' areas of museum work were not just a means of segregating, marginalising and devaluing women's work, but could also allow women to assert new competences and values which affected the entire institution, is a particularly important one which can be applied to the experience of women in British museums as well.

It is also, however, the case that in Britain, museum education did not become as prominent as it did in the USA until considerably later, and women were unable either to build up educational work to the same extent, or to mediate such work into prominent positions within Britain's professional association, the MA. While Kohlstedt found that at the first meeting of the AAM in 1907, four women attended, and one spoke, with women first holding office in the association in 1924, there is little sign of any prominent female membership of the MA in Britain, an older organisation which had been set up in 1889, before the First World War. In the years before 1914 a small number of women either addressed the UK's MA conference or published in the *Museums Journal* and its forerunners, or both. These included Kate Hall and Clara Nördlinger, considered below, along with a Mrs Tubbs who contributed an article on museums and elementary education, and at least one, possibly two Americans, Delia Griffin on the Children's Museum in Boston, of which she was founding Director, and a Mrs Roesler on instructors at the American Museum of Natural History.[25]

Although women were raising similar themes, and were focusing on education, at both the MA and the AAM (and in one case it was even the same woman), they had less impact in Britain than in the USA; educational and outreach programmes and displays were admired but introduced in a much more piecemeal fashion in Britain. This may partly be explained by the MA initially inviting curators and members of governing bodies to become members, two categories which were almost entirely male during this period; additionally, voluntary society museums were over-represented in the early years of the MA and such museums and their parent societies had also been a traditionally male milieu, with more explicit barriers to women's participation than existed at publicly funded museums.[26] Thus, despite the fact that museum educational work was a prominent topic in the early years of the MA as it was in the AAM, women were much less able to establish it as a female niche.[27] Women's experience of museum work, therefore, was also heavily influenced by the national culture in which they found themselves.[28]

In order to understand women's work in museums in England, therefore, I examine all aspects of women's involvement, including education, research, 'assisting' in all its forms, and volunteering. I start with an examination of the only woman who had sole charge of a museum during the period; moving onto an examination of women in university museums. I will then examine women's employment in assistant and non-curatorial roles; and finally I will look at women volunteers and consider the relationship between volunteering and paid museum work for women.

Kate Hall – a female curator

The woman who may be considered to have established her museum professionalism most clearly by working in museums during this period was Miss Kate Marion Hall (1861–1918). She was the curator of the Whitechapel Museum from its opening in 1894 till 1909, and also the founder of the Nature Study Museum, a branch of the Whitechapel Museum which opened in 1904, containing mainly living specimens, and was housed in a disused chapel of St George-in-the-East church (see Figure 1). She was, as far as can be ascertained, the first paid woman curator in the country, though there had been assistant curators before her. Her career reveals a pragmatic and fluid movement between what might be termed 'masculine' and 'feminine' modes of curating.

Miss Hall's father had been a successful animal painter, and she had attended University of London classes without taking a degree. She was one of the first women members of the Linnaean Society, and published scientific papers in learned journals. She was an extremely energetic lecturer at her museum, and at others such as the Horniman Museum (up to a total of forty in one week), and also donated specimens to other museums.[29] Her obituary suggests that the Whitechapel museums she ran were loosely associated with the Toynbee Hall project, set up by the Barnetts to bring high-minded university graduates to live in the East End of London and undertake educational and other work. Samuel and Henrietta Barnett, considered further in Chapter 7, were well-known social reformers in latenineteenth-century east London, amongst other

Figure 1 Children at St George's Nature Study Museum, Whitechapel, *c.* 1910.

projects setting up the Whitechapel Art Gallery.[30] Miss Hall had worked at Toynbee Hall, because, apparently, of her 'love and sympathy for working people', and had formed a close friendship with the Barnetts. However, Miss Hall's own account of her museum, delivered to the MA conference in 1901, did not make many references to Toynbee Hall, and instead stressed the credentials of the museum as the first museum supported by local taxation in London.[31]

Kate Hall's career can therefore be read through different lenses. One perspective sees her as a scientist; her obituary stressed her powers 'of exact observation', and that she had 'the true scientific mind'.[32] The other, which her involvement with Toynbee Hall and friendship with the Barnetts highlighted, focused on her commitment to the diffusion and communication of knowledge and suggests she was particularly able to empathise with the working class and with children. By highlighting her association with the Toynbee Hall project, which despite its focus on a masculine idea of 'brotherhood', also included key female reformers such as Henrietta Barnett herself, Beatrice Webb, and Octavia Hill, Hall was aligned with a branch of female philanthropy which focused on ameliorating the lives of the poor in both voluntarist and professional approaches.[33] This ambiguity in the way she was positioned and positioned herself was, I suggest, typical of women in museum work, who needed to be able to present themselves in multiple ways depending on the context.

The pioneering nature of her appointment must be stressed; but it is also evident that the one museum which was under the sole charge of a woman was small and not at all well known, and focused on serving its impoverished community, and especially children, rather than on advancing scholarship or building a noteworthy collection. In contrast with children's museums in the USA, therefore, where it is argued that women fundamentally changed the nature of the museum, it might be more accurate to suggest that women developed the activities of museums but that these developments were not valued to the same extent as 'masculine' museum areas, and only found space on the periphery of the museum world, seriously limiting their visibility and influence.

It seems, therefore, that women as curators chose not to compete with men on the same ground, but focused on – and were encouraged towards – areas where they were acknowledged to have strengths. They built on their experience of mediating science to children and a popular audience developed as illustrators and popularisers in science publishing, and thus asserted a complementary professionalism to masculine professional curatorship; but they still tried to keep their credentials for 'proper' curating visible. This was because the places which offered opportunities for feminine-style curating were smaller, local museums with low salaries and little prospects.[34]

Women on the curatorial staff

Other women achieved positions within the curatorial staff of museums, though these tended to be assistant roles, and not till about 1890. These roles reveal the necessity for women to be flexible in their strategies for becoming museum workers, and show that neither emulating men nor enacting distinctive feminine approaches to curating were entirely successful approaches. Manchester Museum was a particularly welcoming place for women workers during this period; women were increasingly able to secure positions, sometimes as a result of studying at the university to which the museum was attached. Thus at Manchester, Margaret Hager was employed as a temporary assistant in 1899–1900; Grace Wigglesworth became the assistant keeper of botany in 1910; and Winifred Crompton became the assistant keeper of Egyptology in 1911. These women benefited both from their new ability to study at advanced level, and from their familial networks: Wigglesworth had a degree from Owens College, the forerunner of Manchester University, and Crompton had studied Egyptology, though Hager had no academic qualifications that can be found. Crompton was the sister of Alice Crompton, at one time Head of the Women's House at the University Settlement in Manchester, who had taken a first in Classics from Manchester University in 1889.[35] Winifred had initially been employed as the museum's printer.

The links between women's progress in accessing higher education, and their improving ability to gain curatorial work are also shown by the careers of Margaret Murray and Marie Stopes, both active at Manchester Museum. Margaret Murray, a lecturer in Egyptology at University College London, worked very visibly at Manchester Museum when she undertook the unwrapping of a mummy, one of the 'Two Brothers' excavated by Petrie and his team. Figure 2 shows the unwrapping, in 1908, which took place in front of an audience of 500 students. In addition to the unwrapping, Murray also contributed to the cataloguing of Manchester's Egyptology collection; though it should be noted that she took on much work of this nature to supplement her rather meagre income.[36] Murray benefited from Amelia Edwards's work to support Egyptology, and the prominence of women in Egyptology, and archaeology and anthropology more widely, are considered in Chapter 6. In turn, Murray mentored Winifred Crompton, corresponding with her about how best to work with Egyptological material and advising her to publish her research.[37]

Marie Stopes was a lecturer in palaeobotany at the University of Manchester from 1904 to1907, and according to Alberti, 'researched and arranged specimens in the Museum'.[38] She provides a particularly interesting and rare example of museum worker as research scientist. She was the first female lecturer at Manchester University, and because of her subject, engaged with the museum as researcher and teacher. The role at Manchester was part of her developing academic career, whose pioneering nature should not be underestimated. She amassed an impressive number of 'firsts' for women: first woman in Munich to take a PhD in botany, first woman lecturer at the University of Manchester, and youngest doctor of science in Britain.[39]

Figure 2 Margaret Murray unwrapping one of the 'Two Brothers' mummies at Manchester Museum, 1908. William Flinders Petrie is the bearded figure on the right.

The increasing accessibility of higher education for women was thus important, but not the only factor in making museum work possible for women. This is partly because right up to 1914 it was entirely possible to build a curating career without academic qualifications; however, in order to do so, the right connections and family were usually important. This was just as well, because although provincial universities, the University of London and Oxford and Cambridge were admitting growing numbers of women, who were looking to put their qualifications to work in some suitable employment, women were still much less likely to have full qualifications even if they attended university, and often still faced parental opposition to university study.[40]

Manchester Museum was by some margin the most welcoming museum to women as curatorial staff of those museums examined here. This can be attributed to a number of factors: it had already welcomed an unusually high number of women volunteers working on the collections (see below); it was 'fed' by a provincial university reasonably open to women; and its intellectual networks were quite open. Here, while some women employees followed feminine paths in acquiring positions described as 'assistant', and in relying on a family member or other male mentor to vouch for their abilities, others, notably Marie Stopes, did not. While Owens College, the forerunner of Manchester University, hardly rushed to provide opportunities for women (indeed the question remained a vexed one for some time), they were admitted to classes from 1883 and the first degrees were conferred on four women in 1887.[41] Women were beginning to out-number men in the Faculty of Arts from 1904 to 1905, though this is largely because of the number of women undertaking teacher training. Women had access only to the 'women's department', a small, chilly and dingy building, outside of teaching sessions, and could not even enter the library (a maid apparently fetched books for them).[42] It is interesting to note that the first women's common room was adjoining the museum, necessitating close contact with mummies and stuffed animals. On the other hand, with the right support women could become prominent at Manchester; Alice Cook became assistant lec-turer in history there in 1893.[43]

The case of Manchester Museum supports the findings of Wyse Jackson and Spencer Jones that university museums were relatively open to women. At University College London (UCL), Professor Johnston Garwood, the chair of geology in the early twentieth century, encour-aged women to attend his courses, teaching Marie Stopes among oth-ers, and benefited from the research assistance of several women who went on to develop careers in geology and palaeobotany. He also appointed Edith Goodyear as his assistant, and she looked after the col-lege's geology museum.[44] It is suggested that by the early twentieth cen-tury, museum work had come to be seen as inferior to more rigorous or ground-breaking experimental work in laboratories so in universities there was little competition for the job of looking after the collection, and women benefited from this.[45] However, there is also reason to sug-gest that some relatively new higher education institutions saw part of their modernity and utility as lying in their openness to women. While UCL's claims to have pioneered women's access to higher education may depend on a slightly partial reading of events, and it certainly also offered women a distinctly second-class experience, it was clearly experienced by women as a liberating environment, as Margaret Murray's description of her time there makes clear. The women undergraduates and staff all put substantial effort into improving the facilities and the opportunities they enjoyed there.[46] It seems likely, therefore, that women's perception of some universities as modern and committed to improving female educa-tion encouraged them to seek work there; while these institutions also actually offered them greater opportunities, if only by default, as they filled the positions men did not want.

There were also some openings for women at national museums. At the Museum of Science and Art in Dublin, Matilda Knowles was employed as a temporary assistant, from 1902, and then a full assistant in 1907; while Jane Stephens was employed as a technical assistant from 1905. Stephens did become the assistant naturalist but had to resign in 1920 upon marriage.[47] Meanwhile, at the British Museum (Natural History) (BM(NH)) in the late 1890s, a young Dorothea Bate apparently walked in with no qualifications and asked for a job; which she did in fact get, though for decades her employment was temporary and for her entire career she remained largely paid by piece rate (she worked preparing bird skins and other specimens). She went on to publish widely in mammalian palaeontology and archaeozoology, but never had the job security her eminence might have been expected to bring. And indeed, the BM(NH) did not employ any other women until after the First World War, when they were taken on in increasing numbers as assistants.[48]

In most cases, then, 'assistant' figured prominently in women's job titles in national and university museums.[49] This was certainly a good indicator of museums' views of women's roles. However, we should not necessarily accept this valuation as a description of what they actually did: Bate clearly undertook the same sort of research which a male curator might have done, and accessed research grants from bodies such as the Royal Society. While university museums were much more open to women than other types of museum, they still structured museum careers so that women's contribution, whatever its actual nature, was seen as being silent assistants to the male curators; and women were clustered in the least desirable jobs. In university science, women gravitated towards museum work not just from choice, but because men were able to monopolise other areas and avoided curatorial positions as they were less desirable than other roles.[50] In many ways, museums came to be seen as having an auxiliary role aiding scientific advances but not producing such advances themselves.[51] Nevertheless, women used these opportunities in distinctive ways, colonising assistant roles in some numbers and undertaking their own research, while ostensibly 'assisting'.[52]

Elsewhere, things were very difficult for women attempting to access curatorial positions, and museums could be characterised as exclusionary in their practices. Kathleen Dearden was engaged as a temporary curatorial assistant at Sheffield Museum in 1886, at a wage of 12s a week. It is worth stressing how low this was; about half the salary of an unskilled attendant, and indeed less than the wage of a male agricultural labourer. Compared to wage levels for women it is less shocking; new governesses without experience or strong qualifications could only expect about £20 p.a. (though of course this included board), but even new assistant school mistresses, an area where there was something of a glut developing by the end of the century, could expect £70 p.a.[53] Her employment seems to have continued on a more permanent basis until 1896, when she was dismissed, according to the Museum Sub-Committee because she 'showed no disposition to qualify herself for scientific work'.[54] By this time, Charles Bradshaw, another curatorial assistant who had been employed since 1876, had attended courses of the Science and Art Department in South Kensington, and at the Sheffield Mechanics' Institute.[55] It is not clear why Dearden had not undertaken such courses; she certainly possessed and maintained an interest in some branches of science, as evinced by the fact that she continued to donate specimens to the museum even after her dismissal.[56] It is possible that as she was the eldest daughter of a widower, she had domestic responsibilities that prevented her; but for whatever reason, her career in curating was over.[57] In the year she was dismissed, Elijah Howarth, the curator of Sheffield Museum, was moved to reflect on the vicissitudes of employing women in museums, when he spoke at the MA's conference. His experience of women workers was, he said, 'not wholly encouraging'. His first female curatorial employee left very quickly to get married, and the second (we may assume this was Kathleen Dearden) could 'paint labels, [but] she could do no other kind of work that was of any use in a museum'. The other members suggested that scientifically trained women did exist, and if one could recruit those, they were good employees.[58]

There is, then, no direct evidence that women faced overt barriers to developing a curatorial career, but there is indirect evidence, in the very small numbers, that it was either not easy for them because of barriers to accessing higher education, or developing the right networks, or was even something they considered, by and large; and if they did their position was likely to be subordinate. The example of Kathleen Dearden further suggests that the standards of the profession, nebulous, implicit and developing though they were, might also be harder for women to keep up with. As Bailkin has suggested, the MA's agenda of professionalisation for curators might be imperilled by the entrance of less educated and extremely cheap women into the field; despite the fact that many men were similarly untrained, they were perceived as more trainable, or as having more informal resources to draw on.[59]

Women in non-curatorial roles

Women were also employed in a number of non-curatorial positions in museums, and were already undertaking work as caretakers and cleaners by the middle of the nineteenth century. This in itself may have enhanced opposition to them as curators; if women were associated with cleaning and such menial tasks, then they would undermine the professional status of curating which was specifically trying to divest itself of servile associations.[60] Preston's museum, which became the Harris Museum and Art Gallery, employed a 'curator' who was clearly mainly a caretaker when it was in its first location. Miss Barton, the appointee, was the librarian of Dr Shepherd's Library; most curatorial responsibility for the museum lay with the (male) honorary curator. While her duties are not described, census evidence suggests that her sisters were cotton workers, and that the Barton household lived in working-class areas, suggesting that she would have been seen as suitable for a fairly menial role. Curating was open to those from relatively lowly backgrounds at this period, but men, such as Tom Sheppard at Hull, a clerk who had left school when he was 14 years old, usually came to it through substantial involvement in local natural history societies, and there is no evidence Miss Barton had any such involvement.[61] The museum of the Sussex Archaeological Society was looked after by a husband and wife team. Both in Sussex and Preston, these positions seem to have involved cleaning, lighting fires, locking up and opening the building, and similar tasks. The husband and wife at Sussex Archaeological Society's museum did also show visitors around, although not always in an appropriate way.[62] So these were probably jobs akin to 'housekeeping' for the museum, which were traditionally undertaken by women. Women continued to act as cleaners in museums, though this role was rarely mentioned in museum records.

Women also took on other support roles. Brighton Museum and Art Gallery employed a woman as a clerical assistant, and in Sheffield women were employed as attendants at High Hazels branch museum (paid just over half the wages of male attendants).[63] The extent to which women could be identified with support roles and colonise them heavily is shown by Figure 3, which is a photograph of Manchester Museum staff in 1898 with the curatorial staff (all male) in the back row and the two women employees, Freda Ede, the printer, and Clara Nördlinger the secretary, in the front row. Thus women's employment in support roles sometimes preceded and paved the way for their employment in curatorial roles, though it could equally reinforce ideas about the limits of women's possible contribution.[64]

Figure 3 The staff at Manchester Museum in 1898. The curatorial staff are in the back row; the women in front are the secretary, Clara Nördlinger, and the printer, Freda Ede.

Service occupations were important in establishing a foothold for women within the museum, and moreover were not necessarily conceived of by women as distinct from and subordinate to the curatorial roles. Not only did Winifred Crompton move from the role of printer to that of assistant keeper of Egyptology in 1911; Clara Nördlinger, the secretary, was a substantial donor as well, so contributed in multiple ways to the museum. In fact, Nördlinger was also the first woman to contribute to the *Museums Journal,* and in two articles articulated distinctive ideas about women and museums. In 1896, an article emerging from her contribution to a discussion at the MA's conference, on women in museums, was published. The article dealt specifically with her visit to Schleswig-Holstein where she met the director of the Museum of National Antiquities, Miss Johanna Mestorf. Mestorf, who was in charge of the museum from 1891 to 1909, was the first female museum director in Germany and probably much more widely; certainly no British woman achieved such an important role in our period.[65] The discussion, published in the *Museums Journal,* among mainly male museum staff, as Bailkin argues, focused on women's lack of training. But it was overall far from hostile to women's employment in museums, highlighting their suitability for 'fine and delicate' work, especially cleaning specimens, and also their cheapness, which is certainly borne out by the salary of Kathleen Dearden and also Bertha Hindshaw (which will be discussed in Chapter 7).[66] One curator even argued that one could obtain 'gratuitous help from ... ladies', though it was also asserted that women were 'decidedly underpaid'. It is interesting to note that W. E. Hoyle, the director of the Manchester Museum, the museum with the most female employees, declared that he 'considered museum work a suitable field for the employment of women'.[67]

The other article by Nördlinger, published in 1898, dealt with the issue of cleaning in museums, reclaiming it as an area of feminine expertise – 'essentially feminine' – and suggesting not just that women cleaners should form a separate department under the lead of a woman, but that 'lady inspectors' should include museums in their rounds.[68] Her writing suggests even more strongly the importance of service and auxiliary roles for women, and that women themselves realised this; Bailkin suggests that Nördlinger's intervention attempted to draw museums into a more domestic sphere where virtues of cleanliness and housekeeping were valued above curatorial knowledge, and where ladies' philanthropic visiting was a better model than professionalisation. What is notable, though, is that by stressing the importance of the areas where women had found it relatively easy to find employment, she was opening up opportunities for women to follow her path of undertaking support roles within museums, while also pursuing curatorial activities. On the other hand, women's involvement in cleaning museums, while crucial to the their running, should not be seen as particularly liberating; working-class women cleaners, along with men working as attendants, tend to emerge into records of the middle-class world of the curatorial staff only when they were dismissed for drunkenness.[69] Nördlinger, daughter of a wealthy German-Jewish merchant, seems to have left the museum and other translating work on her marriage in around 1900, which may also indicate the limits of the service occupation route into museums.

There are grounds, then, for suggesting that women's vision of 'professional' roles was based on the idea and the practices of service, as Shales' examination of women working in libraries in the USA around 1900 found. Shales' women librarians were both radical and embodied tropes of femininity; their careers followed some norms of female philanthropy while also constituting paid (albeit badly paid) employment. They carved out a distinctive role for the female professional by stressing the similarities between the work they were doing, and the most highly praised feminine qualities, of nurture, selflessness and even housekeeping. It was part of a range of vocations described as 'municipal housekeeping', and thus made acceptable. Librarianship came to be seen as an ideal feminine vocation which allowed women to serve and in some ways act as wife and mother to their community.[70] In museums, similarly, women took on paid roles which suggested feminine qualities of serving, assisting, nurturing. However, as already suggested, roles and job titles which seemed to emphasise the assistance and nurturing nature of women, in opposition to the freedom and initiative of men, did not always demonstrate the full range of activities which women actually did, and may have acted more as smokescreens than as determinants of their roles. As Wyse Jackson and Spencer Jones show, women certainly contributed to the production of knowledge, but this contribution was not acknowledged.[71]

Volunteers

Also important in creating space for women in the museum was volunteering; again, though, the prominence of women as volunteers enforced the sense that they were a threat to the professionalisation of curating. Men also volunteered in substantial numbers, as I have argued elsewhere; the role of the Reverend Henry Higgins at Liverpool Museum was extremely substantial, despite his having no official connection to the museum except his familiarity with its collection.[72] High-status gentlemen had social standing, wealth and connections to recommend them to museums which were generally glad to share in these assets. For men with some leisure time, volunteering gave them probably more freedom of action than actual employment might do, with the added bonus that curators, especially early in the period, might be regarded socially as rather lowly and subordinate men.

This explains why the MA was so keen to raise the status of curators, and to demote volunteers to a strictly auxiliary position; this in turn was why they feared the employment of under-educated, unserious women. Even to be accepted as volunteers, women sometimes needed the professional expertise of a male relative to vouch for them; some of the Egyptological collection at Manchester Museum was catalogued by Miss Griffith and it was noted 'with peculiar satisfaction' in the Annual Report that she was the 'sister of the college lecturer in Egyptology', Francis Griffith.[73] However, volunteering was a particularly important route in to involvement with the museum throughout the period, both for those whose social and or marital status meant that it was considered inappropriate or unnecessary for them to take paid employment, and for those who did, in fact, aspire to a paid position within the museum.

For many women, paid employment was not really a goal. A marriage bar was officially in place at the larger museums, and in de facto operation everywhere. Volunteering was an important opportunity for married women, as their prominence among the volunteers supplying and arranging wild flowers at Manchester and Bristol Museums shows. Several museums had displays of fresh wild flowers, or Wardian cases with living plants in them, which were usually stocked and tended by a group of volunteers. Women, married and unmarried, figure very heavily in these groups; at Manchester Museum they formed between 60 and 100 per cent of the group, while at Bristol Museum the Wardian cases were 'under the sole charge of Miss Ida Roper FLS', and those contributing to them were mainly female.[74] Wardian cases and wild flower displays can be seen as an area of female control and expertise. Botany had long been an acceptable feminine hobby and even the site of articulation of a feminist counter-science.[75] Women involved in this work may therefore be seen as attempting to make space for themselves in the public places and institutions of science by inserting feminine practices alongside those of men; this allowed them to claim a small part of the museum as female.[76]

For women of high social status, as for men, there was no particular reason to seek paid employment, even if it had been acceptable: there was much more freedom and opportunity in not having a paid position. Moreover, weaknesses in the process of professionalisation continued to allow considerable scope to volunteers, right up to the end of our period, particularly in smaller, provincial museums which were unlikely to have much in the way of paid staff. The example of Nina Layard, at Ipswich, demonstrates this: because of her social position, and also because of the size of the collection she gave to the Museum, she was able to have complete control over the display of her objects. Layard, a relative of the ceramics collector and important museum donor Lady Charlotte Schreiber, and also of the archaeologist and politician Sir Austen Henry Layard, undertook a number of important prehistoric and Anglo-Saxon excavations in and around Ipswich, and donated most of the finds to Ipswich Museum.[77] With the support of the leading archaeologist, Sir John Evans, Layard tried to enter the world of the London learned societies, with mixed success; she was an early female member of the Linnaean Society but the Society of Antiquaries would not let her deliver a paper on her Anglo-Saxon finds, even with Evans as her sponsor, so he delivered it on her behalf.[78]

In the rather more impressionable milieu of the town council in Ipswich, she did, however, acquire considerable intellectual authority, outstripping that of the male, paid curator. She gave her collections to the local museum on the condition that she would still have access to them, and could arrange them herself and remove any object if she wanted to use it in a lecture. She complained to the council's museum committee that the curator, Frank Woolnough (an active member of the MA) had been handling her material, and the committee backed her up to the extent that the collection was put in a separate room to which only she had the key.[79] This episode indicates that particularly at smaller, local museums, social status and connections could still trump an as yet embryonic professional authority; and also goes some way to show why there might be divisions between men and women on the issue of professionalisation of museum work. It might well help women of a certain class if the role of volunteers remained central.

This was not always the case, however, and there could be problems for women in developing this kind of volunteer expertise. It is recorded in Bristol Museum's Sub-Committee Proceedings that in 1880 the curator proposed to delegate to 'a lady' a revision of the Mollusca collections. The Committee, though, preferred 'that the work be undertaken by the curator himself'.[80] By the early twentieth century, Bristol Museum seemed more open to the idea of women volunteers playing a substantial role. In the Report for 1906–07, it was said that 'Miss Roper has given much of her time during the year' to classifying the Herbarium and mounting the collection of mosses; she had already taken responsibility for the Wardian cases.[81] While Miss Nora Ward also worked at a volunteer at Bristol in 1913–14, however, no more than these two are recorded there beyond the Wardian cases team. Many museums recorded no female volunteers at all (though this does not necessarily mean there were none), and at Brighton, Ipswich and the Pitt Rivers Museum just one each is recorded (though two of these were particularly significant, Nina Layard at Ipswich who in fact became an honorary curator of the museum, and Barbara Freire-Marreco at the Pitt Rivers who was an early woman anthropologist). At Manchester Museum, by contrast, six women volunteers are recorded, over a period dating back to 1890.[82] While women volunteers might well be under-recorded by curators jealous of their professional authority, therefore, there were also variations apparent between museums in the apparent levels of volunteers present.

Volunteering in the museum could be a precursor to gaining professional curatorial employment at the museum, rather than an alternative to it. Given the very small numbers in actual curatorial roles, we cannot see this phenomenon at work very often. A crucial example, though, comes from Manchester Museum. Grace Wigglesworth, who was to be appointed assistant keeper of botany there in 1910, later becoming full keeper, began by donating specimens, and then volunteered to catalogue the herbarium. After our period, in 1934, she acquired her own (female) assistant, Annie Higginbotham.[83] Wigglesworth's career appears to show that by donating women could demonstrate the expertise necessary to become volunteers, and then use this to gain paid employment.[84] This route was not exclusive to women, but it was especially important as other paths open to men were more difficult for them.

Volunteering was thus a crucial part of museum work for women, whereas men who had additional channels through which to become involved with their local museum, such as through the council's committee in charge of it, or as leading figures in local scientific societies, or increasingly through formal education and training, had less to gain by volunteering. While not without difficulties for women, volunteering was increasingly acceptable as a feminine role, and even played to women's strengths in some ways. It would be overly reductive, though, to say that a masculine process of professionalisation was in conflict with a feminine model of volunteering, as women deliberately moved between the two types of museum work, and were happy to present themselves as lady philanthropists or serious scholars, depending on what was called for by the context.

Finally, women might also be present in the museum as lecturers. Kate Hall, the curator of Whitechapel Museum, gave public lectures at the Horniman Museum in 1909, as did Miss, later Dr Delf (Miss Delf became Dr Delf in 1913, and had regularly lectured at the Horniman in the intervening years). Marie Stopes lectured there in 1912.[85] However, although women could undertake the public role of lecturing to a mixed-gender audience, they rarely did so, and those who did so had, or were in the process of developing, the professional authority to be able to speak publicly. Moreover, it may be significant that of the museums studied here, only the Horniman recorded women delivering lectures, and these were all in its Saturday afternoon popular lecture series. The Horniman Museum, as Coombes has demonstrated, took a particularly proactive approach to connecting with a popular audience, and thus may have included more women lecturers because of their presumed natural ability to communicate with subordinate groups.[86] For other museums, though, scholarly authority, which was identified as male, took precedence over the accessibility of public lectures.[87]

Conclusion

Women, then, undertook a range of roles within the museum, including paid employment, both curatorial and other, but also including voluntary work. It was very hard for women to attain curatorial employment, and this became harder the more senior the curatorial position was. For many women, however, paid curatorial work was not the main goal (and for some it was an impossible goal because of the marriage bar), and they make use of all opportunities, such as volunteering or working in service occupations, to become involved in museum work in other ways. And those who were, in fact, seeking curatorial positions used these same roles, especially volunteering and lecturing, in order to build expertise and authority.

Some British women undoubtedly followed the model outlined by Kohlstedt, of building a niche which reflected their experiences and concerns, and thereby influencing the development of museums as a whole. Women such as Kate Hall did focus on education and communication, and did spark some interest in fellow museum workers as a result; male members of the MA spoke of the importance of the work she was carrying out in Whitechapel.[88] Equally, the importance of roles which were feminine in their domesticity, service-oriented nature and which suggested an amateur status were also championed by women. However, too binary an approach does not serve women well, as Bailkin also suggests when she argues that this 'was neither a story of women reinventing the museum as a "private" institution nor one of women being recrafted as "public" beings by means of their participation in the arts and sciences'.[89] Women inhabited extremely fluid identities and presented themselves very differently in different situations.

It is insufficient, therefore, either to see museums as exclusionary, or as welcoming to women. Museums were in the middle of a complex process of professionalisation which women were perceived to threaten in a number of ways, though they also were seen to have qualities which museums valued. By the second half of the nineteenth century women were categorised as poorly educated, and as being uncommitted to museum work which they fitted in when could. On the other hand, they were also seen as good at the housekeeping and service aspects of museum work, good at fine and repetitive work, and as very cheap; a set of characteristics which smaller museums especially found quite compelling.

Nor is it enough to say that women and men had a different view of how museums should work, with men focusing on new knowledge and women on popular engagement as well as record-keeping and other ancillary activities. Rather, the fluidity of women's work inside the museum needs to be acknowledged. In particular, it is clear that the label attached to a woman's role might obscure a great deal of what they actually did, either deliberately or through chance and opportunism; it did not always matter whether women were volunteers or paid; assistants, curators or secretaries; authors, illustrators or donors; sisters or daughters or wives of scientists; whether they had studied at university or not, and whether they had a base in the museum or largely worked from home. They used a number of routes to access the 'inside' of the museum, and once within the museum developed a 'feminine' view of what museums could be, as well as, where possible, a 'masculine' career. They were both professional and amateur, and despite the professionalisation of science and museums, or because of it, they found opportunities there which they could not find elsewhere. In this sense, not only did women make museums through their emphasis on education and the importance of the domestic side of the museum, but museums made women by offering an arena which was both about knowledge and communication. Museums allowed women to act in public and in private, to be professional and amateur, and to stress both the creation of new knowledge and the importance of mediating that knowledge to audiences of children, the working class, and others.

On the other hand, there is no doubt that museums could exclude, or at least segregate women. The exclusions ranged from explicit marriage bars, to more subtle mechanisms meaning that men had both better connections and better qualifications (although it was far from clear what qualifications or connections were needed for most museum jobs, despite the MA's best intentions). Women were much less likely to have either full degrees, or the sorts of training courses apparently offered at South Kensington and at local colleges; they were much more likely to have domestic commitments or parents unwilling to see their daughters working; they were almost certain to be paid much less than men (though this latter might recommend them to employers, it did make it hard to survive in such a job). Women were rarely considered for jobs thought to require the ability to produce new scientific knowledge, and never for jobs requiring the supervision of male staff. Perceptions of women as, on the one hand, dilettanti dabblers, and on the other, domestic beings who were naturally suited to communicating with children and the poor, and helping men, meant that women were channelled into particular roles, and away from the most prestigious roles in the most scholarly museums.

Women recognised the value of having 'niches' within museums, in the same way as did women in museums in the USA; they could build on work as popular communicators in science, and could assert expertise which men did not have. However, women also took on more 'masculine' roles in a covert way (and certainly without recognition or financial reward). They were thus poised between embracing and developing a particular set of 'feminine' roles and competences within museums, and resisting this gendering of museum work which sometimes served to ghettoise them. Their self-presentation and strategies within the museum were designed to maintain a fluid identity which could take advantage of any possibility. As we will see in subsequent chapters, such fluidity was characteristic of women outside, as well as inside, the museum.

Notes

1 Women museum workers were regarded as 'a bargain' by the US museum director John Cotton Dana in 1928: Lianne McTavish, *Defining the Modern Museum* (Toronto: University of Toronto Press 2013), p. 147.

2 P. N. Wyse Jackson and M. E. Spencer Jones, 'The quiet workforce: the various roles of women in geological and natural history museums during the early to mid-1900s', in C. V. Burek and B. Higgs (eds), *The Role of Women in the History of Geology*, Geological Society, London, Special Publications 281 (2007), pp. 97–113; Ezra Shales, *Made in Newark, Cultivating Industrial Arts and Civic Identity in the Progressive Era* (New Brunswick, NJ: Rivergate Books 2010), p. 84.

3 Madsen-Brooks uses feminist standpoint theory to some extent in her article, for this very reason. However, she concludes that it is of limited use in examining women working in museums; but usefully stresses that women's focus on education and community engagement was not inherently 'feminine', but produced by their standpoint. I value the emphasis on working from women's lives, and considering socially produced aptitudes, interests and practices that standpoint theory suggests, while not pursuing the theory more fully. Leslie Madsen-Brooks, 'Challenging science as usual: women's participation in American natural history museum work, 1870–1950', *Journal of Women's History* 21: 2 (2009), pp. 13–14; Sandra Harding, *Whose Science? Whose Knowledge? Thinking from Women's Lives* (Ithaca, NY: Cornell University Press 1991), pp. 14, 19–50.

4 Kate Hill, *Culture and Class in English Public Museums 1850–1914* (Aldershot: Ashgate 2005), chapter 4; Samuel J. M. M. Alberti, *Nature and Culture, Objects, Disciplines and the Manchester Museum* (Manchester: Manchester University Press 2009), chapter 2.

5 In the 1980s, Perkin placed this process as stemming from the 1880s; he also saw professionalisation as a fundamentally meritocratic process which offered a much improved measure of equality to women. This has been refined and contested since by studies of particular professions and their gendering, most fully probably in science, but history, medicine and art among others have also been examined. Harold Perkin, *The Rise of Professional Society: England since 1880* (London: Routledge 1989); Samuel J. M. M. Alberti, 'Amateurs and professionals

in one county: biology and natural history in later Victorian Yorkshire', *Journal of the History of Biology* 34 (2001), pp. 115–147; James Mussell, 'Private practices and public knowledge: science, professionalisation and gender in the late nineteenth century', *Nineteenth-Century Gender Studies* 5: 2 (2009), online, available at www.ncgsjournal.com/issue52/mussell.htm, accessed 22 October 2012; Heather Ellis, 'Knowledge, character and professionalisation in nineteenth-century British science', *History of Education* 43: 6 (2014), pp. 777–792; Philippa Levine, *The Amateur and the Professional: Antiquarians, Historians and Archaeologists in Victorian England 1838–1886* (Cambridge: Cambridge University Press 1986); S. E. D. Shortt, 'Physicians, science and status: issues in the professionalisation of Anglo-American medicine in the nineteenth century', *Medical History* 27: 1 (1983), pp. 51–68; Gordon Fyfe, 'Auditing the RA: official discourse and the nineteenth-century Royal Academy', in Rafael Cardoso Denis and Colin Trodd (eds), *Art and the Academy in the Nineteenth Century* (Manchester: Manchester University Press 2000), pp. 117–130.

6 D. E. Allen, *The Naturalist in Britain: A Social History* (Princeton, NJ: Princeton University Press 1976), pp. 113, 124, 150–152; Ann B. Shteir, *Cultivating Women, Cultivating Science: Flora's Daughters and Botany in England 1760–1860* (Baltimore, MD: Johns Hopkins University Press 1999).

7 This is argued by Jordanna Bailkin, *The Culture of Property: The Crisis of Liberalism in Modern Britain* (Chicago, IL: University of Chicago Press 2004).

8 Geoffrey Lewis, *For Instruction and Recreation: A Centenary History of the Museums Association* (London: Quiller Press 1989).

9 The later development of competing gendered visions of the museum professional in Canada has been examined by Lianne McTavish. In her analysis, it was not so much that professionalisation excluded women from museums, as that radically different masculine and feminine museum professionalisms developed, and certainly before the 1950s, both had institutional bases and significant support. McTavish, *Defining the Modern Museum*, chapter 5.

10 Women were involved in laboratory work as Claire Jones has shown, but the characterisation of such work as masculine was much more marked than museum work. Claire G. Jones, *Femininity, Mathematics and Science, c.1880–1914* (Basingstoke: Palgrave Macmillan 2009), esp. chapter 5.

11 Gillian Sutherland, *In Search of the New Woman* (Cambridge: Cambridge University Press 2015), p. 114.

12 Shteir, *Cultivating Women*, p. 165; B. T. Gates and A. B. Shteir (eds), *Natural Eloquence: Women Reinscribe Science* (Madison, WI: University of Wisconsin Press 1997), pp. 8–9.

13 Shteir, *Cultivating Women*, p. 237; B. T. Gates, 'Those who drew and those who wrote: women and Victorian popular science illustration', in A. B. Shteir and B. Lightman (eds), *Figuring It Out: Science, Gender and Visual Culture* (Hanover, NH: Dartmouth College Press 2006), p. 193.

14 Bernard Lightman, 'Depicting nature', defining roles: the gender politics of Victorian illustration' in A. B. Shteir and B. Lightman (eds), *Figuring It Out: Science, Gender and Visual Culture* (Hanover, NH: Dartmouth College Press 2006) pp. 226–232.

15 Alberti, *Nature and Culture*, chapter 5.

16 There is a wide and growing literature on the history of English museums. On local museums see Hill, *Culture and Class*; on university museums see both Alberti, *Nature and Culture*, and Chris Gosden and Frances Larson, *Knowing Things: Exploring the Collections at the Pitt Rivers Museum 1884–1945* (Oxford: Oxford University Press 2007). Much work on national museums has tended to the chronicle or even celebration, but on the British Museum see M. Caygill and J. Cherry (eds), *A. W. Franks: Nineteenth-Century Collecting and the British Museum* (London: British Museum Press 1997) and Stephanie Moser, *Wondrous Curiosities: Ancient Egypt at the British Museum* (Chicago, IL: University of Chicago Press 2006).

17 Jordanna Bailkin, *The Culture of Property: The Crisis of Liberalism in Modern Britain* (Chicago, IL: University of Chicago Press 2004), p. 131.

18 Lewis, *For Instruction and Recreation*, p. 9.

19 McTavish, though, suggests that in the mid-twentieth century at least, the AAM enshrined 'masculine' ideas about the ideal curator, based on specialist knowledge, not the ability to communicate widely. *Defining the Modern Museum*, p. 151.

20 Alberti, 'Amateurs and professionals', pp. 115–147; Mussell, 'Private practices'; Kate Hill, '"He knows me … but not at the museum": women, natural history collecting and museums, 1880–1914', in S. Dudley, A. Barnes, J. Binnie, J. Petrov and J. Walklate (eds), *Narrating Objects, Collecting Stories* (Abingdon: Routledge 2012).

21 Harding, *Whose Science?*; David Allen, 'The women members of the Botanical Society of London, 1836–1856', *British Journal for the History of Science* 13 (1980), pp. 240–252.

22 Wyse Jackson and Spencer Jones, 'The quiet workforce', p. 98.

23 Sally Gregory Kohlstedt, 'Innovative niche scientists: women's role in reframing North American museums, 1880–1930', *Centaurus* 55: 2 (2013), 153–174; Madsen-Brooks, 'Challenging science as usual', pp. 11–38.

24 Kohlstedt, 'Innovative niche scientists', pp. 164–166.

25 On Delia Griffin, see Kohlstedt, 'Innovative niche scientists'; Geoffrey Lewis, *For Instruction and Recreation: A Centenary History of the Museums Association* (London: Quiller Press 1989), pp. 1–13; Mrs Tubbs, 'The relation of museums to elementary education', *Proceedings of the Museums Association* 8 (1897), 69–74; Mrs Roesler, 'The work of an instructor in the American Museum of Natural History', *Museums Journal* 8: 10 (1909), pp. 303–313; Delia Griffin, 'The Children's Museum of Boston, USA', *Museums Journal* 14: 6 (1914), pp. 201–204.

26 Allen, in 'The women members', pp. 247–249, suggests that the Botanical Society was extremely unusual in being so open to women members compared to other societies. See also Hill, '"He knows me"'.

27 Kohlstedt, 'Innovative niche scientists'; Lewis, *For Instruction and Recreation* pp. 23–24.

28 Another way in which the American and British contexts differed was in the prevalence of women's auxiliary or volunteer groups which in both the USA and Canada contributed substantial amounts of fundraising and other assistance; such groups were more or less completely absent in Britain. Kohlstedt, 'Innovative niche scientists'; Ann Whitelaw, 'Women, museums and the problem of biography', in Kate Hill

(ed.), *Museums and Biographies: Stories, Objects, Identities* (Woodbridge: Boydell and Brewer 2012).

29 'Nature study museum', St George in the East Church, available at www.stgite.org. uk/naturesstudy.html, accessed 9 September 2011; Beatrice Harraden, 'Obituary, Kate Marion Hall', *Proceedings of the Linnaean Society of London*, 130th Session, 1917–1918 (1918), pp. 61–63; London County Council, *Annual Report of Horniman Museum 1908* (London 1909).

30 Seth Koven, 'Barnett, Samuel Augustus (1844–1913)', *Oxford Dictionary of National Biography* (Oxford: Oxford University Press 2004), online, available at www. oxforddnb.com/view/article/30612, accessed 23 September 2011.

31 Kate M. Hall, 'The smallest museum', *Museums Journal* 1: 2 (1901), pp. 38–45.

32 Harraden, 'Obituary'.

33 See Chapter 7 for more discussion of the Toynbee Hall circle, its gendering, and its effect on museum development.

34 Cf. V. Turner, 'The factors affecting women's success in museum careers', *Journal of Conservation and Museum Studies* 8 (2002).

35 Anon., 'News: Miss Grace Wigglesworth', *Nature* 154 (August 1944), p. 234; Mabel Tylecote, *The Education of Women at Manchester University 1883–1933* (Manchester: Manchester University Press 1941).

36 Samuel J. M. M. Alberti, *Nature and Culture, Objects, Disciplines and the Manchester Museum* (Manchester: Manchester University Press 2009), p. 68; Max Mallowan, 'Murray, Margaret Alice (1863–1963), Egyptologist and folklorist', rev. R. S. Simpson, *Oxford Dictionary of National Biography* (Oxford: Oxford University Press 2004), online, available at http://oxforddnb.com/view/article/35169, accessed 14 October 2011. Murray was also a donor to museums, giving modern Egyptian and Indian objects to the Pitt Rivers Museum, and after our period, when her interest in folklore and witchcraft was developing, she also gave them a 'witch in a bottle'. Alison Petch, 'Margaret Murray', The Other Within, online, available at http:// england.prm.ox.ac.uk/englishness-Margaret-Murray.html, accessed 14 October 2011. It should be noted that Murray did not in fact have any formal academic qualifications, though she had studied under Flinders Petrie at UCL; he had asked her to start teaching beginners' Egyptian hieroglyphics before she had finished her degree: Margaret Murray, *My First Hundred Years* (London: William Kimber 1963). See also Chapter 6.

37 Kathleen Sheppard, 'Margaret Alice Murray and archaeological training in the classroom', in William Carruthers (ed.), *Histories of Egyptology: Interdisciplinary Measures* (London: Routledge 2014), pp. 123–125.

38 Alberti, *Nature and Culture*, p. 36.

39 L. A. Hall, 'Stopes, Marie Charlotte Carmichael (1880–1958)', *Oxford Dictionary of National Biography* (Oxford: Oxford University Press 2004), online, available at www. oxforddnb.com/view/article/36323, accessed 9 September 2011.

40 Carol Dyhouse, *No Distinction of Sex? Women in British Universities 1870–1939* (London: UCL Press 1995); Tylecote, *Education of Women*, chapter 1.

41 Tylecote, *Education of Women*, chapter 1.

42 Tylecote, *Education of Women*, p. 33; see also Peter McNiven, 'Manchester University archive collections in the John Rylands University Library of Manchester', *Bulletin of the John Rylands Library* 71: 2 (1989), pp. 205–226, p. 211.

43 Tylecote, *Education of Women*, p. 96.

44 Wyse Jackson and Spencer Jones, 'The quiet workforce', p. 101. Goodyear held a BSc in Geology from UCL, graduating in 1903. After the war she held a number of positions at UCL. M. Ogilvie and J. Harvey (eds), *Biographical Dictionary of Women in Science* (London: Routledge 2000), pp. 1051–1052.

45 Madsen-Brooks, 'Challenging science as usual', pp. 12, 13. On the importance or neglect of museums in anthropology and archaeology, see chapter 6.

46 Dyhouse, *No Distinction of Sex?*, p. 12; Murray, *My First Hundred Years*, chapter 9: University College.

47 Wyse Jackson and Spencer Jones, 'The quiet workforce', pp. 102–103.

48 Wyse Jackson and Spencer Jones, 'The quiet workforce', p. 107; K. Shindler, 'Bate, Dorothea Minola Alice (1878–1951), palaeontologist', *Oxford Dictionary of National Biography*, Oxford: Oxford University Press 2004), online, available at www.oxforddnb.com/view/article/67163, accessed 9 September 2011.

49 This shows clear parallels with women's experience of working in higher education. Again, Margaret Murray's autobiography shows how 'assisting' professors was not only considered suitable for women, but was shunned by more ambitious men who understood how it might adversely affect their career: Murray, *My First Hundred Years*, p. 153. There is evidence, though, to suggest that career-minded women might start with jobs which might be shunned by men, and from them move into academic posts: Dyhouse, *No Distinction of Sex?*, p. 135.

50 Madsen-Brooks, 'Challenging science as usual', p. 14; Kohlstedt, 'Innovative niche scientists'.

51 Madsen-Brooks, 'Challenging science as usual', p. 12.

52 This is not quite the same as the educational roles explored by Kohlstedt but the principle, that occupying a niche role is not simply a question of exclusion from the key roles, but offers opportunities to negotiate new ways of doing things, is very similar. Kohlstedt, 'Innovative niche scientists'.

53 This is largely because men were assumed to be supporting a large family on their earnings while working women were presumed to be single. Nevertheless, the disparity between pay for male and female professionals is startling. For wages for agricultural and other labourers, see Arthur L. Bowley, *Wages in the United Kingdom in the Nineteenth Century* (Cambridge: Cambridge University Press 1900); on women's pay in education, see Kathryn Hughes, *The Victorian Governess* (Rio Grande, OH: Hambledon Press 1993) p. 199.

54 Sheffield Museum, Minutes of the Museum Sub-Committee, 5 December 1896.

55 Samuel J. M. M. Alberti, 'Field, lab and museum: the practice and the place of Life Science in Yorkshire, 1870–1904' (unpublished PhD thesis, University of Sheffield 2000)', pp. 79–80.

56 See, for example, Sheffield Museum, Minutes of the Museum Sub-Committee, 16 May 1901.

57 Census for England 1891, online, available at www.ancestry.co.uk, accessed 9 September 2011.

58 C. Nördlinger, 'Visit to Miss Mestorf, directress of Schleswig-Holstein Museum of National Antiquities', *Proceedings of the Museums Association* 7 (1896), 132–138.

59 Bailkin, *Culture of Property*, p. 130.

60 Hill, *Culture and Class*, p. 64.

61 Hill, *Culture and Class*, p. 65; census records for 1861 and 1871, online, available at ancestry.co.uk, accessed 6 April 2012.

62 M. A. Lower, and R. Chapman, 'The Antiquities Preserved in the Museum of Lewes Castle', *Sussex Archaeological Collections* 18 (1866), 60–73; Thomas Sutton, 'The Library and Museums', *Sussex Archaeological Collections* 85 (1946).

63 Brighton Public Library, Museums and Art Galleries, *Annual Report of the Director for the Year ending 1906*, Brighton 1906; Sheffield Council, Minutes of the Museum Sub-Committee, 17 April 1902.

64 Alberti, *Nature and Culture*, figure 2.6, p. 48.

65 Nördlinger, 'Visit to Miss Mestorf'.

66 Bailkin, *Culture of Property*, p. 131.

67 Nördlinger, 'Visit to Miss Mestorf'.

68 Bailkin, *Culture of Property*, p. 132.

69 See, for example, National Portrait Gallery Heinz Archive and Library, NPG82/2/2 Warding and Security Staff Duty Reports, Report 18 November 1909.

70 Shales, *Made in Newark*, pp. 73–74.

71 Wyse Jackson and Spencer Jones, 'The quiet workforce', pp. 99–100.

72 Hill, *Culture and Class*, pp. 44, 62–63, 75.

73 Manchester Museum, *Annual Report 1902–3* (Manchester: Cornish 1903).

74 Manchester Museum, *Annual Reports 1911–12, 1912–13* (Manchester: Cornish 1912, 1913); City and County of Bristol, *Report of the Museum Committee 1910–1911* (Bristol 1911).

75 Shteir, *Cultivating Women*, pp. 158–159.

76 Manchester Museum, *Annual Reports 1911–12, 1912–13* (Manchester: Cornish 1912, 1913); City and County of Bristol, *Report of the Museum Committee 1910–1911* (Bristol 1911).

77 Steven J. Plunkett, 'Layard, Nina Frances (1853–1935)', *Oxford Dictionary of National Biography*, Oxford: Oxford University Press, 2004; online edn, January 2008, www.oxforddnb.com.proxy.library.lincoln.ac.uk/view/article/58931, accessed 11 November 2013.

78 S. J. Plunkett, 'Correspondence of Nina Frances Layard (1853–1935), transcribed and collected by Steven J. Plunkett', 1992/3, typescript at Ipswich Museum.

79 See Ipswich Corporation Museum Accessions Register and Ipswich Corporation Museum Minute Books for these years. See also Letters between E. Ray Lankester (of the BM (NH)) and Nina Layard, October 1907–July 1908, S. J. Plunkett, 'Correspondence of Nina Frances Layard (1853–1935) transcribed and collected by Steven J. Plunkett' 1992/3, Ipswich Museum. On 29 July 1908, Lankester wrote, 'I am astonished to hear that Mr Woolnough [the curator] has been allowed to even enter the room ... except as one of the general public'.

80 Bristol Museum and Library, *Report of Proceedings at the Annual Meeting, 1880* (Bristol 1881).

81 City and Council of Bristol, *Report of the Museum Committee, 1906–7* (Bristol 1907).

82 Manchester Museum, *Annual Report 1890–94, 1898–9, 1902–3, 1910–11, 1912–13* (Manchester: Cornish 1895–1913).

83 Manchester Museum, *Annual Report 1906–7, 1910–11* (Manchester: Cornish 1907 and 1911); Alberti, *Nature and Culture*, pp. 40, 48.

84 Wigglesworth did have academic qualifications, but the striking thing about her career is the way that following academic study she spent a number of years becoming more fully connected to the museum through voluntary means before achieving a paid position. Anon., 'Miss Grace Wigglesworth', *Nature* 154 (1944), p. 234.

85 London County Council, *Eighth Annual Report of the Horniman Museum, 1909* (London 1910); London County Council, *Eleventh Annual Report of the Horniman Museum, 1912* (London 1913).

86 A. E. Coombes, *Reinventing Africa: Museums, Material Culture and Popular Imagination in Late Victorian and Edwardian England* (New Haven, CT and London: Yale University Press 1994), pp. 113–117.

87 Some other museums which focused primarily on a popular, working-class audience, and where women were involved in lecturing to an audience which was not thought to be suitable for a scholarly approach, are considered in Chapter 7.

88 See the discussion recorded at the end of Kate M. Hall, 'The smallest museum', *Museums Journal* 1: 2 (1901), p. 45.

89 Bailkin, *Culture of Property*, p. 132.

2

Outside the museum: women as donors and vendors

While Chapter 1 examined women who established some sort of place inside the museum institution, this chapter examines women whose relationships with museums were much more accidental or incidental; women who would not necessarily have thought of themselves as part of a museum, but who were nevertheless important for museum development. They did not have an insider role at a museum, and their relationship with museums tended to happen through an intermediary or at a remove. Primarily, in fact, this chapter deals with women who made a small donation or donations to a museum during the late Victorian or Edwardian period, and women who sold objects to museums during the same period.

I chose to investigate women donors because our understanding of museums has been hugely enhanced in recent years by the concept of the distributed museum. Museums cannot be thought of as consisting just of the physical building and the people who work within it. Rather, as Gosden and Larson have suggested, museums consist of a set of relationships linking people, objects and institutions, and these relationships spread out in a network across the world.[1] In this formulation, relationships between people and travelling objects create agency; museums no longer seem like institutions formed and directed by curators, but rather ones whose meaning comes from the specific ways in which objects are delivered into the museum and particular people are endowed with the authority to explain certain objects. Similarly, Byrne *et al.* insist that museums are simultaneously material and social assemblages, so that to understand the museum object, we have to understand the whole complex network of people through whose actions the object came to be a museum object; and equally, that the network of people has no meaning without the agency of the objects shaping them. Moreover, they also show that in such networks, useful analysis works from the assumption that there are no natural starting places, or hierarchies, within the net-work.[2] Thus, and despite the titles of my chapters, the idea of museums having an 'inside' and an 'outside' dissolves on a closer view; there are rather different degrees of density of involvement in museum networks.

These conceptualisations of museums as dispersed people–object networks mean that we can see women's relationships with, and agency in, museums more clearly than if we focus only on the more visible agents such as curators. Women as donors or vendors of small collections or sin-gle objects did, I argue, exert influence in museums, and even when they did not set out to change museums, their cumulative actions did. And this change was primarily because their relationships with objects and people, formed through feminine social practices, changed the mean-ings of museum objects. Conversely, women's relationships with objects which changed status to become museum objects changed women them-selves, allowing them to grow in confidence and assert the value of the feminine domestic in a wider public setting.

This chapter and the next, therefore, are focused on women's dona-tions and sales to museums, based on an analysis of the acquisition records of a number of museums between 1880 and 1914.[3] Although, as I have said, museums are important because they are simultaneously social and material assemblages, for the sake of coherence I have divided my analysis between two chapters. The next chapter focuses on the material assemblages: the objects they donated, considered as 'women's objects', and the effect they may have had on museums. However, this one focuses on the *social* assemblages: the women donors and vendors, who they were, what motivations they had for, and what the effects were of, their donation. It argues that women donors worked to make domes-tically based social networks visible in the museum; and that the domes-tic material strategies identified by Hamlett, whereby women used exchanges of objects to mark relationships, assert their position within the family, and pursue emotional goals, were also thereby visible among donors, and made public. The two chapters are therefore an examination of the ways in which particular people–object–museum networks devel-oped, focusing as much as possible on women who donated a few, usu-ally low value, objects, and who are not as well known as major donors often became.[4]

There is very little surviving evidence about most donations except a name, the donation itself, and sometimes an address. This encourages a focus on the minority of important donors who gave so much that they often established a close relationship with curators, and their letters and other documentation thus survive. Equally, these are often the women for whom biographical information is relatively easy to find. However, feminist scholars argue convincingly that such an approach can obscure rather than illuminate women's particular concerns and approaches: it echoes rather a male approach to biography which valorises the individual and the individual's achievements.[5] A methodology which seeks to do justice to women's collective engagement with museums has to find a way adequately to represent and account for a broad mass of 'average' donors. Collective, not individual, biography is seen as an important approach for women's history insofar as it can recover women's relationships: networks, rather than isolated individuals.[6]

I try, therefore, to uncover the donating patterns of the majority of women donors. By examining who gave to museums, and in what sorts of ways they did so, we can start to ask the following questions: what were the social patterns underlying women's donations to museums? What relationships were created and effaced by such donations, both for women and museums? How did donating allow women to perform particular roles, and were these gendered? And what 'work' did women's donations do for them? I argue that very distinctive relationships and strategies emerge through women's donations; women's domestic and familial networks were brought into public view. The kinds of material strategies that historians have established women used within the home were transferred to the museum through the mechanisms of donation and selling. Moreover, such material strategies have been linked to the development of the women's movement towards the end of the nineteenth century; women's confidence was both boosted by and reflected in their increasing assertiveness about their control of the material and familial networks of the home. Through donation, women pushed the feminine domestic into the public, and asserted a wider national value for familial emotions and practices.

Donating patterns

In order to understand women's donating patterns, I collected all instances of women donors from the accession registers and annual reports of a number of museums between 1880 and 1914. The museums studied represent only a sample of those in existence in the period, but cover municipal, university, national and voluntary society museums of different sizes, as well as a geographical area from Brighton to Sunderland, Ipswich to Bristol.[7] The vast majority of women donors to museums were and remain just a name in the accession book of the museum. Women were universally recorded with their title of Miss or Mrs (occasionally

Lady), so in many cases we have no first name, or only an initial, or their husband's name. Some museums, but not all, recorded an address, or at least a location, for the donor, which allows a small amount of biographical information to be recovered. Any attempt to analyse the patterns of women as donors is complicated by the varied practices of recording donations; at Sunderland Museum the stock book contains entries such as 'some shells' and 'bottle of reptiles', and elsewhere imprecise quantification such as 'large collection of …' can be found.[8] Moreover, where annual reports are the main source of information, they tended to roll up all donations in the course of a year into one record, while accession registers detail donations separately even if they were only a week apart. In fine art, each object donated was treated as a separate donation, while natural historical donations tend to be recorded lumped together as a collection.

Women were always in a small minority among donors, but the proportion of women did vary between museums. Some museums were a more exclusively masculine environment, whereas others were more open to contributions from anyone. Voluntary society museums appear to have had the smallest proportion of women donors; at Whitby, there were years at a stretch with no female donors at all, reflecting the masculine nature of such societies.[9] Meanwhile at Liverpool Museum, women donors formed only 4.5 per cent of the total number of donors between 1880 and 1910, with the highest level of 8 per cent being reached in 1910; and at the Harris Museum in Preston, they formed just under 13 per cent.[10] There are several indications that university museums were among the most open to women in a variety of ways. While in many cases only 10 per cent or fewer of museums donors were women, at the Pitt Rivers Museum this figure was 16 per cent (although this figure includes donations up to 1939).[11] At Manchester Museum, more women made repeat donations than elsewhere (and see Chapter 1 for a discussion of women working at that museum). Of seventy-six donors at Sunderland Museum, only ten made more than one donation (and none made more than two) (13 per cent), but at Manchester, out of 166 women donors, thirty-three made more than one donation (20 per cent), and of these, five gave more than four times.

With small numbers (seventy-seven in total at the Harris, for example), the usefulness of these statistics is limited, but it is certainly the case that women were a small minority of donors. And it is not always possible to say that women donors increased as a percentage over time. As suggested by the figures of the Pitt Rivers Museum and Liverpool Museum, this was often the case, but in other instances, women donors were at their highest level around the years the museum opened, and declined thereafter. In Sunderland, for example, there were twenty-four women donors in the 1880s, nineteen in the 1890s, and twenty-three in the first decade of the twentieth century, during which period donations as a whole increased slightly.[12] Thus, although women were always a small proportion of donors, museums varied in the extent to which women contributed to them. Some museums were identified with an old-fashioned masculine scientific milieu, whereas others were seen as, and probably were, clearly more progressive in their openness and organisation.

It is also clear that most women made only one donation to a museum, with no more than 20 per cent making repeat donations anywhere. Among men, too, repeat donation was not the norm, though less noticeably so: work on the Pitt Rivers Museum shows that around 50 per cent of donors gave only one object, and 95 per cent gave fewer than 100 objects, although we do not know in how many instalments.[13] Frequency of donation is a better measure of the significance of donors to museums, and of their relationship with museums, than simply number of objects given. As Chris Wingfield says, making the same point, 'Underlying apparently similarly sized collections can be various patterns of activity that might indicate quite different underlying relationships', and he proposes instead the idea of 'acquisition events', individual acts of acquisition.[14] Although in the records I have studied, there are a few instances of collectors donating or bequeathing their entire large collection in one go, in most cases important collectors made significant donations over time as well as giving their 'main' collection before or after death. While few donors made more than one donation, the ones who did, and particularly the ones who gave four or more times, clearly built a relationship with the museum staff and committee, which could be parlayed into a voluntary or paid position at the museum. An even smaller number donated to more than one museum, and these women are almost all notable figures in their field. Wingfield also found that those individuals who had the strongest relationships with a museum were not only involved in donation, but in sales, loans and swaps with the museum as well.[15] My study confirms this, and I will return to women who sold objects to museums later in this chapter. Wingfield's point here is that the more contact individuals had with a museum, the more they were able to influence the formation of that museum; they were less 'outside', and more 'inside' the museum.[16] It is, therefore, important to analyse the density of women's donating relationships to museums, and most women, it seems, had sparse donating relationships and were thus definitively 'outside' museums.

A significant comparative finding from the Pitt Rivers Museum is that although women formed 20 per cent of donors between 1880 and 1939, in most categories of donor (especially field collector, where the donor acquires the object from its original context themselves, rather than at second- or third-hand), they formed less than this; but in the category of 'other owner and donor', women formed a much more substantial 45 per cent.[17] In other words, women were much more likely to donate objects someone else had originally acquired and of which they had subsequently become secondary owners. This is, perhaps, not surprising, particularly for the Pitt Rivers Museum, where a substantial proportion of objects was acquired in the field in distant countries. But it holds true more widely that women were less able to access directly the objects wanted by museums. However, as we shall see below, women were nevertheless creative and assertive in their donation of these second-hand objects.

There was no clear preponderance of either married or unmarried female donors in my study, and no discernible change following the Married Women's Property Acts (MWPA).[18] Marital status therefore does not appear to have affected either women's economic power to acquire and assert ownership of objects, or the propriety of their donating to public institutions. However, there are indications that women might seek to disguise their identities when donating to museums – several donations came from 'a lady'.[19] There are also a number of cases where women donated through a male intermediary, either anonymously ('a lady per Mr XXX') or by name; there were also women donating through female intermediaries, and a very few men donating through women, but women through men is the predominant form.[20] These together suggest that there was a sense that the public donation of objects to a public museum was something that women should avoid if possible. Clearly, this sense was not very strong, and not felt by many women (at least among donors; we have no way of knowing what non-donating women thought).[21]

Where a clear occupation or other indicator of social status is given, the range is extremely wide. There were a large number of titled donors, donating to most of the museums.[22] It is unsurprising that in areas where fashion and connoisseurship could create very high prices, those who had collections or objects important enough to be accepted by museums would be from social elites.[23] There was no urban bias, as many of the donors lived in rural areas, in what might be termed the 'catchment area' of civic museums. However, there was a solid base in the middle-class suburbs of towns, among a professional group, and in the urban elites of the period, whose menfolk were instrumental in many initiatives of a new urban culture. These were families like the Gurneys in Norwich, the Ransomes in Ipswich, and the Frys in Bristol, who could be relied upon to provide donors to the local museum.[24] These were the same people behind the foundation and growth of municipal museums, and this is reflected in the fact that a large number of female donors were the wives or daughters of museum committee members, such as the Misses Bunce and Mrs Feeney in Birmingham, and Mrs Robson in Ipswich.[25] Insofar as religion can be established, there were a disproportionate number of Quakers, such as the Ransomes, the Gurneys and the Frys, and the wives and daughters of 'reverends' of unknown denominations were also heavily represented, probably reflecting the substantial involvement of clergymen in natural history and antiquarian collecting. There was also an over-representation of groups who had more opportunities than most to acquire objects which might be of interest: wives of diplomats, colonial administrators, military families, and missionaries.[26] A nurse was identified by occupation, but this is the only woman whose occupation is given, apart from some of those whose career was closely linked to their collecting and donating activities, considered in more detail below.[27] Additionally, there were some donors whose occupation is known, such as Dorothea Beale, the educationalist and schoolmistress, at Cheltenham, and Ellen Terry, the actress, at Brighton.[28] Broadly speaking, therefore, women donors reflected the social hierarchy visible in male involvement in museums, especially municipal ones, where the civic elite attempted to use museums as a space for display and legitimation.

I focus in this chapter on the relationships underlying women's donations, and the extent to which they are transcribed into the museum; they reveal the ways in which donation was affected by and in turn created women's social networks, and in so doing uncover the ways in which private and public were entwined in women's relationships with museums and materiality.

Women as part of a couple donation

The most basic fact of women's private existence was their family relationships, which exerted an extremely powerful effect on their donation patterns. Women enacted family relationships in public, rejecting the individualist stance of the male public figure. This is most notable with their marital relationship. Women often donated with their husbands, and it is important to state at the outset that it is hard to unpick women's specific contributions to these donations from the accession register. The actual practices underlying and producing such donations are almost impossible to reconstruct; official documentation tends to understand the contributions of a husband and wife to a joint collection through the lens of pre-existing understandings of male and female collecting, assuming the man was the instigator and leading figure in the partnership.[29] Women certainly had a range of levels of involvement in the acquisition and donation of these collections, from donations initiated by the husband, to genuine joint projects, and those where the wife was the driving force. And the ownership of collections was not always straightforward; were they owned jointly, or by the husband or the wife, or, in practice, by the entire household in an undifferentiated way?

This is indicated by the example of Mrs Smith, who appears in the records of the BM(NH). She collected fossils in the mid-nineteenth century, buying from quarrymen and other collectors but also collecting herself. After her death, her collection passed to her daughter, but both the daughter and daughter's husband also died fairly quickly, leaving the collection in the hands of his second wife (Mrs Smith's son-in-law's second wife, that is), who after about a year sold most of it to the BM. However, her husband had bequeathed a small part of it to another museum, and the second wife kept another part of the collection. She also kept the catalogue for another fourteen years.[30] This shows that ownership of such collections, within a household, was fluid. Within the home, collections and parts of collections moved between spaces and display furniture, and among family members.[31] Thus it will never be possible to be definitive about whether a donation has come primarily from a man or a woman, or jointly from a couple, and probably many women collectors are unrecorded in their husbands' donations. Some of these donations can, therefore, best be thought of as coming from a household, rather than from specific individuals.

In some cases, collecting and donating was a shared habit between husband and wife. Possibly the most prominent example of this is the Schreibers, Lady Charlotte and her younger second husband Charles (who will be discussed more fully in Chapter 5). Of them, it has been said, 'collecting [ceramics] … was a partnership which enhanced and gave meaning to their relationship', although evidence suggests that it was definitely instigated, at least, by Lady Charlotte.[32] Even when donations were not recorded in the name of both husband and wife, it was common for women donors' husbands also to be recorded as donors of separate items. Sometimes these were similar donations, but on other occasions they were not; the collecting habit was shared, but not the specific interest.

There appears to be a neat demarcation between the donations of General and Mrs MacNair to Ipswich Museum in 1909–10, though they clearly have a similar source. He gave Indian buffalo horns shot by himself; she gave a collection of dried specimens of Indian ferns. The traces of a life in India are clear; these traces suggest gender-differentiated pastimes undertaken while there.[33] On the other hand, it is hard to reconstruct the relationship and motivations of Mr and Mrs Vieweg, who both donated objects to the Horniman Museum in 1898. Mr Vieweg donated objects from China, India and Burma, which is suggestive perhaps of a career spent in Asia; but Mrs Vieweg gave a German Meerschaum pipe.[34] For both, these were their only donations. Such a bald record gives little away, but suggests that a collecting/donating husband may have encouraged the same for his wife, more than other men.

A particularly significant subsection of husband and wife donors consisted of curators and their wives. Curators were, in many cases during this period, prolific donors to their own museums, as this often represented their best hope of developing a strategic acquisitions policy. Their wives often helped in this aim, though the extent of this involvement varied. Montagu Browne, the curator of Leicester Museum, gave an enormous number of donations to the museum, often in natural history, but also in archaeology.[35] His wife made few donations: on the same day they both gave reed warblers' nests and eggs, clearly the result of a joint outing.[36] It is equally clear, however, that she was not in the habit of collecting with her husband, who undertook hunting trips and opened up barrows to help supply his museum. Mrs Quick, the wife of the curator of the Horniman Museum, made just one donation, an old blackware teapot, which was later sold.[37] Mrs Boyd Dawkins, wife of William Boyd Dawkins (knighted in 1919) who was the curator of the Manchester Museum, donated a hornet's nest and sixty-eight bird skins in 1908, at the time her husband retired (though he continued to sit on the Museum Committee). Mrs C. H. Read, whose husband was the keeper of British and medieval antiquities and ethnography at the BM between 1896 and 1921, gave one box from New Zealand.[38]

Other wives were more active. Mrs Toms, the wife of the curator of Brighton Museum and Art Gallery, gave a number of donations between 1906 and 1910, covering local history and archaeology, and anthropology.[39] Mrs Toms, formerly the French maid of Lady Pitt Rivers, was more actively involved in collecting work with her husband; a series of flint implements which was arranged for display in 1905 was described as found 'by Mr and Mrs H. S. Toms', and she co-authored at least one article with her husband for *Sussex Archaeological Collections*, the proceedings of the Sussex Archaeological Society.[40] The Baroness von Hügel, wife of Anatole von Hügel, first curator of the Museum of Archaeology at the University of Cambridge (later the Museum of Archaeology and Anthropology), was an even more prolific donor, giving a range of objects including textiles and decorative objects from India, and Roman and British antiquities.[41] Additionally, her brother R. E. Froude and a Miss M. E. Froude, who may have been her sister (she was a niece of the historian James Froude), were also significant donors to the museum.[42] Anna Tylor, who was the wife of Edward Burnett Tylor, the keeper of the Oxford University Museum of Natural History from 1882 to 1910, always had a close interest in her husband's work; she attended many of his lectures, and at one of these it was said 'she sat in the front row, watchful for confusion among the specimens. "Oh, Edward dear" she would say, "last time, you said that one was neolithic." But she did not prevent the conflagration when he demonstrated the fire drill, and his long beard became entangled with the bow.'[43] She was, like her husband, a member of the Folklore Society. She donated 246 objects to the Pitt Rivers Museum, just behind E. B. Tylor's total of 293; however, she was not a frequent donor and the objects were given in a relatively small number of 'acquisition events'.[44] This is connected to the fact that, apparently unlike Baroness von Hügel, she was not the field collector of many of these objects; in one case, that of the so-called witches' ladder (see Figure 4), E. B. Tylor collected the object and researched its provenance, but Mrs Tylor donated it in 1911. This was a year after her husband's retirement, at a time when he was becoming confused; one may speculate that she donated it to materialise an expertise which was disappearing from the man himself, to safeguard his reputation.[45] The theme of wives and widows donating as a form of reputation management on their husbands' behalf is one to which I will return.

Of course, curating was a new and developing profession, and the role of curators' wives was as unclear as many other issues. Being able to accommodate unusual objects around the house, as well as to converse with and entertain other museum staff and researchers, was certainly important for curators' wives. Sharing interests and being supportive was evidently thought to be an important element of marriage for these donors, as well as reflecting the fact that such couples may have met through shared interests in natural history, anthropology or archaeology, and that these interests formed a leisure time activity for the husband and wife, as well as the working hours of the husband. Curators' wives became active intellectual participants in their husbands' institutions. While the household mode of production in science and other intellectual fields in

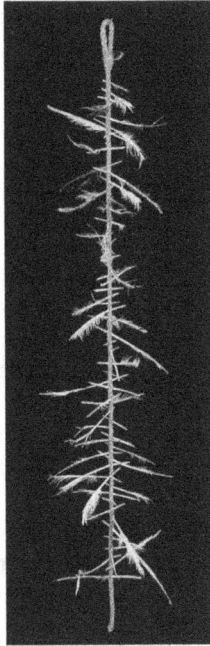

Figure 4 'Witches' ladder' acquired by E. B. Tylor, donated by Anna Tylor
to the Pitt Rivers Museum in 1911.

the nineteenth century was under attack, it is clear that it persisted far
longer than in other fields where it was in decline from the late eighteenth
century.[46] Laboratory science may have been attempting to detach scientific knowledge production from the household but this was far from
complete; in disciplines such as history a household mode of production
was strongly in evidence at least up to 1900, with wives and daughters
acting as secretaries, research assistants, amanuenses and editors for their
menfolk. Despite the attempts of the MA to develop the professional status of curators as qualified people acting in a public institution, it is clear
that many curators depended on an unseen, unpaid workforce of family
members, usually female, throughout our period.[47]

Women who donated alongside their husbands, thus, were in some
way asserting the primacy of the household as the locus of collecting and
knowledge production. It might be overstating the case to see this as an
assertion in opposition to the idea that knowledge production happened
in public, non-familial institutions such as museums and universities;

rather such an assertion emerged naturally from the way in which objects flowed into and out of the home, and women's position within the emotional economy of the family. This is further borne out through the examination of other relationships visible among donors.

Widows, daughters, sisters and mothers

A large proportion of female donors, the largest proportion for which we have evidence, were those passing on collections and possessions of (usually) male family members after their death. This emerges as an important theme, whereby family members are memorialised and their achievements made more public; it could function as an active mode of reputation management, and as a way for women to develop and enlarge their family role. In this material practice, women undertook the apparently feminine strategy of using objects to mark or create intimate relationships. Such a strategy can be discerned in women's autobiographical accounts and in their testamentary practices, as well as appearing in children's prescriptive literature, and has been widely studied by scholars.[48] The key point here, as Hamlett shows, is that this was both born of necessity and offered particular advantages to women; it was instrumental rather than essential. They experienced family relationships and the objects associated with them in ways that were different to men, and also often experienced different types of ownership of goods. This latter aspect was not just an effect of women's legal status within marriage and the passing of the various MWPA; women's legal right to necessaries, moral right to particular other goods, and tendency to transfer ownership informally were prominent before the Acts, and even after their passage married women were still less likely than men to own high-value goods or make wills.[49] Throughout the second half of the nineteenth century, Hamlett importantly draws attention to women's frequent responsibility for dividing up and allocating the personal effects of deceased family members, items which were not valuable enough to be specified in wills, but which were felt to be important enough to family members as material testimony to the deceased to need distribution.[50] Thus the commemorative practices of families were often (though not exclusively) in the hands of women. Similarly, women donors to museums used control over their dead relatives' possessions in order to assert their position as inheritor of their relatives' life's work and guardian of their memory.

Many donations were made by the widows, daughters, sisters or mothers of the field collector after his (usually – but occasionally her) death. In 1893, Bristol Museum was given both a large geological collection formed by the late Reverend G. Hope Dixon, by Mrs G. H. Dixon, and a large collection of British and foreign shells, British echinoderms and fossils, collected by the late Mr Montague W. Smith, by his mother Mrs William Smith.[51] In 1902, Mrs Norgate offered a number of flint implements and a few birds' eggs, all collected by her brother in the Argentine Republic, to the Horniman Museum. At the BM in 1890, Mrs J. W. Robinson donated an 'ancient British cinerary urn and remains' excavated by Canon Greenwell and her late husband, and later that year 'expressed a desire to present to the museum one of the most costly objects in the collection, a bronze sword … purchased by Mr Robinson for £60 or more'.[52] Sometimes widows and daughters held onto the collections they had inherited until their own death, so the objects came into the museum as a bequest; this was the case with Miss Swindells, whose father's collection of minerals and other geological material was received by Manchester Museum from her executors.[53]

In fact, the recording of family relationships in the transmission of objects was an important part of establishing a provenance for them, and curators seem to have relied on this heavily at times. For example, in 1911 Brighton Museum and Art Gallery recorded the donation of the skull and horns of a Cape Buffalo, from Mrs Bonny. The accession register noted that the items were 'brought over with other relics of the Livingstone expedition by Mr Bonny's uncle, Charles Mellor Esq., who was doctor to the expedition'.[54] This collection had therefore been passed on at least twice within the family before entering the museum. George Steka and his sister Miss Steka made available fifteen birds (curator to select) from their father's collection to Brighton Museum. They asked that the birds not selected be packed up again and sent on to Miss Steka's house in Lewes. The curator, in compiling the accession register, also copied out the part of their letter which described their father's biography, especially his precocious mastery of taxidermy and his own shooting of the birds collected.[55]

We can, therefore, develop Hamlett's insights about the way in which women made the meaning and relationships of their deceased relatives material through the process of distributing their possessions among the family. Women also gave the possessions of deceased relatives to museums, either by themselves, or as part of a joint decision on the disposition of such goods with their siblings, parents and children. In doing so, they breached the boundary between private and public, using objects to mark out their family relationships in public institutions. In this sense, museums functioned as an extension of, and more public version of, domestic space. This is partly owing to the fact that for urban elites, local museums were more than purely public institutions. Rather, they were parts of municipal space to which urban elites had privileged access and which in many ways acted as convivial, family and leisure spaces for them; they treated such museums as extensions of their drawing rooms and studies.[56] For women in particular, this enabled them to assert the importance of their husband or son's collecting hobby, and to claim public space for such collections, in so doing memorialising their family and ensuring their role as the repository of family memories was acknowledged.

It should not be assumed that widows were always 'merely' passing on their husband's collection; in exercising stewardship over the collection, they could become experts themselves. In this sense, widowhood offered them new opportunities for intellectual development and public engagement. Mrs Percy Sladen gave her husband's large zoological and fossil collection to the BM(NH) and Exeter Museum after his death. This collection cannot simply be seen as her husband's. Although when they married she did not apparently have natural history interests, she became involved in his work; four years after his death she became one of the first women to join the Linnaean Society. She used his collection to become knowledgeable in natural history, and may have contributed to its classification.[57] It is noteworthy that her acquisition of expertise took place after his death. Widows were relatively free agents among middle-class women. While there was always the possibility of being left in a precarious financial situation, if they had a decent income they could probably please themselves in what they did, to a greater extent than married women. It is, therefore, unsurprising to find them so prominent among donors. The strategy outlined here, therefore, is one whereby widows used donations of things produced by or belonging to their husbands to memorialise, build reputations and find themselves a new public role.

It was, similarly, common for the likeness or the artistic production of the deceased to be donated by a surviving female family member to a museum. This functioned as a form of reputation management by widows, and was particularly noticeable in the case of artists. Mrs George Cruikshank donated various pamphlets, drawings and autographs by her late husband to the BM in the late 1880s.[58] This was just part of a concerted campaign on Eliza Cruikshank's part to promote the reputation of her husband, despite the fact that he had left his entire estate to his mistress: she also bought up a stock of his work, which she gave to the South Kensington Museum (SKM), and attempted to endow a George Cruikshank prize at the Royal Academy.[59] She stipulated that the works she had given to the BM be called the George

Cruikshank Collection.[60] Similarly, Miss Emily Stannard bequeathed work by her father, Joseph Stannard, her mother, Mrs J. Stannard and her grandmother, Mrs Coppin, as well as medals won by Mrs Stannard and Mrs Coppin, to Norwich Museum in 1894, an unusual example of an attempt to memorialise women artists as well as men. The intention to build an image of a matrilineal artistic dynasty is clear.[61] Mrs Redgrave gave an oil painting by her late husband, Richard Redgrave, to Birmingham Museum and Art Gallery in 1890; while their daughter Miss Redgrave gave drawings and etchings by him to the BM in 1891, and Mrs Watts donated photographs after paintings by G. F. Watts there in 1912.[62] Mme Pissarro also gave a number of etchings by Camille Pissarro to the BM in 1907, and Lady Burne-Jones donated a manuscript copy of an illustrated edition of Fitzgerald's *Rubaiyat of Omar Khayyam*, designed by her husband and William Morris, in 1909.[63] Georgiana Burne-Jones was also the biographer of her husband, and so, as Morse suggests, invested significantly in the public presentation of herself as the selfless and devoted wife and widow upholding her husband's work. Equally though, such work on her husband's legacy offered her intellectual challenge, achievement and independence.[64] It was a way both to be a good wife and widow, and simultaneously to transcend the limitations of such a role.

One of the most energetic widows who sought to use strategic donations to museums to enhance her husband's reputation was Mrs Edwards, the widow of artist Edwin Edwards; she gave his work to Norwich Castle Museum, Birmingham Museum and Art Gallery and the BM.[65] She also presented a double portrait of herself and her husband, by Henri Fantin-Latour, to the National Gallery in 1904.[66] Elizabeth Edwards has been described both as a 'devoted supporter of her husband's career' and also as a leading art dealer: she was the British agent of Fantin-Latour.[67] Again, in a similar way to Georgiana Burne-Jones, her exploitation of the wifely role may have helped her to establish herself as a successful independent art expert. She was reported to have acted out an almost parodic version of the self-denying wife, allegedly assisting her husband in such matters as clearing condensation from the windows to improve his light. She was portrayed by Fantin-Latour as her husband's inspiration and 'guardian angel', but after his death she brokered the division of his works among a number of institutions in such a way as to boost his reputation, and her own career as a dealer and a publisher of prints, editing and publishing the last two volumes of his series on English inns after his death.[68] Here the domestic relationships of women were used to provide them with the credentials to take on a public role.

It was not, however, always the case that donations which passed on family members' collections worked to memorialise or enhance the reputation of family members. In 1901, a donation was made to the Horniman Museum by Mrs Baskerville, of her father's collection of minerals. A note from the curator reads, 'as the lady is moving out of her house on Monday next, she wished the things moved away by Saturday ... Of course, she says, the Committee may do just whatever they like with them.'[69] It is hard to avoid the conclusion that the purpose of this donation was to clear out unwanted objects from the house. Similarly, when Mrs A. M. Favarger gave some birds to the museum it was clearly stated that 'there is no sentiment attached either to the birds themselves or to the way in which they were mounted – kindly therefore deal with them as you think fit'. This is interesting for a number of reasons. First of all, the correspondence was all undertaken with her husband though it was made clear that Mrs Favarger was the donor ('My wife has asked me to answer your letter'). Secondly, the assumption seems to have been that such objects would normally have had sentiment attached to them for this donor, and it is possible that the gender of the donor played some part in this assumption.[70]

While not every donation of family possessions may be identifiable, therefore, evidence suggests that women did donate such objects, and in doing so, simultaneously affirmed the importance of family ties, exhibited their adherence to appropriate gender roles, and stretched those roles to incorporate the public promotion of their husband, or other male relative.[71] Women's donations to museums emerged from their existing social and especially family networks, particularly those which gave urban middle classes and elites coherence through a system of practices which spanned the public and the private. The extent to which municipal museums were seen as an extension of the drawing rooms and studies of the urban elite, and the extent to which intellectual and artistic occupations were still carried out as household activities, firmly enmeshing women in the work of their menfolk, all meant that women's donations would tend to insert family relationships into public knowledge. Women further used museum donation as a way of inscribing family and domesticity in the public realm, and thereby asserted a public value for their domestic material practices.

Women as vendors of museum objects

Women also sold objects to museums. These women ranged from dealers, who made a living primarily through such sales, to more casual vendors, whose sales were either secondary to their own collecting, or entirely fortuitous. It is not always possible to identify the extent or nature of women's sales to museums, and the reasons for their particular dealing activities were complex and various; moreover the marketplace for sales varied with different types of object. It seems, though, that women's contribution to museums through object sales was small but distinctive, adding to the change in museums created by women donors. It is important to include analysis of this route whereby women outside museums contributed to their development because, as Wingfield has shown, people who had the most dense relationship with museums usually included selling objects in the ways they contributed; though it is not therefore true that people who sold objects to museums always had a close relationship to those museums.[72] Moreover, although women donors nearly always gave objects which had been in their home, highlighting their role within a family economy of materiality, women who sold objects sometimes came from a commercial world concerned only with the public sale and purchase of goods, though they might equally be domestically based, amateur collectors. One might, therefore, expect to see a different kind of social network expressed through female vendors to museums; in fact, though, family ties and domestic objects feature heavily in the activities of women who sold objects to museums.

By the middle of the nineteenth century, it was not unknown for working-class women to work as collector-dealers in some scientific areas, especially geology and fossils; though there is much less evidence for women who worked purely as dealers, middlemen so to speak, in these areas. Knell notes the advice for geology collectors that they could buy specimens from poor women and children, and describes a 'proletariat of fossil gatherers'. Thus, he shows that geology was not at all as masculine as has been assumed, but also suggests that women's contribution to it is hard to uncover.[73] This is despite the existence of some well-known female fossil hunters and sellers. Mary Anning (1799–1847) was both the first to discover some major fossils, the proprietress of a fossil shop, and a celebrity who had close relationships with a number of important scientists such as Henry de la Beche.[74] In following this trade so successfully, she benefited from living in Lyme Regis, the fossil hot spot, and from the low regard in which field collecting was held in the early nineteenth century. Middle-class male collectors preferred to buy their specimens, rather than undertake the unpleasant, uncomfortable and occasionally dangerous activity of gathering bits of rock, plant or dead animal.

By the second half of the century, natural history dealing was a more complex field. Scientists, collectors and museum curators were much more likely to wish to undertake their own field collecting, and museums undertook collecting expeditions in order to be able to document the contextual information around specimens more fully.[75] Although dealers were still to be found, they were more often collectors, either selling their whole collection, or selling parts in order to finance more collecting. This meant that it could be harder to define a dealer in natural history; a minimal definition of someone who sold natural history specimens would include many who did not primarily make a living from such sales, and women vendors were often particularly hard to pigeonhole. Collectors had reasons to sell objects in order to raise money for further purchases of their own, and also frequently engaged in exchanging duplicate objects, again to enhance their own collection. A good example of this is Miss Hele, a very active natural history collector in the Bristol region, who donated, exchanged, and sold specimens to the Museum there. In 1883, it was recorded that the curator was empowered by the Museum Committee to purchase fossils from her to the value of £2.[76]

Dealing in antiques, curiosities and fine art was a different area.[77] It tended to be more straightforwardly a commercial activity, because the goods had higher values and the market for such sales was more developed. To some extent, it developed out of the masculine occupation of cabinet making, though women, and men, could also emerge into antique dealing through the occupation of second-hand clothes dealer.[78] From the middle of the century when the market began to segment, women dealers tended to be concentrated in the less profitable parts of the market and were more likely to be described as 'curiosity' dealers, than the more up-market 'antique dealer'. Where women dealers specialised, it was in 'feminine' objects such as antique china, prints or works of art, and lace. Such women dealers as are recorded were highly likely to have inherited the business from a husband or father, and then to pass it onto a son when they came of age.[79] These women dealers' relationships with museums demonstrate that they were most successful when they specialised in feminine goods, and utilised family networks.

Thus, when John Pollen from the SKM, who was on a collecting trip, visited the shop of Mrs Oven in Cirencester in 1864, he described it as large, with a 'promiscuous stock'. J. C. Robinson, back at the museum, decided nothing Pollen had described from there was worth having.[80] Women, when part of an unspecialised, downmarket curiosity trade, especially in the provinces, faced difficulties in establishing themselves as knowledgeable and well connected enough to trade in valuable antiques. On the other hand, Miss Clarke, who dealt in lace and ceramics from the 'Antique Lace Warehouse', a well-known and respected business, did sell a number of objects to the SKM in 1854, including a porcelain teapot and a number of specimens of lace.[81] Specialisms such as lace, which were widely acknowledged to be part of a feminine realm of expertise, brought significant benefits to women dealers.

Eva Cutter, who dealt in ethnographic curiosities and antiquities in Bloomsbury, London, is another woman dealer known to have sold objects to museums. According to Alison Petch she specialised in 'Antique needlework, samplers, antiquities and curiosities', and she sold a small number of English objects and a larger number of foreign objects to the Pitt Rivers Museum.[82] She also sold natural history objects from Mauritius, Costa Rica, India and West Africa to Leicester Museum, and both natural history and ethnographic items to the Horniman Museum.[83] She came from a family of well-known dealers, who had sold many ethnographic objects to the BM (or at least to A. W. Franks, who then donated them to the museum), and like so many other women dealers, took over the firm, apparently on her father's death. She developed a personal and business relationship with W. D. Webster, another well-known dealer in ethnographic objects, who was already married; after his death in 1913 she began to use the name 'Mrs W. D. Webster', and continued in business until 1926.[84]

Many women followed a similar pattern in dealing. Like Eva Cutter, Mrs Brazenor came from a family of dealers. She was the daughter-in-law, or possibly sister-in-law, of Robert Brazenor, who founded the firm of Brazenor and Sons in the 1860s. They were described on their trade label as 'Naturalists, Osteologists and Furriers to the Brighton Aquarium and Museum', and undertook both taxidermy and the mounting of skeletons for the Museum. There was apparently a gendered division of labour within the business; wives and daughters worked in the furrier shop while the men undertook the skinning and stuffing.[85] Quite how this led to Mrs Brazenor selling African ethnography to Brighton Museum for fifteen shillings in 1914 is not clear, but presumably if she acquired such material she had a ready route to offer it to the museum.[86] Another vendor of note is Mrs Mogridge, who together with Mr Mintorn sold a number of models of plants which they had made, to Leicester Museum in 1894.[87] Mogridge and Mintorn were in fact sister and brother, and they were leading proponents of flower and plant modelling, supplying models to the BM and the American Museum of Natural History, and published books on wax flower modelling, which was a popular female pastime.[88]

Beyond these commercial dealers, other women who sold objects to museums are not always fully recorded; annual reports mainly focused on thanking donors, and day-to-day acquisition books have not always survived. There does seem, however, to have been a very wide variation in the number of women vendors at different museums, which cannot be attributed to factors such as the size of the museum. Thus of the museums where data was available, the Horniman Museum made the most purchases from women, followed by Leicester Museum, while Ipswich, Cheltenham and Bristol made hardly any. In very few cases can these vendors be identified as actual dealers; rather in several cases it is clear that they were selling collections and objects belonging to deceased husbands and fathers. Mrs Sargent sold a large collection of fossils which had been collected by her late husband to Leicester Museum for an unknown sum in 1908, while Mrs Hodge sold 121 mosses collected by her late husband to Warrington Museum for £10 in 1913. Meanwhile, Mrs Howard sold the Horniman Museum African objects up to a value of £30 'on condition that at least one of the descriptive labels should be inscribed with the words – "part of the collection of H. J. Hodgson, Esq".'[89] Additionally, as museums started to become interested in new sorts of object, this could open up possibilities for women to sell items which belonged to them. At the Pitt Rivers Museum, the interest in lace bobbins, not for instruction in production techniques but as social historical documents, led to the purchase of such items from elderly pillow-lace makers in the early twentieth century. One such bobbin is shown in Figure 5; it was purchased from Mrs Butler in 1903, by Henry Balfour. She was then 76 years old and had been a lace maker from at least the age of 13.[90]

In general, purchases from women were for fairly small sums (though of course most municipal museums could only make purchases for small sums, given their budgets), from as little as one shilling for a 'witch ball' purchased by Warrington Museum in 1914, usually up to a few pounds. The one exception to this is Mrs Bogle, who sold an oil painting to Cheltenham Museum and Art Gallery for £75 in 1914.[91] This underscores the casual nature of women's sales to museums, as well as the fact that they tended not to have valuable objects to sell. The small numbers of female vendors to museums during this period, then, were responding to different constraints and opportunities. Unlike men, they were generally unable to mediate collecting activity into either a viable ongoing business, or a large one-off sum (though it is worth noting that many men did not do so either). However, they did continue businesses created by their husbands and fathers; and showed a tendency to specialise in areas where their gender was a positive bonus, such as lace and its production. In doing so, they contributed to a shift in the nature of the museum object around 1900.[92] In addition, they used sales to museums to finance further collecting, and to involve themselves further with

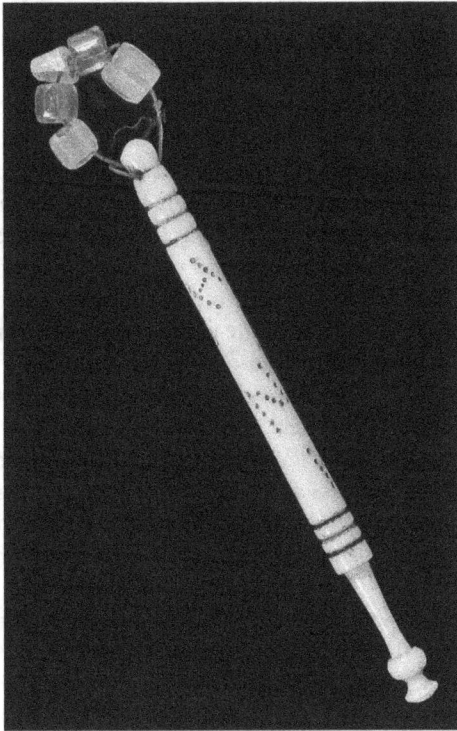

Figure 5 Lace maker's bobbin bought from Mrs Butler by the Pitt Rivers Museum in 1903.

the mission of the museum; selling objects was a way of pursuing serious collecting on their own behalf. They also undertook opportunistic sales of objects they had acquired accidentally, finding them or inheriting them from relatives.

Conclusion

This chapter has investigated the role of women who were not 'part' of the museum, but rather contributed to it via donation and sales of objects. In contrast to the women in Chapter 1 who were officially part of the museum institution, even if in many ways a subordinate part, these women 'outside' the museum contributed mainly from a domestic setting. Unsurprisingly therefore, their actions reflected and shaped their domestic relationships. However, it may be more accurate to say that the division between public and private was blurred in and by these cases; the model of the domestic mode of production remained a key one for artists, curators, collectors and dealers, so the public and private aspects of knowledge production and the circulation of objects were hard to separate. Although there are traces of the existence of this household mode of knowledge production in the way that daughters and wives are known to have offered significant amounts of assistance to scholars, this analysis of donors and dealers shows that it was widespread also in other occupations, and that the advances of male professionalisation did not necessarily sweep it away.

Moreover, this analysis shows women taking on a particular role in relation to the material culture of the family. Women's strong attachment to small and low-value household objects has been shown by Hamlett, Logan and Wynne to have been closely associated with their attempts to build and control family relationships, especially when disposing of the possessions of the dead.[93] Women engaged with museums as a way of commemorating and asserting authority over the legacies of their male relations; and in several cases, particularly for the widows of artists, such a private practice enabled them to assert a public role as mediator between the deceased and the public. Not only was a public/private divide not always visible for women because of their enmeshment in a household form of intellectual production, therefore, but they actively used donation as a way of further blurring the boundary between the two spheres, and of bringing private, or domestic and familial, valuations and relationships into public view, and thus of creating wider value for them.

The social networks underlying women's donations and sales to museums, then, existed alongside male networks. Male networks also bridged the public and private, in that most donors were amateur collectors whose collections were held in their home and who undertook collecting activities in their spare time. However, for much of the nineteenth century the most important male donors to local museums were members of local voluntary societies; the networks which underlay their engagement with museums were all-male and non-familial.[94] So women's social networks reveal different strategies to engage with public institutions, which rested on their strengths within the home and family, and also served to enhance and expand those strengths. Although it has been shown that the MWPA did not produce much clearly identifiable change in women's attitudes to or behaviour with domestic goods, it seems significant that in the second half of the century, women donors were increasingly marking their authority on and custody of the things of their family and home; this may be a cause, rather than an effect, of the MWPA. Cohen has also suggested that the growth of women's rights was associated with an increasing female investment in the things of the home.[95] Women's use of museum donations to make public and develop their familially based social networks, therefore, both reflects the expansion of their rights over material goods, and is evidence of a female strategy to develop their public presence further.

In asserting their control over the material legacies of the family, and in claiming public space for such legacies, women donors were developing a new social presence which did not emulate (though it occasionally overlapped with) masculine trajectories of professionalisation and demarcation between the public and the private. Their actions served to develop the idea that home and family were at the heart of public value, and that the purpose of museums was as much to display family relationships as it was to show off disembodied knowledge. In the next chapter, I show how this strategy worked in terms of the donations themselves.

Notes

1 Chris Gosden and Frances Larson, *Knowing Things: Exploring the Collection at the Pitt Rivers Museum 1884–1945* (Oxford: Oxford University Press 2007), p. 11.

2 Sarah Byrne, Anne Clarke, Rodney Harrison and Robin Torrence, 'Networks, agents and objects: frameworks for unpacking museum collections', in S. Byrne, A. Clarke, R. Harrison and R. Torrence (eds), *Unpacking the Collection: Networks of Material and Social Agency in the Museum* (New York: Springer 2011), esp. pp. 4, 15.

3 The museums covered were Birmingham Museum and Art Gallery, Brighton Museum and Art Gallery, Bristol Museum, the BM, Cheltenham Museum and Art Gallery, the Horniman Museum and Gardens, Leicester Museum, Manchester Museum, Norwich Castle Museum, Sunderland Borough Museum, Warrington Museum, and Whitby Museum; chosen largely on the basis of their foundation date and the continued existence of their pre-1914 records. The selection was also made to encompass local authority museums, university museums, voluntary society museums and national museums. Where possible, the Annual Reports and the Accession Registers, or equivalent, were consulted; for the British Museum, the Book of Presents was consulted. In addition the online catalogue and analysis of acquisitions undertaken by researchers at the Pitt Rivers Museum have been used – see http://objects.prm.ox.ac.uk/, http://history.prm.ox.ac.uk/, and http://england.prm.ox.ac.uk/.

4 Some major donors are considered instead in Chapter 5.

5 This case is put forward in relation to the art historical canon by Kristen Frederickson, 'Introduction', in K. Frederickson and S. Webb (eds), *Singular Women: Writing the Artist* (Berkeley, CA: University of California Press 2003), p. 2. See also Dianne Sachko Macleod, *Enchanted Lives, Enchanted Objects: American Women Collectors and the Making of Culture, 1800–1940* (Berkeley, CA: University of California Press 2008), for the argument that a small number of case studies allows her to 'listen more closely to the stories' of the women she does examine; pp. 2–3.

6 See Krista Cowman, 'Collective Biography', in S. Gunn and L. Faire (eds), *Research Methods for History* (Edinburgh: Edinburgh University Press 2011); Ann Whitelaw, 'Women, Museums and the Problem of Biography', in Kate Hill (ed.), *Museums and Biographies* (Woodbridge: Boydell and Brewer 2012).

7 See note 3.

8 Sunderland Borough Museum Stock Book, October 1879, September 1881.

9 On the early years of nineteenth-century societies, see R. J. Morris, 'Voluntary societies and British urban elites, 1780–1850: an analysis', *Historical Journal* 26: 1 (1983), 95–118; on the gendering of such societies, see Leonore Davidoff and Catherine Hall, *Family Fortunes: Men and Women of the English Middle Class, 1780–1850* (London: Hutchison 1987), chapter 10.

10 Liverpool Museum, Minutes of the Museum Sub-Committee, Corporation of Liverpool; Harris Museum, Minutes of the Free Public Library Committee, Corporation of Preston, all between 1880 and 1910.

11 Pitt Rivers Museum, Relational Museum Project, 'Statistics: field collectors', *The Relational Museum*, online, available at http://history.prm.ox.ac.uk/page_74.html, accessed 1 April 2011.

12 Sunderland Borough Museum Stock Book 1880–1910.

13 http://england.prm.ox.ac.uk/analysis-4.html; see http://england.prm.ox.ac.uk/englishness-acq.events1.html for a discussion of the difference between donations and acquisition events.

14 Chris Wingfield, 'Donors, loaners, dealers and swappers: the relationships behind the English collections at the Pitt Rivers Museum', in S. Byrne, A. Clarke, R. Harrison and R. Torrence (eds), *Unpacking the Collection: Networks of Material and Social Agency in the Museum* (New York: Springer 2011), pp. 126–127.

15 Wingfield, 'Donors, loaners', p. 134.

16 Wingfield, 'Donors, loaners', p. 133.

17 'Statistical information, all individuals associated with PRM collections', The Relational Museum, online, available at http://history.prm.ox.ac.uk/page_72.html, accessed on 1 April 2011.

18 The MWPA, between 1870 and 1893, gradually gave married women more legal control of their property. Their enactment was a key aim of the women's movement at the time, but there is some evidence to show that although they improved women's position in some way, those women with extensive property had already found ways to protect it before the acts; and of course they had little benefit for those without property. On women's property relationships before and after the Acts, see Mary Beth Combs, ' "A measure of legal independence": the 1870 Married Women's Property Act and the portfolio allocations of British wives', *Journal of Economic History*, 65: 4 (2005), pp. 1028–1057; Margot Finn, 'Women, consumption and coverture in England, c. 1760–1860', *Historical Journal*, 39: 3 (1996), pp. 703–722; Morris, *Men, Women and Property*; Deborah Wynne, *Women and Personal Property in the Victorian Novel* (Farnham: Ashgate 2010).

19 Ipswich Corporation Museum Accession Register 1894–1911, June 1898.

20 Whitby Literary and Philosophical Society, *Eighty-seventh Report of the Whitby Literary and Philosophical Society, 1909* (Whitby 1910); Brighton Museum Accession Register January 1891; Sunderland Borough Museum Stock Book January 1892.

21 Claire Wintle has found, later in the twentieth century although in donations from a woman born in the mid-nineteenth century, a distinctive feminine donating style – self-effacing in comparison to men's more ostentatious donations. As suggested by the anonymous donations I cite above, there is some reflection of this in my findings, but it was by no means universal among women donors before 1914. Claire Wintle, *Colonial Collecting and Display* (New York and Oxford: Berghahn 2013), pp. 94–95.

22 For example, Lady Leighton Warren at Manchester: Manchester Museum, *Annual Report 1904–5* (Manchester: Cornish 1905); Lady Greenall at Warrington: Warrington Museum Receiving Book January 1911; Baroness Berners at Norwich: Norwich Museum Accession Registers, June 1896. The Duchess of Mantua was listed as a donor to the BM and sold objects to the Horniman Museum – she was not, however, an actual duchess, but rather Ann Groom, the mother of a somewhat delusional man (but substantial collector) who believed himself to be the Prince of Mantua and Montferrat. Richard Davenport-Hines, 'Groom, Charles Ottley (1839–1894)', *Oxford Dictionary of National Biography* (Oxford: Oxford University Press 2004), online, available at www.oxforddnb.com/view/article/54058, accessed 1 April 2011.

23 Anne Eatwell, 'Private pleasure, public beneficence: Lady Charlotte Schreiber and ceramic collecting', in Clarissa Campbell Orr (ed.), *Women in the Victorian Art World* (Manchester: Manchester University Press 1995), p. 129.

24 See donations from Miss P. A. Fry to Bristol Museum in 1900, Bristol Museum and Library, *Report of Proceedings at the 27th Annual Meeting, 1900–1* (Bristol 1901); and from Mrs Gurney to Norwich Castle Museum: Norwich Museum Accession Register, December 1888, April 1891.

25 See, for example, Birmingham Museum and Art Gallery Master Inventory 1906–1915, 1912. For the role of Feeney and Bunce in the development of Birmingham see Kate Hill, *Culture and Class in English Public Museums 1850–1914* (Aldershot: Ashgate 2005); Birmingham Museum and Art Gallery, *John and Christina Feeney, Benefactors* (Birmingham 1985). Mrs Robson's donation was in 1887: Ipswich Corporation Museum Minute Book, 2 March 1887.

26 Sunderland Borough Museum Stock Book, August 1910.

27 Norwich Castle Museum Accession Registers, February 1892.

28 Cheltenham Museum and Art Gallery accession register, vol. 1, May 1907; Brighton Museum Accession Register, November 1897.

29 Paul Martin, *Popular Collecting and the Everyday Self: The Reinvention of Museums?* (London: Leicester University Press 1999), p. 72.

30 E. R. Lankester (ed.), *The History of the Collections Contained in the Natural History Departments of the British Museum*, vol. 1 (London: British Museum 1904), p. 327.

31 Susan Pearce, 'Making up is hard to do', *Museums Journal* 93: 12 (1993), p. 25–27; Martin, *Popular Collecting*, p. 71.

32 Eatwell, 'Private pleasure, public beneficence', p. 138.

33 Ipswich Corporation Museum Accession Register 1894–1911, June 1909 and July 1910.

34 Horniman Museum Accession Registers, January 1898.

35 See Leicester Museum Accession Register from 1880, when he became curator.

36 Leicester Museum Accession Register, June 1889.

37 *Horniman Free Museum, Sixth Annual Report, 1896* (London 1897).

38 Manchester Museum, *Annual Report 1908–9* (Manchester: Cornish 1909); British Museum Book of Presents Supplement, vol. 2 (1890–1896), April 1895.

39 For example, Brighton Museum Accession Register June 1906, March 1910, October 1910.

40 Alison Petch, 'Herbert Toms', Rethinking Pitt Rivers (2011), online, available at http://web.prm.ox.ac.uk/rpr/index.php/article-index/12-articles/695-herbert-toms, accessed 16 October 2011; Brighton Public Libraries, Museums and Art Galleries, *Annual Report of the Director for year ending 1905* (1906); Herbert Toms and Christina Toms, 'The Cissbury Earthworks', *Sussex Archaeological Collections*, 67 (1926), pp. 55–84.

41 Peter W. Allott, 'Hügel, Anatole Andreas Aloys von, Baron von Hügel in the nobility of the Holy Roman empire (1854–1928)', *Oxford Dictionary of National Biography* (Oxford: Oxford University Press 2012), online, available at www.oxforddnb.com. proxy.library.lincoln.ac.uk/view/article/103702, accessed 14 July 2015.

42 Museum of General and Local Archaeology, *First Annual Report of the Antiquarian Committee to the Senate* (Cambridge 1885); *Seventh and Eighth Annual Reports* (Cambridge 1892), Appendix 1: Accessions to 1891; Appendix 3: Accessions to 1892.

43 J. L. Myres, 1953, cited in Petch, 'Edward Burnett Tylor', The Relational Museum project website, available at http://history.prm.ox.ac.uk/collector_tylor.html, accessed 25 February 2011.

44 'Individuals that contributed more than 100 objects to the Pitt Rivers Museum's English collections by size of collection', England, The Other Within: Analysing the English Collections at the Pitt Rivers Museum, online, available at http://england. prm.ox.ac.uk/analysis-6.html, accessed 14 February 2011.

45 Petch, 'Tylor'.

46 See, for example, Louise A. Tilly and Joan W. Scott, *Women, Work and Family* (London: Routledge 1989, 2nd edn).

47 It is notable that a few 'curating dynasties' emerged in the nineteenth century, such as the Wallises; this suggests the importance of family support for male curators. Hill, *Culture and Class*, pp. 63–64; J. L. Teather, 'Museology and its traditions: the British experience 1845–1945' (unpublished PhD thesis, University of Leicester 1984).

48 See Macleod, *Enchanted Lives, Enchanted Objects*; Beverley Gordon, *The Saturated World: Aesthetic Meaning, Intimate Objects, Women's Lives 1890–1940* (Knoxville: University of Tennessee Press 2006); E. Hall (ed.), *Miss Weeton's Journal of a Governess*, 2 vols, vol 2: *1811–1825* (New York: Augustus M. Kelly 1969), p. 325. On testamentary practices, see David Green, 'Independent women, wealth and wills in nineteenth-century London', in Jon Stobart and Alastair Owens (eds), *Urban Fortunes: Property and Inheritance in the Town, 1700–1900* (Aldershot: Ashgate 2000); Jane Hamlett, *Material Relations: Domestic Interiors and Middle-Class Families in England, 1850–1910* (Manchester: Manchester University Press 2010), chapter 5; R. J. Morris, *Men, Women and Property in England, 1780–1870: A Social and Economic*

History of Family Strategies Amongst the Leeds Middle Classes (Cambridge: Cambridge University Press 2005).

49 Hamlett, *Material Relations*, p. 200; Morris, *Men, Women and Property*, chapter 6.

50 Hamlett, *Material Relations*, pp. 182–188.

51 Bristol Museum and Library, *Report of Proceedings at the 22nd Annual Meeting, 1893* (Bristol 1894).

52 British Museum Book of Presents, November and May 1890.

53 Manchester Museum, *Annual Report 1911–12* (Manchester: Cornish 1912).

54 Brighton Museum Accession Register, 1911.

55 Brighton Museum Accession Register, 1914.

56 Hill, *Culture and Class*, p. 128.

57 D. Nicholls, 'A biography of Percy Sladen (1849–1900)', *The Linnaean* Special Issue 4 (2003), pp. 5–29.

58 British Museum Book of Presents, December 1887, July 1888.

59 Robert L. Patten, 'Cruikshank, George (1792–1878)', *Oxford Dictionary of National Biography* (Oxford: Oxford University Press 2004), online, available at www.oxforddnb.com/view/article/6843, accessed 16 December 2015.

60 British Museum Book of Presents Supplement, vol. 2 (1890–1896).

61 Norwich Museum Accession Registers, December 1894.

62 Birmingham Museum and Art Gallery Inventory, vol. 1, 1885–1905, 1890; British Museum Book of Presents, September 1891, January 1912.

63 British Museum Book of Presents November 1907, July 1909.

64 Elizabeth J. Morse, 'MacDonald Sisters (act. 1837–1925)', *Oxford Dictionary of National Biography* (Oxford: Oxford University Press 2004), online, available at www.oxforddnb.com/view/article/76071, accessed 29 September 2009.

65 Norwich Museum Accession Registers, January 1898; British Museum Book of Presents December 1898.

66 Tate Collection online, entry for 'Mr and Mrs Edwin Edwards' by Henri Fantin-Latour, ref N01952, online, available at www.tate.org.uk/servlet/ViewWork?cgroupid=999999961&workid=4223&searchid=11948, accessed 4 March 2011.

67 Anne Pimlott Baker, 'Edwards, Edwin (1823–1879)', *Oxford Dictionary of National Biography* (Oxford: Oxford University Press 2004), online, available at www.oxforddnb.com/view/article/8536, accessed 4 March 2011; 'Elizabeth Ruth Edwards, ca 183–d.1907', The Correspondence of James McNeill Whistler, online edition, available at www.whistler.arts.gla.ac.uk/correspondence/biog/display/?bid=Edwa_Mrs, accessed 4 March 2011.

68 Tate Collection online; Baker, 'Edwards, Edwin'.

69 London Metropolitan Archives (LMA), LCC Historical Records and Buildings Committee Minutes, 23 April 1901.

70 LMA, LCC Historical Records and Buildings Committee Minutes, 17 January 1903.

71 Wintle suggests that donations which passed on objects redolent of now-deceased relatives, especially spouses, onto museums, also show women dealing with the painful memories embedded in the objects by moving them out of the home and into the

public space of the museum, where they were still safe and not discarded, but out of sight. Wintle, *Colonial Collecting*, p. 101.

72 Chris Wingfield, 'Acquisition events: examining regular sources', England, The Other Within; Analysing the English Collections at the Pitt Rivers Museum, online, available at http://england.prm.ox.ac.uk/englishness-acq.events6.html, accessed 8 June 2015.

73 Simon Knell, *The Culture of English Geology, 1815–51: A Science Revealed Through its Collecting* (Aldershot: Ashgate 2000), pp. 3, 6.

74 H. S. Torrens, 'Anning, Mary (1799–1847)', *Oxford Dictionary of National Biography* (Oxford: Oxford University Press 2004), online, available at www.oxforddnb.com/view/article/568, accessed 30 June 2011. See also Torrens, 'Presidential Address: Mary Anning (1799–1847) of Lyme; "the greatest fossilist the world ever knew"', *British Journal of the History of Science*, 28 (1995), pp. 257–284; Judith Pascoe, *The Hummingbird Cabinet: A Rare and Curious History of Romantic Collectors* (Ithaca, NY: Cornell University Press 2006), chapter 5.

75 See, for example, Liverpool Museum's collecting expeditions: Hill, *Culture and Class*, p. 83.

76 Bristol Museum and Library, *Report of Proceedings at the Annual Meeting, 1883* (Bristol 1884).

77 This may, however, have become the case more towards the end of the nineteenth century. On the development of antique and second-hand dealing, see Clive Edwards and Margaret Ponsonby, 'A Desirable Commodity or Practical Necessity? The Sale and Consumption of Secondhand Furniture 1750–1900', in M. Ponsonby and D. Hussey (eds), *Buying for the Home: Shopping for the Domestic from the Seventeenth Century to the Present* (Aldershot: Ashgate 2008), pp. 117–139; on 'curio' dealing which became more clearly anthropological see H. Waterfield and J. C. H. King, *Provenance: Twelve Collectors of Ethnographic Art in England 1760–1990* (Paris: Somogy 2006).

78 Mark Westgarth, 'A biographical dictionary of nineteenth century antique and curiosity dealers', *Regional Furniture*, 22 (2009), p. 4.

79 Westgarth, 'Biographical dictionary'.

80 Westgarth, 'Biographical dictionary', p. 145.

81 Westgarth, 'Biographical dictionary', p. 80.

82 Alison Petch, 'Sellers' relationships with the Pitt Rivers Museum Part One', England, The Other Within: Analysing the English Collections at the Pitt Rivers Museum, online, available at http://england.prm.ox.ac.uk/englishness-Sellers-relationships-with-PRM-Part-1.html, accessed 30 August 2011.

83 Leicester Museum Accession Books, September 1895; Horniman Museum Accession Registers June and July 1902.

84 Waterfield and King, *Provenance*. While the business was owned by Cutter's father, Beatrix Potter visited: Leslie Linder (ed. and transcr.), *The Journal of Beatrix Potter from 1881 to 1897* (London and New York: Frederick Warne & Co. 1966), p. 114.

85 'The Booth Museum and Brighton taxidermy', Royal Pavilion and Brighton Museums blog, online, available at http://rpmcollections.wordpress.com/2011/05/12/the-booth-museum-and-brighton-taxidermy/, accessed 9 September 2011; 'Natural history – taxidermy trade labels', Haslemere Museum website, online, available at www.haslemeremuseum.co.uk/birdtaxidermy.html#TL3, accessed 9 September 2011.

86 'Booth Museum and Brighton taxidermy'; 'Natural history – taxidermy trade labels'.

87 'Booth Museum and Brighton taxidermy'; 'Natural history – taxidermy trade labels'.

88 A. B. Shteir, '"Fac-similes of nature": Victorian wax flower modelling', *Victorian Literature and Culture* 35 (2007), pp. 649–661, 659.

89 Leicester Museum Accession Books February 1908; Warrington Museum Receiving Book 10 July 1913; LMA, LCC, Minutes of the Historical Records and Buildings Committee, 26 November 1903, LCC/MIN/7235.

90 Nicolette Macovicky, 'Lace maker's bobbins', The Other Within, online, available at http://england.prm.ox.ac.uk/englishness-lace-makers-bobbins.html, accessed 17 October 2011.

91 Warrington Museum Receiving Book March 1914; Cheltenham Museum and Art Gallery Accession Register vol. 1, July 1914.

92 See Chapter 3.

93 Hamlett, *Material Relations*, chapter 5; Wynne, *Women and Personal*; Thad Logan, *The Victorian Parlour: A Cultural Study* (Cambridge: Cambridge University Press 2001).

94 See, for example, Hill, *Culture and Class*, p. 61.

95 Deborah Cohen, *Household Gods: The British and Their Possessions* (New Haven, CT and London: Yale University Press 2006), pp. 104–113.

3

Outside the museum: women's donations, materiality and the museum object

We have seen that women's social networks, formed and expanded by their donation to museums, were rooted in domestic relationships, but also acted to link the domestic with the public. But what actual things did women give and sell to museums? What meanings did such things make in the museum, what sort of museum did they create, and how did they produce their meanings and effects? Women's donations and sales not only emerged out of domestic and feminine networks, they produced new regimes of value for the museum, contributing to a shift in museum focus from a classificatory logic to one which also acknowledged memory and affect. This chapter, then, is fundamentally concerned with the question of whether women's things formed a distinctive category, and in what ways they might resemble or differ from men's museum objects.

The gendering of materiality is an increasingly popular topic, and there has been a move away from investigating what are conceived of as relatively static systems of gender difference in materiality to an understanding of a dynamic, historically situated and fluid interaction between materiality and gender. As Macleod in particular insists, women's things had the capacity to change the women who came into contact with them and interacted with them in particular ways – even while as women's things became identifiably feminine because of their emergence from a particularly feminine environment and set of practices, they also helped women to change and expand their environment and competences.[1] The ways in which historical processes both align women with particular things and material practices, and allow them to reframe or transcend that alignment, are a key focus here. A number of scholars have found that women's use of particular objects in the domestic space for emotional and relational purposes was widespread in the nineteenth century, and have also suggested that such private material assemblages were linked to women's increased assertiveness in public life. In other words, women were increasingly associated with the collection and valuation of specific objects which were seen as gendered female, not male; but this was a creative process stemming from women's own experiences, which allowed them to articulate a feminine contribution to public life.[2] This chapter broadly follows this argument but additionally looks at the power and agency of women's objects in public, in the museum.

The focus here, then, is a particular subset of objects, namely, those donated to museums. The nature of the move from private possession to museum object is a complex one, epistemologically. How far are objects reshaped by the museum, and how far do they retain their earlier meanings in the new setting? Recent work has suggested that museums' processes were directed towards suppressing all object qualities and meanings except those sanctioned by the museum itself, but I am sceptical of museums' ability to do this.[3] What is notable about the objects contributed by women is that they refused to conform to the alleged increasing systematisation of the material culture of knowledge during this period. The objects considered here were both constitutive of various modern disciplines, and also valued for more affective qualities. They were both metaphors and metonyms; they established 'scientific' relationships between orderly things, and also invoked imaginative and unsystematic links with the invisible world of the past, the dead, and the 'ideal'.[4] This chapter suggests that donations modified the organisation and very conception of knowledge possible in museums; understanding museums as distributed allows us to see the agency of women's donations more clearly.

One way of investigating the meanings of donations is to consider the lives of the objects. Object biography is a qualitative approach which has become popular within museum studies and anthropology, and offers the valuable benefit of developing an understanding of the changing meaning of things as they pass through different hands.[5] It can also shed light on objects' abilities to affect their own journey, and bring new meanings into different contexts. However, it is dependent upon the presence of a great deal of documentation surrounding an object, and few of the objects donated by women in this period have more than a few sentences of documentation. There is a risk with object biography that, as with biographies of people, only the 'stars' will be considered. In this chapter, therefore, I attempt something more akin to a collective biography of objects, working with scraps of information, and trying to elucidate the relationships surrounding and animating the group of objects.[6]

The evidence presented here suggests that there were distinct 'women's things', whose distinctiveness stemmed from their roots in women's experiences; this meant they did not fit easily into existing regimes of value, categories and meanings of museum objects. Not all of this distinctiveness survived the process of becoming a museum object, but some of it did; and this was partly because of the slightly protean nature of many museums before 1914; they had little in the way of acquisition policies, a pressing need for objects, and a tendency to accept anything that was offered to them.[7] By contributing their donations to museums, women altered the nature of the publicly valued object, and made a space for femininity, as well as for feelings and memories, in institutions of knowledge. Thus, the distinctive nature of women's objects set the twentieth-century museum on its course to become a place of memory, nostalgia and sensation as much as it was a place of knowledge and classification.[8]

Quantitative analysis of women's objects

In order to understand women's donations, we must first try to establish what objects women gave, and in what quantities. This question raises some fundamental methodological problems of counting, comparison and classification. It was much more common for natural history objects to be given in very large quantities than fine art objects; and within natural history, botanical and entomological donations would probably consist of more objects than mammalian zoology. It is, perhaps, better to analyse objects in terms of 'acquisition events', that is, occasions when donations were made, rather than in terms of absolute numbers of objects donated.[9] However, although this is useful for analysing donors, it is unsatisfactory for the donations themselves; mixed donations were very common, and the variation in recording practices across different museums makes any conclusions tentative.

A major division into 'natural' and manufactured objects is relatively unproblematic, though there certainly were objects which crossed that line. However, any attempt at subdividing the donations further is immensely fraught, particularly as I argue below that these objects in many ways disrupted and subverted the existing classification system, which was itself in flux. Deciding what category manufactured objects fit into is very difficult, not least because so little information is sometimes recorded about them. The same object could easily be seen as applied art or ethnography; the dividing line between ethnography and local or social history could be blurred; and it can be equally hard to decide if an object is local history, applied art or archaeology; and all these categories were changing during the period anyway.[10] I have, however, retained such an analysis despite its problematic nature, because it does offer some insight into relative proportions of, broadly speaking, different types of object. The category of fine art, though in some ways relatively easy to define, is complicated by the fact that in some places, such as Manchester, there were separate institutions collecting fine art, while in others, such as Birmingham, everything came to one institution. As a majority of municipal institutions collected fine art as well as other objects, it has been retained within the analysis. The overall level of manufactured donations, therefore, is a safer category than the sub-disciplines within it, though I think the broad proportions are valid.

The following analysis, then, is based on accessions to those museums which apparently had the broadest acquisition policy, and where the recording of accessions was most reliable, namely Ipswich, Whitby, Brighton, Bristol, Cheltenham, Warrington, Manchester, Birmingham and Sunderland. The BM was not included because the economy of donation was significantly different here; neither was the Horniman, which during this period specialised solely in natural history and ethnography. Manchester Museum was included, although in some ways it operated a restricted acquisitions policy; as Alberti has shown, donors were active in developing the collections there in ways which were not necessarily foreseen or wanted by the staff.[11] Birmingham Museum, although initially focusing very much on fine and decorative art, had a natural history section by the end of our period. Figure 6 shows the proportions of the main categories of object in women's donations. This is not a perfect analysis, but it gives some idea of relative levels of donations in different types of object, and does reveal some useful patterns.

It is to be expected that natural historical objects dominate the donations in these museums. Municipal and civic museums were by and large based on natural history collections, although there is evidence that from around 1900 interest in these museums was moving towards the manufactured.[12] Moreover, natural history was a very widespread hobby in the nineteenth century, with many middle-class children inculcated in such collecting as an 'improving' pursuit, much popular literature dedicated to it, and a network of local societies with a much greater female membership than the national societies.[13] Anyway, natural historical objects were the most likely of museum objects to be acquired 'accidentally' as people came upon plants, rocks and dead animals (or killed the animals themselves).[14] Both of these factors were particularly important for women as donors, and there are a number of donations, often of insects, spiders and

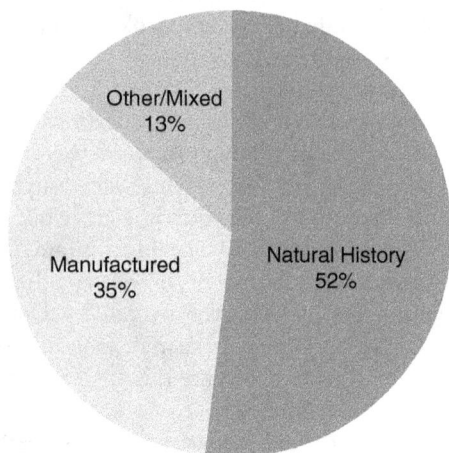

Figure 6 Women's donation events by main discipline.
(Data from accession registers and annual reports, 1880–1914.)

birds, where the comment 'found in donor's garden', or 'found in pantry' is recorded.[15]

The number of manufactured donations is, however, higher than might have been expected. This reflects a growth of interest in all areas of human study including history, archaeology, anthropology and the arts and crafts.[16] Museums, especially municipal museums, moved decisively towards manufactured objects, particularly local history and archaeology, towards the end of the period, for reasons encompassing both the politics of the locality and reflecting changing interests of the public at large.[17] University museums expanded and diversified their archaeological holdings, while national museums which already specialised in archaeology or applied art, such as the BM and SKM, also developed their collection significantly during the period.[18] A. W. Franks, at the BM, paid much more attention to British antiquities and also to anthropology (it was also Franks who encouraged Lady Charlotte Schreiber to donate her playing cards and fans to the museum) and thus diversified the museum away from its primary focus on classical material; while at the SKM, although a commitment to objects which could educate the artisan and raise standards of public taste, as mandated by Henry Cole, was still publicly adhered to, the collection of historical objects had gone so far as to suggest to many a growing connoisseurial approach.[19]

Donation events by sub-discipline

189   136   96   52   174   100   60   132   101   55   79   95

Vertebrate zoology · Botany · Geology · Shells · Other natural history · Art · Archaeology · Ethnography · Social and/or local history · Applied art · Mixed · Other

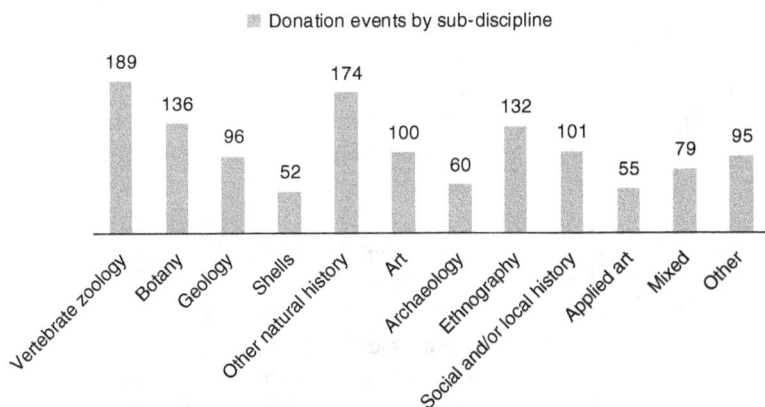

Figure 7 Women's donation events by sub-discipline.
(Data from accession registers and annual reports, 1880–1914.)

In fact, one might say that such disciplines were particularly attractive to and offered particular opportunities to women to explore the overlap between knowledge and affect; this suggestion will be explored further in Chapter 6. Women gave so many of these objects because they already owned them, and they thought them to be objects with value. Women, I argue, were not just following a trend towards the human sciences, but were in fact driving it.

Figure 7 represents the attempt to subdivide both natural and manufactured donations further. Within natural history, I have not included all possible categories, but singled out both the biggest categories, and those which are known to have been seen as appropriate for women, such as botany and conchology. The 'Other natural history' category mainly contains invertebrates, as well as a substantial number of mixed donations which are entirely composed of natural history.

Given the emphasis on botany in popular collecting literature aimed at women, the preponderance of vertebrate zoology is a little surprising.[20] However, vertebrate zoology is among the most 'displayable' of natural history categories; botany, though almost universally covered by museums at this period, was hard to display – most accessions were in the form of albums of pressed, dried plants, and while developments in botanical display were taking place, they were not universally adopted. Vertebrate zoology tended to account for the greatest amount of display space within the natural history rooms of museums. Within this category, by far the most numerous type of specimen was birds, including eggs and nests. Such objects were reasonably common within Victorian homes; egg and nest collecting was an accepted part of 'nature study', and undertaken by women as well as men.[21] However, women were also more viscerally involved with vertebrate zoology; some women shot their own donations, and stuffed them.[22] Thus both the museum's priorities, and the gendering of natural history collecting, exerted an influence on the donations made to museums; these might be described as supply and demand factors. Museums made their most significant efforts to shape donation in the field of natural history, issuing advice to potential donors in the form of pamphlets and other publications.[23] Natural history donations show us where women's possessions and museums' agendas overlap.

Yet such an overlap does not guarantee that objects had the same meaning for women and museums, as a consideration of geological donations shows. We know that geology and fossil hunting were both carried out by women for profit, as well as by leisured women. Moreover, such collecting, by the second half of the nineteenth century, overtook the collection of shells, which had earlier been seen as appropriate for women because of their decorative nature.[24] Geological collections could be used for decorative purposes, and women donated polished specimens which clearly had aesthetic as well as scientific value.[25] Geology's popularity may thus be explained by the ease with which objects valued in a domestic setting for their aesthetic properties could become valuable in a museum setting for scientific reasons. Thus, objects which were particularly multivalent facilitated the relationship between women and museums.

Although a quantitative analysis of women's donations reveals, therefore, that such objects both responded to and expanded museums' own developing plans for their collections, and showed some continuity with women's interactions with objects in the earlier nineteenth century, it is unable to take us much further than this. In particular, in order to see how objects acted as agents in the development of feminine identities and museums, we need to examine particular objects, or particular groups of objects, in more detail. The next section, therefore, examines groups of objects which collectively brought feminine values most clearly into the museum and undermined its norms of value.

The nature of women's objects – collective object biographies

What follows is not object biography in the usual sense of life story of an object or case study of significant or representative thing. Rather, I am trying to understand the routes through which women's things came into the museum, and the effect this had on their meaning, collectively. In tracing the paths which sets or types of objects travelled in order to become museum objects, and the ways in which they might come to be associated with women, I am not merely interested in the different significances which people placed on those objects at different times; rather, I hope to uncover the ways in which objects' previous lives were carried with them into new contexts, and thus enabled the objects to remake the contexts as much as vice versa. Objects on the move might change status and meaning, or they might bring meanings with them. And in doing so, they might remake or revalue their owners. Object or collection biographies can highlight how things have produced identities and emotional states, as well as bringing people and institutions into relation.[26]

Women's donations were almost always things which their owners had lived with in their homes prior to donation, though their field origin might have been far away. They were, thus, domesticated objects, with their original meaning overlain with familial and memory connotations. This is often true of men's donations as well, especially to smaller local museums, though their donations also came out of non-domestic settings such as clubs and societies. But how far did objects' residence in a domestic setting affect their public valuation? This depended partly upon the type of object; museums strove to make objects of science, scientific and not domestic. However, they were more prepared to embrace the domestic origins of social and local history objects, and relics, which we might term objects with an aura of authenticity; domesticity could be an important part of such objects' guarantee of authenticity. Authenticity, it has been suggested, was an increasingly problematic but desirable quality with the advent and development of modernity.[27] The humble, domestic, historical object appeared to be the antithesis of the mass-produced, alienated and alienating modern object.[28] A space was thus opened up for a debate around the valuation of historical objects which, as I will show, ascribed gendered qualities to those objects and even to the nature of authenticity itself. Beyond this, I argue that the biographies and meanings of women's objects coming from a domestic setting meant, in fact, that they could not easily be placed into the categories and classifications of the museum, and indeed undermined and destabilised these categories. Below, I examine textiles and clothing, souvenirs and relics, and 'old things': a selection of categories imposed retrospectively (some of them were used by museums at the time but inconsistently) because they are relatively well documented and have particular relevance to the issue of gendered (and gendering) objects.

Textiles and clothing

In considering both textiles and clothing, I echo the dichotomy identified by Lou Taylor, who argues that male collectors and institutions began to value and collect textiles in the nineteenth century, but it took considerably longer for clothing to be collected or displayed in a systematic way by museums. Taylor suggests that this is because clothing was perceived as too closely aligned with fashion, consumption and retail; with feminine things, essentially. Thus it did not fall easily into the mould of the decorative arts which was being fashioned by people such as Henry Cole. He envisaged an all-encompassing pedagogical system for the design of manufactures which did not respond to fashion but rather communicated timeless principles.[29] Moreover she points out that women were instrumental in initiating the collection of clothing, citing pioneering women curators in the twentieth century such as Thalassa Cruso at the Museum of London in the 1930s, or Doris Langley Moore who set up the Museum of Costume in Bath in 1963; they turned the display of clothing from something frivolous and ephemeral to something which could be seriously studied.[30] This suggests that for women the association with fashion, consumption and ephemerality was not problematic; and maybe even that this dichotomy between the serious and the frivolous object was not always recognised by women.

There is certainly much validity in Taylor's argument. 'Mere' fashion was seen as unsuitable for the museum by commentators such as Cole, and textiles lent themselves more easily to deriving the type of knowledge which museums were increasingly looking to produce and display with applied arts: surveys of historical development and demonstrations of techniques. On the other hand, there is evidence that major historical clothing collections were driven by (male) artists who collected them as props for their paintings, as Petrov's work on the collections at the Victoria and Albert Museum (V&A) (as the SKM was renamed), and the Guildhall Museum, the forerunner of the Museum of London, has shown.[31] This was in advance of Taylor's women collectors. The study of donations in regional museums allows us to look beyond the London collections and also to push the start of clothing collecting even earlier; some sorts of clothing were being collected well before the First World War. These collections suggest that the centrality of sewing to ideas of femininity had led women to invest textiles, sewing paraphernalia and clothing with a distinct significance which was recognised, sometimes valued and sometimes resisted by museums.

Textiles and clothing, of course, had for some time been bound up in the memory practices of women, especially within the family.[32] Family memory here was bound up in the material minutiae of everyday life; and women were the custodians of this memory. Gordon has shown how the production, exchange and collection of textiles were used by women in the formation and consolidation of friendships.[33] Textiles and needlework were part of the everyday life of almost all women for much of the nineteenth century, in a way that they were not for men. It is equally important, though, to recognise that by the end of the nineteenth century, domestic needlework had already changed and was still rapidly transforming, largely because of the growth of the ready-made clothing industry. This did not necessarily diminish the symbolic value of needlework as a feminine attribute, which was still widely undertaken by women and played a significant part in the formation of feminine identities well into the twentieth century.[34] Needlework was recognised by men and women as producing objects whose significance came from their dense invocation of emotional, relational and memory-based qualities.[35]

In addition, the growth of 'art needlework' affected the way in which textiles were seen. Ancient tapestries were collected by the SKM from an early stage, and were conceptually indistinguishable from other historical artefacts; they were studied by scholars and connoisseurs to inform an art historical discourse.[36] William Morris led the development of modern art needlework, which was seen as valuable art; but the products of his company often evinced a gendered divide where men developed the design, and women executed it, though a few women such as May Morris were able to move into design with some success.[37] In some sense, then, textiles and clothing can be seen as areas where there was some conflict between men and women over who determined the meaning and significance of the artefacts. Thus it is crucial to examine the particular objects that women donated.

In fact, textiles were outnumbered by clothing among women's donations (though of course there is not a clear dividing line between the two, as Taylor makes clear).[38] Among textiles were some important donations of art needlework, historical or contemporary. At Birmingham in 1912, needlework dating to around 1780 was donated, along with a Morris & Co. tapestry designed by Edward Burne Jones; Hungarian and Moravian embroidery was also donated.[39] Tapestry was given to Norwich Museum in 1908.[40] There were also, however, textiles and needlework whose claim to art status is unclear. The noteworthy subscription of sixty-three Leicester ladies to the purchase of a needlework picture, which was then donated to the museum, is one such. It was a copy, in needlework, of a late seventeenth-century Italian painting; thus it certainly did not conform to Morris's ideals for needlework.[41] Instead, it celebrated female ingenuity and skill.

Most of the other donations relate to domestic, rather than art, needlework. Thus, at Leicester, donations include a sampler in 1908, and a needlework picture of unknown manufacture or subject matter; at Warrington women gave a needle case, a pin cushion, a knitting sheath and a sampler; while in Norwich the donation of at least five samplers between 1912 and 1914 was recorded, as well as a knitting sheath and a bodkin.[42] The inclusion of domestic needlework equipment here is particularly striking.[43] The symbolic and emotional valuation of domestic needlework was shared by men as well as women; as Pettitt notes, Dickens endowed Peggotty's workbox with powerful emotional significance for David Copperfield as symbolic of Peggotty herself.[44] Women, however, had a head start in the ownership of such objects: the female donor of a knitting sheath to Warrington Museum noted that it was used by her grandmother up to 1879.[45]

Surprisingly large amounts of clothing were donated to museums. At Leicester, such acquisitions included a tippet, and a waistcoat; at Warrington a muslin neckerchief, a Khartoum cap, two bonnets and a dress box; at Norwich a mayor's robe, two waistcoats, two parasols, three shawls, a spencer (short, close-fitting jacket), several collars and a fichu (women's small triangular shawl), a surplice, three military caps, other items of military uniform, and numerous items of children's clothing including babies' bonnets and caps, christening gowns and shirts. At Cheltenham, a shawl was given, while at Bristol a military uniform was donated.[46] There were, therefore, two main categories of clothing: domestic and female or infant, and official, male clothing, often uniforms. The official, male clothing, both civic and military, functioned more as memorial than illustration of the history of costume; in all cases the name and position of the man who wore the uniform was given. Other clothing, however, was for women and children, and generally had no individual associated with it (though occasionally the *maker* of the artefact was identified, usually as a female relative of the donor). In other words, there was a different reason for valuing women's and children's clothing. Men were remembered by women as individual, public figures through their official clothing; women's donation of feminine items of clothing was designed rather to highlight feminine domestic needlework and its role in the development of family relationships and feminine selves.

There are instances of women's offers of textiles, needlework and clothing items being refused by museums, highlighting the lack of consensus over the meaning and value of such items. In Bristol, the loan of antique embroidery was turned down in 1896; while at the Horniman Museum, seventeenth-century needlework, offered for sale, was refused in 1903.[47] This indicates that there was still some uncertainty over the value of these objects, even art needlework, and that the reluctance to display them noted by Taylor could be found. Women's attempts to introduce objects which suggested both an art historical agenda and a desire to value objects which were resonant with memory, gendered identity and intimate relationships, were only partly successful.

Thus far, then, we can see that women's objects often complicated existing museum categories. The second half of the nineteenth century was a period when attempts were being made to co-opt domestic, personal items into a systematic art historical framework. The origins and drivers of such attempts were complex, deriving from the design reform principles of Cole, the Morrisian assertion that hand crafting could be art, and the connoisseurial approach to decorative objects visible at the SKM by 1900.[48] What united this masculine approach was the sense that the objective, scientific value of such objects was separate from their subjective, affective meaning, and that in order to make the objects meaningful such emotional associations needed to be stripped away. For women, this division was not so meaningful and they were more likely to highlight the affective and intimate side of such objects, as well as to highlight the feminine traditions of making and using which gave them an expertise distinct from those of the masculine approaches highlighted above. They had some success in inserting this value system into local museums, but still found that sometimes it was not accepted.

Souvenirs and relics

A substantial number of what can only be described as relics were donated by women during our period. These include what was alleged to be the Earl of Warwick's chair, a letter from James Watt, gloves from the Franklin expedition, Edward II's hair, and a pillion on which the donor's grandmother allegedly rode behind Sir Isaac Newton.[49] Coleridge's hair was given to Bristol Museum in 1902, along with a letter and autograph poem; and a plaster mask of Napoleon was given to Leicester Museum in 1882.[50] In most cases, the story whereby the relic object came into the donor's possession was recorded; in many ways the basic requirement to make something a relic is that its relationship to the person or event being remembered can be demonstrated (though there is no record of why the hair was believed to have come from Edward II). Family and the domestic environment seem to have been either the major reason for the acquisition of such relics by the museum, or at least the best way of offering some measure of authenticity to these relics. Thus, donors and museums recorded family traditions as essential to the meaning of objects.[51]

Pascoe argues that the collection of relics, especially those of poets, was a characteristically Romantic way of engaging with materiality. She describes the relic market of the early nineteenth century as 'founded on literary embellishment and speculative half-truth'.[52] Relics were widely displayed at attractions like William Bullock's Egyptian Hall, and Madame Tussaud's.[53] By the later nineteenth century, a certain illegitimacy therefore surrounded such relics, and new civic museums were keen to stress instead their pedagogical and scientific credentials. Yet Pascoe also documents the continuation of this trend, noting the late nineteenth-century collector Edward Silsbee, obsessed with relics of the poet Shelley, and the author Henry James, who retold Silsbee's story in *The Aspern Papers*, and whose writings often evinced an interest in the potential of physical relics to promote contact between past and present, or even to project their possessor back in time.[54] The voracious collector Henry Wellcome also made a point of tracking down as many relics of important figures in the history of medicine as he could, though he subjected them to what he felt was a rigorous process of verification, and saw them as scientific objects.[55] What this suggests, therefore, is that the power of relics was popularly felt as strongly as ever, but that legitimate, and especially publicly run institutions like museums had to be very careful in acquiring and displaying them, particularly when they did not relate to literary figures whose importance was acknowledged to be based on affective power; they were slightly embarrassing objects for professional museum curators. The relics donated by women came from figures who were already well established as appropriate for relic collecting, such as Coleridge, as well as from newly popular events, for example the Franklin expedition, and scientists such as Newton.[56]

A similar group of objects derived their power from the fact of their journey round the world to the museum, and again reveal how women's objects could disrupt and undermine the categories of the museum. Many objects were, in some form or another, souvenirs, collected to mark the owner's actual presence in a particular location. While the souvenir predated the nineteenth century, according to Marius Kwint it did not predate it by much; he suggests that 'today's souvenir was certainly constituted in the eighteenth century under the immense influence of the Grand Tour; and around 1775 the word was first applied to an object, rather than a notion'.[57] In this specific form, then, the souvenir is a product of the modern world, and reflects a sense of transformation in time and space which underlay ideas of modernity.

The souvenir is a particularly important type of object for this study, both for its emergent gendering, and because souvenirs in museums combined intimate and individual significance with public value and display. Thus it shows how public space could be inflected by the intimate, and how men's and women's ways of collecting and living with objects produced quite different meanings for those objects. The souvenir is not a category of object which can be strictly defined; nor is it a stable identification for an object. It is more a mode of signifying or meaning, which an object can take on in certain contexts or for certain people.[58]

Witcomb suggests that souvenirs do not carry meaning in a representational way at all; 'these objects simply "were"'.[59] As she and Kwint both argue, souvenirs can in fact combine representational modes where meaning can be read, with sensory modes where the object's significance comes from its bodily, physical effect. Souvenirs thus work by moving 'away from the traditional binary oppositions of subject-object and mind-body, and focus instead on the space in-between, the space of engagement between people and the material world which surrounds them and of which they too are a part'.[60] Thus women's donations of souvenirs, like their textile and clothing donations, both partake of and resist museum schemes of knowledge.

Harrison's study of the movement of souvenirs through a number of locations including museums shows how much these particular objects can tell us about the way individuals and institutions were connected. He suggests that individual objects were 'splinters of memory' which, when assembled and reassembled in different ways in Britain, told stories about its Empire. As he suggests, this means that the distinction between souvenirs and collections is not at all stable, but depends rather on how individual objects were successively assembled in different times and places.[61] It also suggests that souvenirs can be examined, not just as individual objects with individual meanings, but collectively as part of networks, producing meanings which are more widely dispersed.[62]

The souvenirs which I explore here were not generally purpose-made; rather they were found or repurposed objects often just picked up, but sometimes bought, in the course of overseas travel of various sorts.[63] The result is that souvenirs are hard to identify in museum collections, largely because of poor surviving documentation in nineteenth-century collections.[64] The purchase and collection of souvenirs abroad expanded with tourist travel. As the persona of the tourist developed in the later nineteenth century, there were signs that touristic souvenir collecting was starting to be seen as an unserious feminine practice; or at least, one which was so closely associated with affective bonds of family and friendship so as to be totally at odds with a masculine, objective project of knowing the world through collecting. Men who had any pretensions to scholarly status were less likely to present themselves as souvenir collectors. Such a gendered division between female souvenir collectors and male 'scientific' collectors, in perceptions at least, is strongly suggested by Shaun Garner's account of the travels and collections of Merton (later Sir) and Annie Russell-Cotes in Asia and Australasia, especially Japan, in the late nineteenth century. Although their collecting showed features which were both scientific (especially Annie's botanical collecting) and touristic (a bank manager in Japan advanced them cash to buy curios, which he assumed they, like all British travellers, would be buying in large quantities), on their return to Britain Merton Russell-Cotes used his collections to assert expertise in Japanese culture, become a founding member of the Japan Society, and present himself as an explorer.[65]

Among the bald records of accession books and annual reports, some potential souvenirs can be identified. Kabyle ornaments which were given to Warrington Museum in 1908 came with the comment from the donor, 'Algiers, 1870', and it is hard to see this as anything other than the record of the donor's own presence in a particular place which gave the objects meaning to her. In the same way, Mrs and Miss Weekes gave what were described as 'curios' to the Horniman Museum in 1897 noting their origins as 'Azores, 1866'.[66] The model of the Leaning Tower of Pisa given to Bristol Museum in 1909 seems highly likely to have been acquired as a souvenir, though by whom, and even when, is not clear.[67]

Other souvenirs testified to the travelling, not of the donor, but of other family members, such as the model of a Swiss chalet bought in Switzerland in 1844 by Mr Sancroft Holmes, and donated to Norwich Museum in 1880 by Mrs Sancroft Holmes. The 'feather flowers brought from Madeira' in 1840 seem to be souvenirs, but as they were donated in 1909–10, were probably not originally acquired by the donor. Several souvenirs testify to the military or Imperial service of the menfolk of the donor's family. Thus at Brighton Museum in 1910, a finger ring obtained during the first Zulu War was acquired, while in 1913, objects were acquired from Miss Stewart which were collected during the Punitive Expedition to Benin in 1897; and in the same year, a helmet worn by 'one of the six hundred' at the charge of Balaclava was presented to the museum by Mrs James Barker.[68]

Women's souvenir and relic donations were likely to have spent quite some time, around 30 years, in the donor's house, between field collection and donation. It is this, I argue, that gave them their particular meaning, as they were domesticated and immersed in the intimate relationships of the home.[69] Furthermore, they therefore represented their women owners as custodians of the material memories of their families. Men collected objects as souvenirs of their military travels, and relics of historic events, and brought them back to the (British) home, where women incorporated them into domestic material assemblages. Women might feel deeply ambivalent about such objects, which both embodied members of their family, and, in the case of military souvenirs, symbolised a highly masculine environment.[70] The ambiguity may be evidenced in the fact that these objects were ultimately given to museums; they were removed from the home, but their sacred qualities as family souvenirs meant that they needed to be placed somewhere suitable, and not sold or thrown away.[71]

The gendering of souvenirs and relics thus works in a number of ways. While the initial gathering of the objects was not always strongly gendered, it functioned to bring them into a familial, domestic regime of value, so that souvenirs did not simply tell an individual's life, but rather that of a family. In addition, men were more likely to disavow the status of souvenir or relic for their object, and thus less likely to offer them to museums with such an explicit label; such objects were increasingly regarded as not serious or objective. Women asserted their competence in preserving family material memory, while men were more likely to re-imagine their souvenir or relic as an object of knowledge, as Henry Wellcome and Sir Merton Russell-Cotes show.

'Bygones' or old things

Another group worth examining is one we might call 'old things'. A number of the objects donated by women show signs of being valued primarily for the length of their biography; the signs of oldness are what seems to have been appreciated in this case, rather than historical or archaeological significance more strictly defined. Of course, this is not a new phenomenon; early nineteenth-century antiquarians were mocked for their obsession with the signs of age, and the Romantic period generally found compelling those things which had visibly survived from an earlier period.[72] However, the assumption has tended to be that in the second half of the nineteenth century, antiquarianism reshaped itself as archaeology, and became more concerned with system, context, and the development of a scientifically reliable chronology than it was with age as a valuable quality in its own right.[73] However it is also true to say that more and more old things were becoming desirable in the late nineteenth century, and to more people, building on the growth in the antiques trade throughout the century. This can be seen as another response to the modern which showed increased emphasis on the idea of the authentic; cultural commentators such as John Ruskin and William Morris were influential in ascribing authenticity to pre-industrial modes of production.[74]

The gendering of old things was not clear-cut. Antiques proper, as a specific subsection of old things, were quite robustly male, as the discussion of dealers in Chapter 2 confirms; women made up only fifteen per cent of the clientele of a Bradford antiques dealer and Cohen suggests this was quite typical.[75] The figure of the antiques collector came to be represented as a man who either did not marry, or made a bad husband, because of his absorption in his things; a person whose relationships were solely with his things, rather than with people. Cohen's example of the Cardiff collector Robert Drane, who found antiques far more truthful than people, is telling.[76] But antiques, with their high market value, emphasis on the importance of provenance, and growing literature of appreciation, were not the only kind of old thing to become more popular around 1900. Other, more humble objects, such as family possessions (not heirlooms, but quite everyday things, such as thimbles), and 'bygones' were beginning to be more prominent also.[77]

Bygones, family heirlooms and general 'old things' are less visible in the historical record than antiques, but signs of interest in them can be found. Beatrix Potter, a woman who had a strong romantic attachment to old things, was interested in old family clothes, as well as harbouring an attachment to old furniture. She declared, 'It is extraordinary how little people value old things if they are of little intrinsic value.'[78] At a curiosity shop in Falmouth, she bought 'a white pot head in bone, which was one of the few English curios of any antiquity'.[79] Mary Greg had formed a substantial collection of bygones by 1920, and gave it to Manchester Art Gallery in the 1920s as the Greg Collection of Bygones. Its origins, as far as one can tell, seem to have been quite ad hoc, including gifts, purchases, found items, things worked by her and inherited items. It included such things as keys, old wooden spoons and thimble cases.[80] Although less widespread than antique collecting, an interest in domestic and everyday old things may have been less firmly masculine, and may have developed from the material matrilineal family history described by Styles and Vickery, and possibly traceable as far back as the Renaissance.[81] In endowing old things with qualities of authenticity, women enthusiasts for old things found a relationship that was not only more emotionally satisfying than relationships with new things, but that also created a relationship with the dead; the dead of family history, or of an imagined age of peasant authenticity or genteel sensibility.[82]

Museum acquisition books show many examples of women giving objects whose ability to inform a scientific discourse about the past was minimal, but whose resonant, age-related qualities were prominent. The investigation of objects which could very broadly be designated as local or social history shows many of them embodied a family past, because of their association with particular past family members, or lengthy residence within the family home. In several cases, associations with the donor's family are recorded by the museum; for example a knife and fork that belonged to the donor's grandfather and a neckerchief that belonged to the donor's mother.[83] Such associations may have been useful to the museums for dating and provenance, but could also serve to indicate a kind of emotional authenticity as well.[84] Even where details of family links between the donor and the original owner or maker of objects are not recorded, it is clear that they are present in many cases. A significant number of objects such as babies' bonnets, caps and christening gowns were kept as family objects and then donated.[85] Thus the journey of old things to the museum could be inflected by gender as they emerged from a particular familial, domestic setting, and this journey might be accepted, even celebrated by the museum, rather than being erased.

The value of an object biography approach for my study, then, is that it shows how objects link the donors, their homes and families, and the museums, revealing how the domestic meaning of the objects could persist in the museum. Many of the objects given by women were initially acquired and valued for reasons which were far removed from the rationales of the museum. By preserving, grouping or otherwise indicating the specialness of these objects, the donors gave them a power which persisted into the museum. They resisted and undermined the museum's categories; and asserted instead the multivalent and affective power of domestic things. Women's objects also tended to embody stories, often stories about family heritage; in many ways these were objects which could materialise memories. This led to museum objects which were intensely evocative; one might not have a family link between oneself and the exhibit, but it powerfully suggested universalities of human experience in the past.

Conclusion

The objects donated by women were valued and valuable for reasons which cut across the established rationale for putting objects in museums, both resisting and accommodating museum categories. Items given to museums in small quantities, by women who were in no sense experts, for apparently very personal reasons, were often flexible enough to 'pass' as scholarly objects; while equally often, even the most apparently scholarly of women's donations encompassed more affective, commemorative or ludic valuations of objects. Partly, this is because museums were struggling to develop a scholarly or systematic display approach for many kinds of manufactured object at the time, and were both suspicious of, and drawn to, popular genres of object such as relics. What is particularly significant here, though, is the extent to which such objects gained value from their authenticated transit through a domestic environment. Old objects, relics and even souvenirs accrued meaning, especially when they were given to a museum by their domestic custodian, who could supply information about how and when the object was used, and could attest to its descent across the generations. Textiles and clothing which were not part of an elite material culture were things which were or had been used and produced by women in a domestic setting. Women's material practices within the home thus gained an importance of which they took advantage.

Women's donations often foregrounded a sense of truthfulness in objects; and it is this which drove much of the revaluation of historical objects we see in donations around this period.[86] The idea of authenticity was a critical and contested one in the late nineteenth century; although the Ruskinian and Morrisian concept of authenticity as deriving from persistence through time is clearly influential here, such family souvenirs develop the concept further, tying it more closely both to family continuity through time, and to the identity and nature of the (feminine) person possessing the authentic object in the present.[87]

Women's enhanced roles as the custodians of the affective elements of the home, as the people who were attuned to the qualities of objects, and as the creators and sustainers of a family history based on the domestic, allowed them to assert a leading position in the revaluation of manufactured things evident in the museum around 1900. Women's objects both looked back to romantic and other older modes of valuing things; and constituted a distinctive and 'modern' way of valuing and relating to the material world. They constructed a sense of self and of the self's place in space and time by emphasising the domestic, familial and local, as well as souvenirs and relics which harnessed history and geography to the identity of the owner and their family. Women's objects clearly helped to shape the concerns of the twentieth-century museum; but they also shaped the women who donated them, who through the public display of their objects could assert an alternative type of history and geography, over which they exercised more control. At the very least, these objects allowed women to engage in debate over what were important objects, and why; and to give greater public prominence to qualities of empathy, sensibility and aesthetic effect, which formed much of the basis of their claim to greater involvement in public life.[88] Women did not reject the ideals of objectivity and systematicity, but alongside these, and sometimes interwoven into these, they asserted the value of memory, affect, relational qualities and subjectivity in objects, not just for the private domain of the home, but for public display for a wider national benefit.

The study, therefore, of which women donated, how they donated and what they donated, has demonstrated that women's contribution to museums was much wider and deeper than concentrating on either the museum institution and personnel, or on major donors, would tend to indicate. It is not just that more women were involved in donating than we might think, but that this almost invisible donating contributed to a shift in the things valued by museums. In the twentieth century, museums came to focus more and more on social and cultural history, along with taking on a role within the developing collective memory practices of the modern world; in a sense, they became feminised.[89] Women's difficulty in accessing the 'inner' areas of the museum did not mean that they were unable to be part of the museum project; they were outsiders but they still powerfully shaped museums into their twentieth-century form.

Notes

1 Dianne Sachko Macleod, *Enchanted Lives, Enchanted Objects: American Women Collectors and the Making of Culture, 1800–1940* (Berkeley, CA: University of California Press 2008).

2 See Macleod, *Enchanted Lives*. Also of interest in this context are Maureen Daly Goggin and Beth Fowkes Tobin (eds), *Material Women, 1750–1950: Consuming Desires and Collecting Practices* (Aldershot: Ashgate 2009) and M. D. Goggin and B. F. Tobin (eds), *Women and Things, 1750–1950: Gendered Material Strategies* (Aldershot: Ashgate 2009).

3 Samuel J. M. M. Alberti, 'The museum affect: visiting collections of anatomy and natural history', in A. Fyfe and B. Lightman (eds), *Science in the Marketplace: Nineteenth-Century Sites and Experiences* (Chicago, IL: University of Chicago Press 2007); Samuel J. M. M. Alberti, *Nature and Culture: Objects, Disciplines*

and the Manchester Museum (Manchester: Manchester University Press 2009), chapter 5. See also Chris Gosden and Frances Larson, *Knowing Things: Exploring the Collections at the Pitt Rivers Museum 1884–1945* (Oxford: Oxford University Press 2007), chapter 6.

4 The multivalent properties of objects have been explored by a number of scholars: most prominently Susan Pearce in *On Collecting: An Investigation into Collecting in the European Tradition* (Abingdon: Routledge 1995), who stressed objects' ability to be both metaphor and metonym. Pomian suggests that collecting serves to connect people to the invisible realm but here I am particularly interested in objects' ability to signify both scientific knowledge, and mnemonic and affective states; Krzysztof Pomian, 'The collection: between the visible and the invisible', in Susan M. Pearce (ed.), *Interpreting Objects and Collections* (London: Routledge 1994). Harrison restates the idea that objects may act as metaphor or metonym, but does suggest that objects could and did move back and forth between these modes of signification: Rodney Harrison, 'Consuming colonialism: curio dealers' catalogues, souvenir objects, and indigenous agency in Oceania', in S. Byrne, A. Clarke, R. Harrison and R. Torrence (eds), *Unpacking the Collection: Networks of Material and Social Agency in the Museum* (New York: Springer, 2011), p. 77.

5 The starting point for most studies in object biography is Arjun Appadurai (ed.), *The Social Life of Things: Commodities in Cultural Perspective* (Cambridge: Cambridge University Press 1986), and especially the chapter within it by Igor Kopytoff: 'The cultural biography of things: commoditisation as process', pp. 64–91. See also Chris Gosden and Yvonne Marshall, 'The cultural biography of objects', *World Archaeology* 31: 2 (1999), pp. 169–178. For an example of an object biography which illuminates the changing meaning of an object, see L. Tythacott, 'Classifying China: shifting interpretations of Buddhist bronzes in Liverpool Museum, 1867–1997', in Kate Hill (ed.), *Museums and Biographies: Stories, Objects, Identities* (Woodbridge: Boydell and Brewer 2012).

6 See Lucie Carreau, 'Individual, collective and institutional biographies: the Beasley collection of Pacific artefacts', in K. Hill, *Museums and Biographies*.

7 Kate Hill, *Culture and Class in English Public Museums, 1850–1914* (Aldershot: Ashgate 2005), p. 83.

8 Gaynor Kavanagh, *Dream Spaces: Memory and the Museum* (London: Leicester University Press 2000).

9 Wingfield's concept of 'acquisition events' is discussed in Chapter 2.

10 See Tythacott, 'Classifying China', for an example of how the same object could be classified differently by the same museum at different times.

11 Alberti, *Nature and Culture*, chapter 4.

12 Alberti, *Nature and Culture*, chapter 3; Hill, *Culture and Class*, chapter 5.

13 Lynn Merrill, *The Romance of Victorian Natural History* (Oxford: Oxford University Press 1989); David E. Allen, 'The women members of the Botanical Society of London, 1836–56', *British Journal for the History of Science*, 13 (1980), pp. 240–254; Ann B Shteir, *Cultivating Women, Cultivating Science: Flora's Daughters and Botany in England, 1760–1860* (Baltimore, MD: Johns Hopkins University Press 1996).

14 Women hunted as well as men; a good example is Cara Buxton, who shot quite a few large mammals in East Africa around 1900, which she donated to Norwich Museum. See Buxton, *Adventurous Norfolk Lady: Miss Cara Buxton's Sport in Africa* (St Albans: Fisher Knight and Co, n.d.). This, admittedly, could not exactly be classed as 'accidental', but the point remains that the museum donation was not Buxton's aim, rather it was a by-product.

15 See, for example, Leicester Museum Accession Books, October 1884 and November 1884.

16 See Chapter 6.

17 Hill, *Culture and Class*, chapter 5; Kate Hill, 'Manufactures, archaeology and bygones: making a sense of place in civic museums, 1850–1914', *International Journal of Regional and Local History* 8: 1 (2013), pp. 54–74.

18 Alberti, *Nature and Culture*, chapter 3; Gosden and Larson, *Knowing Things*, chapter 7.

19 Arthur MacGregor, 'Collectors, connoisseurs and curators in the Victorian age', in M. Caygill and J. Cherry (eds), *A. W. Franks: Nineteenth-Century Collecting and the British Museum* (London: British Museum Press 1997); Anthony Burton, *Vision and Accident: The Story of the Victoria and Albert Museum* (London: V&A Publications 1999). On women and decorative art objects, see A. Anderson, ' "Chinamania": collecting Old Blue for the House Beautiful, c. 1860–1900', in J. Potvin and A. Myzelev (eds), *Material Cultures 1740–1920: The Meanings and Pleasures of Collecting* (Aldershot: Ashgate 2009); Sonia Ashmore, 'Liberty and lifestyle: shopping for art and luxury in nineteenth-century London', in D. E. Hussey and M. Ponsonby (eds), *Buying for the Home: Shopping for the Domestic from the Seventeenth Century to the Present* (Aldershot: Ashgate 2008) and Deborah Cohen, *Household Gods: The British and Their Possessions* (New Haven, CT and London: Yale University Press 2006).

20 Shteir, *Cultivating Women*; Merrill, *Romance of Victorian Natural History*.

21 Thad Logan, *The Victorian Parlour: A Cultural Study* (Cambridge: Cambridge University Press 2001), pp. 141–158.

22 Cara Buxton, referred to in note 11 above, prepared her own specimens or at least got her native servants to do so. Buxton, *Adventurous Norfolk Lady*.

23 Hill, *Culture and Class*, p. 83.

24 On conchology, see D. E. Allen, *Naturalists and Society: The Culture of Natural History in Britain 1700–1900* (Aldershot: Ashgate Variorum 2001), pp. 1–9, 395–397.

25 An example is the five pieces of limestone, cut and polished, from Gibraltar, given to Leicester Museum in 1903: Leicester Museum Accession Books August 1903.

26 S. Byrne, A. Clarke, R. Harrison and R. Torrence, 'Networks, agents and objects: frameworks for unpacking museum collections', and Harrison, 'Consuming colonialism', both in S. Byrne, A. Clarke, R. Harrison and R. Torrence (eds), *Unpacking the Collection*.

27 Susan Stewart, *On Longing: Narratives of the Miniature, the Gigantic, the Souvenir, the Collection* (Baltimore, MD: Johns Hopkins University Press 1984), especially chapter 5; Mark B. Sandberg, *Living Pictures, Missing Persons: Mannequins, Museums and Modernity* (Princeton: Princeton University Press 2003); Elizabeth Outka, *Consuming Traditions: Modernity, Modernism and the Commodified Authentic* (Oxford: Oxford University Press 2009).

28 Logan, *Victorian Parlour*, p. 187; Cohen, *Household Gods*, chapter 6.

29 Clive Wainwright, 'The making of the South Kensington Museum II, collecting modern manufactures: 1851 and the Great Exhibition', *Journal of the History of Collections* 14: 1 (2002), p. 29; Kriegel, *Grand Designs*, p. 128.

30 Lou Taylor, *Establishing Dress History* (Manchester: Manchester University Press 2004), chapter 4.

31 Julia Petrov, '"The habit of their age": English genre painters, dress collecting, and museums, 1910–1914', *Journal of the History of Collections* 20: 2 (2008).

32 In the early nineteenth century, a lower middle-class woman writing to her daughter, who was in the custody of her estranged husband, sent her some lace which had been in the family for sixty years, along with ribbon which had belonged to the child's grandmother, 'that you may know something of the history of your mother's family'; and a piece of patchwork 'out of an old quilt I made above 20 years ago ... The hexagon in the middle was a shred of our best bed hangings'. E. Hall (ed.), *Miss Weeton's Journal of a Governess*, 2 vols, vol. 2: *1811–1825* (New York: Augustus M. Kelly, 1969), p. 325.

33 Gordon, *The Saturated World*, pp. 3, 170. For an earlier period and with the emphasis on the mother–daughter relationship, see Rozsika Parker, *The Subversive Stitch: Embroidery and the Making of the Feminine* (London: Women's Library 1984).

34 Carla Cesare, 'Sewing the self: needlework, femininity and domesticity in interwar Britain' (unpublished doctoral thesis, Northumbria University 2012).

35 Clare Pettitt, 'Peggotty's work-box: Victorian souvenirs and material memory', *Romanticism and Victorianism on the Net* 53, 2009, available at www.erudit.org/revue/ravon/2009/v/n53/029896ar.html, accessed 2 May 2011, for the significance of needlework in symbolising a woman to a man. Both Edwards and Logan suggest that women's needlework was important symbolically as well as, or even instead of, functionally: C. Edwards, 'Women's home-crafted objects as collections of culture and comfort, 1750–1900', in J. Potvin and A. Myzelev, *Material Cultures*; Logan, *The Victorian Parlour*.

36 Clive Wainwright, 'The making of the South Kensington Museum III: collecting abroad', *Journal of the History of Collections* 14: 1 (2002), p. 59.

37 Note also the role of the Royal School of Art Needlework in training women as designers: Anthea Callen, *The Angel in the Studio: Women in the Arts and Crafts Movement 1870–1914* (London: Astragal Books 1979), pp. 95–115.

38 Taylor, *Establishing Dress History*, p. 110.

39 Birmingham Museum and Art Gallery Master Inventory 1906–1915, numbers 11, 52–58 (1912).

40 Norwich Castle Museum and Art Gallery catalogue record NWHCM:1908.861:T.

41 Leicester Museum Accession Books, November 1891.

42 Leicester Museum Accession Books, March 1908; Warrington Museum Receiving Book April 1883, December 1906, January 1912; Norwich Museum Accession Registers August 1890, Norwich Castle Museum and Art Gallery catalogue records NWHCM:1890.42:S, NWHCM:1912.97:T, NWHCM:1912.98:T, NWHCM:1914.118B:T, NWHCM:1914.t65:T.

43 Parker argues strongly that samplers, in particular, were emblematic of femininity and were used to inculcate feminine virtues right through to the nineteenth century. Parker, *Subversive Stitch*, p. 130.

44 Pettitt, 'Peggotty's workbox'.

45 Warrington Museum Receiving Book, January 1912.

46 Leicester Museum Accession Books, May and August 1913; Warrington Museum Receiving Books, February 1896, January 1906; Norwich Museum Accession Registers March 1897, Norwich Castle Museum and Art Gallery catalogue record MWHCM:1894.40.2:C, NWHCM:1897.12a:C, NWHCM:1906.14.1:C, NWHCM:1912.15:C, MWHCM:1913.5:B, NWHCM:1913.72.1:C, NWHCM:1913.72. CH1:C.

47 Bristol Museum Curator's report, April 1896; London Metropolitan Archives, London County Council records, Minutes of the Historical Records and Buildings Committee 2 October 1903.

48 Minihan, *Nationalisation of Culture*, p. 163.

49 Leicester Museum Accession Book February 1880, June 1892, February 1896, January 1912.

50 Leicester Museum Accession Book October 1882; City and Council of Bristol, *Report of the Museum Committee 1902–3* (Bristol 1903).

51 For example, in addition to the fact that the donor's grandmother was alleged to have ridden on the pillion, the Earl of Warwick's chair was alleged to have come into the donor's family when one of them was in service with the Earl, and the Coleridge relics came from someone whose grandfather and grandmother knew him personally.

52 Judith Pascoe, *The Hummingbird Cabinet: A Rare and Curious History of Romantic Collectors* (Ithaca, NY and London: Cornell University Press 2006), p. 87.

53 Pascoe, *Hummingbird Cabinet*, covers Bullock's display of Napoleon's carriage, in chapter 3. For Madame Tussaud's, see Richard Altick, *The Shows of London, A Panoramic History of Exhibitions 1600–1862* (Cambridge, MA and London: Belknap Press 1978), p. 335.

54 Pascoe, *Hummingbird Cabinet*, Introduction.

55 Frances Larson, 'The curious and the glorious: science and the British past at the Wellcome Historical Medical Museum', *Museum History Journal* 4: 2 (2011), p. 193.

56 See Kate Hill, 'Collecting and the body in late Victorian and Edwardian museums', in Katharina Boehm (ed.), *Bodies and Things in Victorian Literature and Culture* (Basingstoke: Palgrave Macmillan 2012).

57 Marius Kwint, 'Introduction: The physical past', in Marius Kwint, Christopher Breward and Jeremy Aynsley (eds), *Material Memories: Design and Evocation* (Oxford: Berg 1999), p. 10.

58 Harrison, 'Consuming colonialism'.

59 Andrea Witcomb, 'Using souvenirs to rethink how we tell histories of migration', in S. Dudley, A. Barnes, J. Binnie, J. Petrov and J. Walklate (eds), *Narrating Objects, Collecting Stories* (London: Routledge 2012), p. 43,

60 Witcomb, 'Using souvenirs', p. 44; cf. Kwint: 'Memory connects with the entire body' ('Introduction', p. 4).

61 Harrison, 'Consuming colonialism', p. 76.

62 Harrison, 'Consuming colonialism', p. 59.

63 See Witcomb, 'Histories of migration', pp. 41, 43 for a discussion of 'sample' souvenirs, individual experience souvenirs, and 'salvaged' souvenirs. In fact, my study of souvenirs collected in the nineteenth century suggests that any such classification is inadequate to the improvisational nature of souvenir collecting at the time.

64 Geoffrey N. Swinney discusses both of these issues in 'What do we know about what we know? The museum "register" as museum object', in S. Dudley, A. Barnes, J. Binnie, J. Petrov and J. Walklate (eds), *The Thing About Museums: Objects and Experience, Representation and Contestation* (London: Routledge 2012).

65 Shaun Garner, 'Sir Merton Russell-Cotes and his Japanese collection: the importance and impact of an unplanned trip to Japan in 1885', in A. Shelton (ed.), *Collectors: Individuals and Institutions* (London: Horniman Museum and Gardens/ Museu Antropologico da Universidade de Coimbra 2001); Sir Merton Russell-Cotes, *Home and Abroad: An Autobiography of an Octogenarian* (Bournemouth: private printing 1921).

66 Warrington Museum Receiving Book, February 1908; *Horniman Free Museum 7th Annual Report 1897* (London 1898).

67 City and County of Bristol, *Report of the Museum Committee 1899–1900, 1900–1, 1908–9* (Bristol 1900–1909).

68 Norwich Museum Accession Registers, May 1880; City and County of Bristol, *Report of the Museum Committee 1909–10* (Bristol 1910); Brighton Museum Accession Register January 1910, June 1913, November 1913.

69 Hamlett, *Material Relations*, p. 12.

70 S. J. Harrison, 'Skulls and scientific collecting in the Victorian military: keeping the enemy dead in British frontier warfare', *Comparative Studies in Society and History* 50: 1 (2008), pp. 285–303. The gendered contestation over imperial and military objects in the home is evidenced both by Logan and Wintle. Logan gives the example of a woman marrying a man who had served in India; she was determined not to have her house filled with tusks: Logan, *Victorian Parlour*, p. 185.Wintle describes men and women from the Andaman Islands' colonial community; their domestic interiors, both abroad and back home, showed gendered differences, with men 'litter[ing] … homes with the trophies … of travel', while women's homes 'betrayed little evidence of a life in the colonies'. When a woman did possess colonial objects, they were kept separately from other domestic objects. Claire Wintle, *Colonial Collecting and Display* (New York and Oxford: Berghahn 2013), p. 100.

71 The position of museum objects within a life cycle economy of objects generally has been considered; they are sometimes considered to occupy a kind of afterlife (see, for example, Elizabeth Crooke, 'The "world of objects at rest": memories, material culture and the museum' (2014) online, available at www.academia.edu/7030338/The_world_of_objects_at_rest_memories_material_culture_and_the_museum, accessed 1 October 2014. Compare this with Oliver Douglas who suggests museum objects are dead or in a retirement home (Douglas, 'Upstairs, downstairs: the materialisation

of Victorian folklore studies' (2009), online, available at http://england.prm.ox.ac.uk/englishness-Douglas-paper.html, accessed 2 November 2010). I would suggest that they might alternatively be conceptualised as being in quarantine.

72 Pascoe, *Hummingbird Cabinet*; Robert McCombe, 'Anglo-Saxon artefacts and nationalist discourse; acquisition, interpretation and display in the nineteenth century', *Museum History Journal* 4: 2 (2011), p. 142.

73 This is critically discussed by McCombe in 'Anglo-Saxon artefacts'. A progressive view is found in Susan Crane, 'Story, history and the passionate collector', in M. Myrone and L. Pelz (eds), *Producing the Past: Aspects of Antiquarian Culture and Practice 1700–1850* (Aldershot: Ashgate 1999), pp. 187–188, 191.

74 Chris Miele, 'Morris and conservation', in Chris Miele (ed.), *From William Morris; Building Conservation and the Arts and Crafts Cult of Authenticity* (New Haven, CT: Yale University Press 2005), p. 34.

75 Cohen, *Household Gods*, p. 159. However, for much of the century the figure of antiques dealer was much less distinct from other kinds of dealer where women were more prominent; Mark Westgarth, 'A biographical dictionary of nineteenth century antique and curiosity dealers', *Regional Furniture* 22 (2009).

76 Cohen, *Household Gods*, p. 162.

77 Cohen, *Household Gods*, p. 155.

78 Linder, *Journal*, pp. 78, 90, 109.

79 Linder, *Journal*, p. 215.

80 Manchester Art Gallery archive, Greg Correspondence, letters from 1920 to 1922.

81 J. Styles and A. Vickery (eds), *Gender, Taste and Material Culture in Britain and North America 1700–1830* (New Haven, CT and London: Yale Center for British Art/Paul Mellon Centre for Studies in British Art 2006), p. 13; Marta Ajmar, 'Toys for girls: objects, women and memory in the Renaissance household', in M. Kwint, C. Breward and J. Aynsley (eds), *Material Memories: Design and Evocation* (Oxford: Berg 1999).

82 Kate Hill, 'Collecting authenticity: domestic, familial and everyday "old things" in English museums, 1850–1939', *Museum History Journal* 4: 2 (2011).

83 Leicester Museum Accession Book, September 1914; Warrington Museum Receiving Book, February 1896.

84 Oliver Douglas describes a process whereby valued folklore objects emerged from an ' "entanglement" of historical, individual and social factors'. Douglas, 'Upstairs, downstairs'.

85 For example, Warrington Museum Receiving Book, January 1906; Norwich Castle Public Catalogue records NWHCM:1913.72.CH1:C, NWHCM:1913.72.CH2.C, NWHCM:1914.26:C, NWCHM:1914.26.CH1:C.

86 Jones discusses how objects are felt to build up authenticity and an aura through the accumulation of relationships with people in the past they carry. Sian Jones, 'Negotiating authentic objects and authentic selves: beyond the deconstruction of authenticity', *Journal of Material Culture* 15: 2 (2010), pp. 181–203; Cohen, *Household Gods*, chapter 5.

87 Miele, 'Morris', pp. 34–35. It is clear that for both Ruskin and Morris, a person could only flourish through a relationship with authentic materiality, but the way in which authenticity was apparently articulated through these donations, and set in relation

with personal identities and relationships, was both more specific in its reliance on family souvenirs, and less specific in its invocation of a fuller self.

88 See, for example, Judith Walkowitz, *City of Dreadful Delight: Narratives of Sexual Danger in Late Victorian London* (London: Virago 1992); cf. Macleod, *Enchanted Lives*.

89 Gaynor Kavanagh, *History Curatorship* (Leicester: Leicester University Press 1990); Graham Black, *The Engaging Museum: Developing Museums for Audience Involvement* (Abingdon: Routledge 2005), esp. 'Introduction'.

4

Women visiting museums

If a museum is a distributed entity whose meaning comes not just from the intentions and actions of its curators and governing body, but rather from the networks of relations between people and things, then it must be the case that one of the most important roles women played in museums was as visitors. While a preoccupation with visitors is a key feature of museum studies scholarship today, arguably in museum history the visitors have been sidelined, despite the title of Kenneth Hudson's 1975 book *A Social History of Museums: What the Visitors Thought*.[1] In most cases the enormous asymmetry in evidence between the documents systematically created and preserved by the museum itself, and the sparse surviving records of visitors' reactions, actions and experiences has meant that even when historians set out to document visitors' opinions about museums, they have ended up focusing on how museums sought to shape those opinions. In other cases, scholars have not actually sought to do so; influential Foucauldian readings of museums have tended to see them as mechanisms for producing certain effects, not on the visitors to be sure, but with the visitors.[2] This, together with the current interest in the practices of curatorship, has meant that the visitors seem almost to have disappeared from some museum histories.[3] It is particularly important that we acknowledge women's active role as visitors, and ask, not just what they thought, but how they actively contributed to making the museum and its meanings.

However, visitors have been present in some important work on museums. The way in which people perform their museum visits was highlighted in 1980 by Carol Duncan and Alan Wallach, who suggested that visiting a museum was a ritual, with, essentially, a set script followed by visitors in slightly differing ways, but with a broad pattern. In this way museums could function as ideological institutions propagating national identities and citizenship through the enactment of quasi-spiritual values.[4] Duncan and Wallach certainly showed how the script, the architecture and arrangement, of museums such as the Louvre was orchestrated so as to make certain claims about the nation state and its citizens, but they did not show how far that script was enacted or deviated from, or how far in fact visitors did internalise the ideology embedded in the institution. While nineteenth-century visitors did not always leave much to tell us about their experience of, and conformity to the scripts of museum visiting, there is enough to suggest that scripts were ignored or even resisted, as much as they were followed.[5]

Helen Rees Leahy's recent book examining museum bodies develops this idea. The book examines how institutions sought to inculcate certain practices in visitors, from the way they looked at objects to the way they walked around and discussed objects. It also shows how visitors might ignore such 'rules' in favour of other preoccupations (often with the spectacle of other visitors), be incompetent in performing them, or intentionally resist them for various ends.[6] Moreover, what also emerges are the anxieties felt about admitting the wrong sorts of bodies into museums; female bodies are identified as one of the major categories of wrong body, along with children and the working class – and of course many women were constrained to come with children so were effectively implicated in at least two of the three problematic categories.[7] In highlighting the embodied nature of the museum visit, Rees Leahy draws out one of the key perceptions of those commenting on museum visitors in the nineteenth century: the troubling presence of female bodies in museums was much more remarked upon than male bodies, which, unless obviously working class or otherwise marginal, effaced themselves almost to become disembodied eyes and brains. Women's bodies might be threatening or reassuring, but they were always remarked upon. This might be something which women visitors could take advantage of, as we shall see.

Visiting a publicly funded museum was a new kind of activity in the mid-nineteenth century. If such museums had taken over from the museums of literary and philosophical society museums, this also implied a different audience for the institution.[8] Such a change appears to map directly onto Habermas's assertion of a switch from a culture-producing to a culture-consuming public.[9] Whether or not this adequately describes the change, it does highlight the fact that the nature of 'the public' was to a great extent determined by, and set expectations for, the audience or visitors at institutions such as public museums. In both national and local institutions, the visitors constituted an actual or potential citizenry, endowed with both rights and duties; if they were not yet fully citizens, visiting the museum would offer the opportunity make them so. Women were an important but difficult part of this potential citizenry; their presence was an index of civility and politeness, which might, moreover, tame the uncivilised behaviour of working-class men. But they were also thought to contaminate the public sphere with frivolity, irrationality, bodily pollution and, interestingly in the light of Habermas's view, an association with consumption. More significantly, it also offered them the opportunity to influence the ideals of citizenship being held up for emulation; to challenge, modify or reject the political nation.

In fact, by 1900, museums were not just open to women visitors, but were very largely dominated by them, especially during the week. This chapter will show the growing extent to which women visitors adopted the museum as a space for all sorts of practices. It argues that as concern about disruptive female bodies in museums diminished, women were able to utilise the practical, affective and political possibilities of museum spaces, ignoring or incorporating the official 'script' of the museum performance into more complex enactments of varying identities.

Historians have increasingly shown the extent to which women were present in the public sphere in the nineteenth century.[10] A recognition of the variety of lived experiences as opposed to rhetoric and discourse about public life has been the hallmark of some such work, but perhaps more interesting are approaches which attempt to establish what women were doing when they did things in public: were they creating what might be seen as a competing public sphere, based on different spaces and practices to those of men (and in some ways corresponding to the spaces and practices of a Habermasian 'debased' public sphere[11]), or were they attempting to gain access to the existing, masculine, public sphere? Simon Morgan's study of Leeds between 1830 and 1860 suggested that middle-class women developed 'identities based around notions of civic virtue and public service' and that their sense of worth, such that they should be part of dominant public life, stemmed from this public service.[12] He suggests that 'the public' should be understood as a complex, overlapping and organically developing series of publics, in most of which women were embedded to some degree, and through which they attempted to navigate in order to find positions from which to speak; they both opposed and infiltrated the male public sphere. Smitley posits a distinct 'feminine public sphere' in Scotland between 1870 and 1914, alongside but not the same as the masculine one, suggesting that this, similarly, emerged from 'a commitment to civic life and public service' on women's part, largely through philanthropic activities.[13] On the other hand, Hoberman suggests that before 1914 women's main aim was to be part of the dominant male public sphere, only later becoming disillusioned and seeking to create counter-publics. Before 1914, she suggests, women formed a 'quasi-public' sphere, ambiguous, unstable and volatile.[14] What such work suggests, then, is that women's contribution to public life, being articulated through their special contribution of particular sorts of service, was awkwardly poised between assimilation into existing male models of public life, and carving out a distinctive, separate position and contribution.

However, while women workers in museums stressed service, women did not always, or even usually, *visit* museums out of commitment to public service; in order to understand fully women's museum visiting we have to consider the ways in which their public pleasures, as well as duties, expanded and changed in the decades up to 1900, and the sorts of spaces museums offered. Although as cultural institutions they were public, museums resembled other institutions, from churches, to clubs, to shops; and insofar as they resembled the latter, they did not behave in the same way as classic 'public sphere' institutions.[15] As Erika Rappaport has shown, pleasure and an assertion of women's place within civic life were not entirely separate issues; the women she studied took part in philanthropic activities. but they did this in conjunction with a range of other activities, often consumption related, in public. Shopping, dining and visiting the poor were all equally assertions of women's place in public streets and other, new spaces such as department stores and clubs.[16] Museums, as sites of pleasure in many ways analogous to shops, should not just be seen as places where citizenship and the civic were defined; they were also sociable and fashionable spaces, spaces for intense subjective and aesthetic experiences, and spaces where practical educational goals could be achieved. Rappaport suggests first of all that women did not compartmentalise these different ways of being in public, and secondly that the roles brought mutually reinforcing advantages. She also points out that understandings of women's desires were shaped by (and shaping) feminist and liberal thinking about the public sphere.[17] The implication of this for museums as a public space used by women, is that in visiting the museum they could also stake a claim to a new kind of citizenship; again, one based on women's apparent unique ability to remoralise public life through a superior sensibility. Pleasure and service proclaimed women as feminine citizens.

From before our period, women had enjoyed visiting museums. An interest in the development of science and collecting was shared by both men and women in the eighteenth century; women's alleged more refined sensibility meant they were expected to be attracted to the aesthetic spectacle of the museum.[18] However, not all museums and galleries

were open to women, certainly not on the same terms as men. The asso-
ciational culture of new urban middle classes tended to strictly control
and curtail women's opportunities to take part; Leeds Philosophical
Institute's museum was open to the public only on Easter Monday
and Tuesday, while the Yorkshire Philosophical Institute attempted to
improve its financial position by offering incentives to ladies who sub-
scribed at least £10, though these did not extend to allowing them to
be full members.[19] The more 'serious' a museum, the less likely it was
to welcome women visitors; and conversely, the visiting of a museum
by women was seen as a sign that it was not an institution which dealt
in 'gentlemanly' knowledge.[20] Women's enjoyment of proprietary, commercial museums, such as the Egyptian Museum of William Bullock or
the Leverian Museum, might be seen as a sign of their susceptibility to
sensation, rather than their refined sensibility. Susan Burney's account
of visiting Lever's museum in 1778 is of interest here: her party consisted of four women and a man, and her impressions were of beautiful and strange animals, some 'filthy creatures', posed monkeys 'scarce
fit to be looked at', Pacific artefacts, other ethnographic costumes, and
Oliver Cromwell's armour.[21] The middle of the nineteenth century,
though, brought museums out of the private, voluntary or commercial
world into the public, and publicly funded, sphere, which had important
implications for women as visitors.

This chapter will examine the varying perceptions of women
museum visitors which emerged or developed after 1850, and then will
consider how women visitors used museums during the period, and with
what effects. It will show that women were important, confident and
sometimes disruptive users of museum space. Despite their apparently
passive position as museum consumers, their (usually – but not always)
uncontested occupation of museum spaces allowed them to claim new
pleasures, to become autodidacts, and to insert themselves into the discourse of national citizenship.

Perceptions of women visitors

The 'woman visitor' was not a monolithic figure, but was understood in
a number of different ways in the second half of the nineteenth century.
A number of extremely positive valuations of women in museums were
expressed, along with some concern about women's tendencies in such
spaces; positive and negative views tended to diverge along the class lines
of the women being perceived. The working-class woman visitor was
a cause for some concern, especially in the first half of the nineteenth

century and at the beginning of our period. Two major fears were that she might be a prostitute soliciting for business, and her perceived tendency to nurse babies in any available space.[22] These were particularly problematic for the National Gallery because of its location in central London.[23] Colin Trodd has discussed these perceptions of problematic women as part of a concern with pollution in the gallery; the dirtiness of working-class visitors, male and female, was a common theme in discussions around the widening of access in the middle of the century; but the particular concern with women who were nursing babies is instructive.[24] Gustav Waagen, the respected German art historian, suggested that 'for the mere preservation of the pictures', wet nurses should be excluded from the gallery.[25] Pollution with bodily fluids was something which select committees were extremely concerned about and suspected to be a particularly feminine vice; one witness to a select committee asserted that women were the worst culprits when it came to using public spaces as lavatories.[26]

Such concern additionally highlights the association of women visitors with children, especially infants, and especially for the working-class woman visitor. For many commentators, the question of whether women should visit museums was identical with the question of whether children should visit museums, and their view on one conditioned their view on the other. For some, perhaps a declining number, museums were institutions of science which were diminished by the presence of women who were nursing babies and trailing yet more small and dirty children.[27] Not only were such visitors inimical to the pursuit of scientific understanding or aesthetic experience by others, they also cheapened the nature of the public enactment of the nation, contaminating it with the domestic (and specifically, according Uwins, the assistant keeper of the National Gallery, contaminating it with 'all the little accidents that happen with children, and which are constantly visible on the floors'[28]). Children under the age of eight were not admitted to the BM until 1879. There was also some suggestion of domestic contamination coming from the men and women who picnicked in the National Gallery; or at least contamination by the public house, as when a woman offered Uwins a glass of gin.[29] On the other hand, one witness to the Select Committee of 1841 on National Monuments asserted that statements about working-class nuisance visitors were overdrawn and he complained not of prostitutes or nursing mothers but 'fashionable gentlewomen', who lounged about in large parties, creating noise and distractions.[30] However, all such concerns with the bodily habits and fluids of women of any class were voiced much less frequently after the Great Exhibition and the great increase in freely accessible cultural institutions which followed it; the SKM, of course, specifically included refreshment rooms and late opening in order to appeal to family groups, among others.[31]

Thereafter, some ideas about what the 'feminine' could do in the museum emerged which stressed the universality of feminine virtues rather than the class-based differences between women.[32] The woman visitor of both the working and the middle class was assumed to embody a particular reaction to displays; one often characterised by emotion and sensibility.[33] This was, moreover, believed to have benefits in refining the sensibilities of the men and children who might also be present with them in the museum; Bennett memorably suggests that women became 'culture's gentle handmaidens'.[34] Thus Thomas Greenwood, in describing how family visits to museums could improve the working class, suggested that in a family visit the husband would be refined by his exposure to his wife's reaction to paintings, for example. He emphasised the emotional response to displays as bringing husband and wife together: 'I have more than once seen a wife with a pale, careworn face cling more closely to the arm of her husband as some picture of child life was being looked at, or something else suggestive to them, perhaps, of little fingers lying cold in mother earth.'[35]

Women's claim to importance or significance as visitors, then, could be said to rest upon their sensitivity and emotional response to museum displays, and their ability to raise the moral tone of their menfolk. *Punch* additionally suggested, in Figure 8, that the presence of women was felt to make museums a healthy, because partly domesticated, public space, the 'house of the public', unlike the opposed space of the public house which was too masculine. Women's mere presence brought a portion of the domestic into existence within the public, and created a new public–private hybrid where both masculine and feminine virtues could flourish. Moreover, as views about children in museums changed, so did views about women; the Greenwood quotation also indicates a belief that women were motivated to visit museums largely by their children, in various ways. Increasingly, museums saw small children as an important part of their constituency, and therefore needed to attract their mothers to museums; the main constituency of the problematic visitor shifted from small children to teenagers who tended to visit without their parents anyway.[36]

The civic nature of museums by the later part of the nineteenth century changed the ways in which some women could access them, and simultaneously changed the perceptions and meanings of women visiting museums. Of course, the committees in charge of museums were

THE SUNDAY QUESTION.

THE PUBLIC-HOUSE ;   OR,   THE HOUSE FOR THE PUBLIC ?

Figure 8 'The Sunday question: the public house or the house for the public?'
(*Punch* 1869)

exclusively male, as they were drawn from councillors. But civic museums were transformed into an arena for civic display; conversazioni and soirées were held even more frequently than in society museums, for a wider range of occasions; or they were exported to other settings as their objects were borrowed for conversazioni held elsewhere. For example, a conversazione was held by the Naturalists Field Club in Liverpool's museum in 1868; another, rather grander one was held to mark the opening of the Harris Museum and Art Gallery in Preston in 1893, with about 1,720 guests, music, microscopical entertainment and electrical experiments.[37]

Conversazioni were generally open to the wives and other female relatives of councillors, society members and other local notables; at the Royal Society they were even known as 'Ladies' Night'. They were important social occasions which confirmed the importance of those present, either as cultural, political or economic elites; while also enacting the openness and democracy of the new urban society. They tended to include refreshments, musical entertainment and scientific demonstrations, and reports suggest that they were noisy and convivial events.[38] In fact, the holding of conversazioni was contested on a gendered basis. Some contended that precisely because of the presence of women, they were unsuitable events for allegedly serious scientists; there was 'a little dilettanti science thrown in', they were gossipy and there was too much focus on fashion.[39] For others, though, the presence of women was the whole point of such events, which distinguished a new, open civic culture from an old, corrupt, closed group who did not understand polite culture and its role in promoting a civilised society. Thus, conversazioni and soirées were defended on the basis of their civility and the opportunity they offered for local elites to enact polite, rational discourse as the basis for legitimacy. Women's presence or absence helped to define what a civic museum actually was, and marked its distinction from those voluntary institutions which had preceded it. As with working-class women's ability to exert domestic influences on working-class men in public museum spaces, so middle-class women's socialising in museums reformed public culture by domesticating it.

Perceptions of women visitors, then, began with a strong emphasis on women's bodies, especially the bodies of working-class women, and their problematic, sexualised, polluting nature. However, they showed a tendency to shift towards a concentration on the emotional, domestic and maternal qualities of all women as virtues rather than problems, as well as on the polite and refining nature of middle-class women, towards the end of the century. What is clear, though, is that the presence of women, for good or bad, was seen as a defining characteristic of museums in the second half of the nineteenth century and became emblematic of everything that was right, or wrong, about mass public access to cultural institutions.

Women as students in museums

Students were a distinct and often privileged group within the museum audience, although not always a very firmly defined one. Generally students had to apply for a student ticket which would allow them to be admitted at times specially set aside for such access, when the museum was closed to the general public. While in Sheffield, the curator Elijah Howarth recorded that 'the interest taken in the collections by Students has also steadily increased ... Eighteen students have availed themselves in the past year of the privilege of studying in the Museum on Fridays, when it is closed to the public',[40] the 1887 Report of the British Association for the Advancement of Science stated that 'about fifty' museums reported frequent use by 'local naturalists, archaeologists, and medical and art students', although it also made clear that many museums reported little interest from students.[41] The 'students' envisaged included those enrolled on particular programmes of study at a range of educational institutions, but could also be self-described if clearly from an educated background, and could thus be anyone of a suitable background who chose to apply.

Although little specific information is available about the gender of those claiming student status, there can be no doubt that women and girls were an important component of this group.[42] The emphasis placed upon the desirability of decorative work for women meant that they had a strong claim to student status in order to learn from the historical examples of decorative art in museums such as Birmingham.[43] For much of the second half of the nineteenth century, women who were seeking employment were strongly encouraged into work such as art needlework and decorative work of other kinds, and attended schools of art and design in significant numbers; on at least one occasion a special Loan Exhibition of Decorative Art Needlework was held at the SKM 'in the interests of … the employment of women'.[44] Meanwhile girls who would not need to earn their living also spent plenty of time as students in museums and galleries copying paintings in large numbers, as Beatrix Potter acidly noted ('swarms of young ladies painting, frightfully for the most part'), along with women copyists who sold their reproductions.[45] The ubiquity of women artists working in museums and galleries is further indicated by the fact that when a suffragette attacked a painting in the National Portrait Gallery (see below), the only other people present were two lady students copying works of art.[46] Such lady copyists were not highly regarded and seemed to embody the lack of either serious purpose, or original creativity, of women in museums; they were even suspected of using their public visibility in museums to attract men.[47] Beyond the big London galleries, though, women and girls' use of museum space as students of various sorts was not as problematic as the art student and copyist experience suggests. At the Horniman Museum in south London, it is clear that women's and girls' educational groups made considerable use of the museum facilities. In 1891–92, seven girls' schools visited the museum, out of a total of forty-one organisations and educational groups.[48] It was not, therefore, just 'lady artists' who used museums as students; this was an important and expanding category which women and girls took full advantage of. Though studying art brought up gendered issues surrounding the nature of artistic subject matter and originality as a key component of artistic genius, other types of museum object did not do so to such an extent, and museums formed an important part of the expansion of women's educational opportunities in the late nineteenth century.[49]

Women visitors: pleasures, possibilities and citizenship

For 'ordinary' middle-class women visitors, the museum became important as a space of free access; it was a place where they could just be, where they could perform particular versions of femininity, or where their subjectivity could roam far and wide. Thus, as Mills has argued, women used museum visiting to develop their sense of self. This is both a practical and an affective development. Mills describes the way that art galleries in Rome and Florence filled up with women visitors, women art students, and women art historians from the 1860s onwards; these were places outside the domestic environment where women could go as of right.[50] This is reminiscent of Erika Rappaport's identification of the urban environment in the second half of the nineteenth century as 'a sphere for female autonomy, pleasure, and creativity', and these are the specific aspects of the museum space which female visitors seem to have valued.[51] Museums and new shopping spaces were linked not just through their mutual constitution of a value system for objects, but in the types of space they made available; these spaces, Rappaport argues, transformed notions of bourgeois femininity. Desire became a key characteristic of both the shopping woman and the woman museum visitor; though the nature of the desire might be different. In museums, women valued the sensory and imaginative pleasures afforded them, as well as the availability of knowledge.

Museums were practically accessible and politically loaded spaces; they also formed a space which 'impacts on both the cognitive and affective realms, provoking memory and recognition but also fantasy, desire and anxiety', as Mills put it.[52] She suggests that such affective potentiality was enabled by the multiple possibilities of seeing, which opened up the idea of transformation of the self and of consciousness. In this reading, the experience of visiting museums, galleries and historic buildings in Rome by Dorothea Brooke in *Middlemarch* is portrayed by Eliot as an important psychological tool for unlocking her creative potential. The 'dream state' women could attain in museums was a powerful tool for recognising and evaluating their desires and identities.[53]

This combination of the practical, political and affective possibilities of museums for women is borne out in some of the evidence relating to actual women and their use of museums. Throughout the nineteenth century, women confirmed the myriad attractions of the museum's space, information and visual pleasures, stressing, but not confining themselves to, the pleasures of museum visiting. Jane Carlyle reported that the BM 'charmed my mother, while I myself was affected beyond measure by the Elgin marbles'.[54] Fanny Kemble, meanwhile, seems to have enjoyed 'wander[ing] in ignorant wonderment' through the Ashmolean Museum in 1847; and the 11-year-old Mary Elizabeth Squirrell, visiting Ipswich Museum in 1849, described herself as 'completely enthralled ... instructed as well as gratified'.[55] The simple visual pleasure of variety and interest was noted by women visiting museums, especially by women travellers visiting overseas museums: Hariot Blackwood, Lady Dufferin, said of the museum in Calcutta, 'Here one could spend many days in looking at all the things'; while on a more practical note Anne Brassey recorded the following in her diary of a museum in Melbourne: 'ugly objects are here arranged so as to look pretty, and I gathered many hints for the future arrangement of my own museum at home'.[56]

Women went further and experienced the pleasures of fantasy and imagination. Most strikingly, Matilda Betham-Edwards, travelling in Egypt in 1871 and writing with an eye to publication, found an intensely imaginative experience in a museum there,

> As you wander about you are carried in spirit to the beautiful Biblical pastorals more than three thousand years old ... The mummies around us, men and women, who, perhaps, knew all these things, are silent. When we gaze upon the painted masks, an expression seems to come over them almost as if they read our thoughts. We see their hands and feet protruding from the costly wrappings with a ghostly feeling of expectancy, that in a moment the figure itself will shake off its bindings and discourse with us. But they do not stir.[57]

This intense, mystical experiencing of contact with the past was clearly understood as transformative. A similar pleasure seems to have been experienced by Octavia Hill in Rome, from whence she wrote to her mother of a museum, 'it was wonderfully living and interesting to hear, in so living a way, what all the things were'.[58] The term 'living' here suggests that the attraction of a museum was its ability to make things come alive; a number of women described the pleasure they derived from visiting museums, as offering an imaginative, fantastical experience which captured their interest and enlarged their sense of self.

On the other hand, Ruth Hoberman suggests that the ability to experience such imaginative transcendence of the here and now was a sign of class-based cultural competence which the working class found hard to achieve.[59] By this reading, the women describing their museum experiences above were not, or not only, extolling the expansive and even liberating possibilities and pleasures which opened up to them; they were engaged in an ostentatious display of their aesthetic training, ability to relate object to obscure historical and geographical settings, and ability to move between material and spiritual realms.[60] Thus in women's actual use of museums, though less so in the perceptions of such use, class divisions remained obvious and indeed, middle-class women used museums in specific ways in order to perform both feminine and middle-class identities. This does not, in fact, negate Mills's argument about the liberating pleasures of museum visiting for women; rather it demonstrates how certain performances in museum spaces brought multiple benefits to particular women giving them both a gender- and class-based advantage.

The pleasures of museum spaces: Beatrix Potter

The attraction of museums for women lay not just in their imaginative, fantastical and spiritual possibilities; it also came from the non-domestic spaces they offered. While many commentators saw museum spaces as partaking of domestic qualities, it was their distinctiveness from the home that some women valued. Beatrix Potter is an important example of a woman visitor because her life, prior to her success as a children's author and her marriage, embodied many of the key restrictions facing middle-class women. Her diaries reveal the close control of her parents while she lived under their roof as an unmarried daughter. She visited relatives, holidayed with her parents and went on a limited number of errands for items such as art materials. Other than this, though, both the metaphorical space and the actual space she could access were quite limited, and thus it is revealing to see the role museums played in her life. For Beatrix Potter, the museum was a place where she felt comfortable by herself or with a companion; where she went to view specific items, to draw and study.

She visited a substantial number of museums of natural history and art galleries; her journal references to museums and galleries are too numerous to document individually. As a teenager she went most often to art galleries, including the Royal Academy and the SKM, as well as private galleries and art auctions. It is noticeable that her visits to art galleries gave her the opportunity to form her own opinion, though she only voiced this in her head and to her (encoded) diary: after visiting the National Gallery, she wrote the following: 'No one will read this. I say fearlessly that the Michelangelo is hideous.' She went twice to a museum in Oxford, apparently the University Museum of Natural History, which was 'very interesting'. In a lengthy description of a museum in Salisbury, she notes both the excellence of the flint collection, the 'good' bird collection and fossils, and the curiousness of the antiquities and a 'touching' doll said to have been dressed by Marie Antoinette in prison. Of Owens College Museum, later the Manchester Museum, she said it was 'very cool and quiet among the fossils'.[61]

The place she frequented most often in her twenties and thirties was the BM(NH), and her feelings about it are suggested by the following entries: 'I had a pleasant afternoon'; 'Went to the Museum, very empty and quiet. Studied fossils peaceably, and afterwards the insects again.' However, she was also critical of it, referring to 'museum labelling gone mad', and particularly feeling that she was unable to ask questions of the staff there.[62] She noted, not entirely approvingly, the anonymity of the space and the (gendered) division between visitors and staff – the Director of the BM(NH), Sir William Flower, who sometimes acknowledged her acquaintance on social occasions outside the museum, never did so within it.[63] It thus seems that she valued museums for a number of reasons, from their scientific value, to their ability to provoke curiosity and other emotions, to the physical sanctuary of calm and quiet they provided; but she also thought some of them, especially the BM(NH), overly masculine.

Women's actual use and account of their use of museums, then, suggests that though these spaces might have been created by men, they offered middle-class women practical and pleasurable possibilities which they took up in very large numbers, incorporating museum and gallery visiting in the normal routine of their lives, and often dominating those spaces; in 1887, the *Saturday Review* asserted that 'The Walker Art Gallery on a Saturday is as crowded with the working classes as the Royal Academy with ladies in the month of June', a statement which highlights the ways in which audiences, though heterogeneous, were structured by season, weekday, and time of day.[64] This meant middle-class women could both demonstrate class distinctions and assert feminine virtues and identities. Women also used museums in the way they used other public and semi-public spaces which were open to them in the urban environment, in order to try to build their own mobility and presence within the public spheres of politics and consumption. Museums were, of course, not exclusively female, unlike some elements of the urban environment such as women's clubs or refreshment rooms, and there were dangers to be found there, as indicated by a complaint made to the National Portrait Gallery about a man exposing himself to the complainant's 11-year-old daughter (the girl was visiting with her brother but without parents).[65] However, museums provided an important new space for middle-class women, which was more protected and controlled than some other elements of that environment.[66] Moreover, during much of the week, museums, like the new suburbs, were spaces dominated by non-working middle-class women.[67]

Women behaving badly

However, women were certainly not bound by perceptions and expectations that they would exercise a civilising and moralising role in museums. It is instructive to examine instances where women transgressed the rules of museum visiting; such transgressions took place sometimes jointly with men, and sometimes exclusively among women. Working-class women and girls, in particular, have left intriguing traces of a defiance of the norms of museum visiting. It was working-class women and girls who giggled so much at a reproduction of Michelangelo's 'David' at the Harris Museum in Preston that it was moved to the most distant room, where its nudity could be more successfully framed as art. A more common issue was working-class girls, and lads, apparently using museum and gallery space for courting. Such a criticism, of using the art gallery for 'promenading', was made in Sheffield.[68] For most of the period under study, middle-class women tended not to disregard visiting norms so openly, but in novels and paintings at least, they were prone to finding the experience wearying; Henry James depicts bored and resentful young American women visiting the National Gallery in *The Wings of the Dove*.[69] Such tiredness and boredom, rarely expressed in women's letters or diaries, can be read as passive resistance of the roles and expectations available for middle-class women.[70] It is, of course, impossible to say whether women's reticence on this subject stemmed from genuine interest in every museum or gallery experience, or whether such counter-hegemonic views of museum visiting could only be expressed in fiction; but it is certainly fair to suggest that not all museums were universally found stimulating by women despite a strong mandate or expectation that the natural world and artistic creations would appeal to the female sensibility.

Moreover, it was mainly middle-class women who undertook the most notable and sustained attempt to 'behave badly' in museums; to use their role as museum visitors to disrupt the museum project itself. Such a use of museum space developed slowly and we can see assertions of feminist politics before the physical misuse of the space is apparent. Bailkin finds evidence of women visitors' use of museums as a space to assert a specifically feminist politics in the debate over Holbein's *Christina of Denmark*, on loan to the National Gallery but in 1909 put up for sale by its owner. She points to the way in which public comment suggested portraits of women were unimportant, especially if they were not of beautiful women.[71] Meanwhile, women, especially those involved in feminism, rallied to save the Holbein for the nation; Bailkin suggests this in turn led to fears that the National Gallery was being feminised. Thus, she convincingly shows that 'gender and citizenship [were] enacted in ... museological' spaces.[72]

At the end of our period, some women used museums more directly to further a feminist politics. In 1913–14, a series of attacks on museums and galleries, directed at mainly at paintings but also at other museum objects, was carried out by militant suffragettes.[73] These attacks, on canonical works by Bellini, Millais and Velazquez at the National Gallery, National Portrait Gallery and Birmingham Museum and Art Gallery, as well as on objects including porcelain, jewels and mummy cases at the BM and the Tower of London, led to extraordinary restrictions on women visitors.[74] At the BM, women had to be accompanied by a man or have a letter of recommendation; the National Gallery, National Portrait Gallery and others closed for undefined periods; women were not permitted to carry items such as muffs and bags; and attendants were issued with cards with identification photographs of 'known militant suffragettes', thus demonstrating, as MacLeod suggests, from the way in which militants could so easily 'pass' as normal visitors, the ubiquity of middle-class women in museums.[75] The attack by Mary Richardson on the 'Rokeby Venus' at the National Gallery is the most well-known incident, in March 1914; but attacks had begun in 1913 and they continued until the summer of 1914 when they were overshadowed by the approach of war.[76]

This was part of a campaign to damage a range of public and private property of high value, and to shut institutions such as theatres and galleries. However, some of the paintings and galleries were specifically targeted because of their public endorsement of particular gender constructions: both the Rokeby Venus and Millais's portrait of Thomas Carlyle were understood to symbolically enact established ideals of femininity and masculinity. Moreover, Hoberman notes that Mary Richardson, who attacked the Rokeby Venus in the National Gallery, included a critique of ideas of beauty in her justification: 'Justice is an element of beauty', and therefore paintings of women can only be beautiful if they emerge from a social, political and cultural milieu in which women have parity with men. Thus, as Perry suggests, this was a 'recognition of the galleries as sites in which the gendering of the nation was enacted – and could be challenged'.[77] Other suffragettes indicated either that this was part of a general campaign against property, or referred to unequal valuation of paintings by men and women artists. Annie Hunt who slashed the portrait of Carlyle in the National Portrait Gallery, said at her trial that 'this picture will be of added value and of great historical interest because it has been honoured by the attention of a Militant', showing the ability of the militant suffragette movement to mythologise their own history.[78] Museums and galleries were not just blank slates for such protest; they added 'weight and meaning to [suffrage] protest whilst at the same time amplifying public disapproval'.[79] Museums and galleries both represented patriarchal values to women visitors, and offered them spaces in which to challenge those values.[80]

However, another notable aspect of the suffragette attacks is the reaction of the other women who were present in the museums at the time. When the portrait of Carlyle by Millais was attacked, the only two other people in the room were both young women, art students copying paintings, giving their addresses in court later as in the lower middle-class London suburbs, Dulwich and Camberwell. Both copyists gave evidence against Annie Hunt, and one, Miss Daisy Payne, who was copying a portrait of Tennyson right next to the portrait of Carlyle, seized Hunt's arm in an unsuccessful attempt to stop her, but Hunt pulled away and was only restrained when the attendants arrived.[81] Thus, while some women used the space of the museum to contest the gendering of the nation and of history, others were concerned to defend it for reasons which are not explicitly stated, but can be assumed to result from their investment in the idea of art training as a key to their future. For them the space offered opportunities, even if those opportunities came in a space where the nation was represented as male, and the museum's staff members were also male. This sums up the ambiguity of museums for women in many ways – they offered real new possibilities while simultaneously denying equality.

Conclusion

Women were enormously prominent among both the imagined and the actual visitors to museums. Their behaviour within museums was initially seen as a cause for concern, and as embodying all the reasons why public life should be dominated by adult, male, middle-class citizens; but was swiftly reconceived as helping to remoralise and civilise urban recreation; in Bennett's words, women were 'enlisted as an accomplice' in the project of reforming the working class, because of their very domesticity in public.[82]

Yet, it is far from clear that this is what women actually did in museums. They copied works of art and drew fossils, enjoyed imaginative reveries where they travelled to the past, showed off their clothes, visited with husbands and children, disobeyed the rules and even attacked the exhibits. This is a long way from the public service often seen as women's contribution to and claim on public life, especially in the mid- to late nineteenth century. Municipal and national museums, though civic institutions, were not part of a classic public sphere; they were about consumption, viewing a spectacle, and offering a social space which privileged emotion and fashion over the formation of public opinion. Moreover, insofar as they did constitute national or local citizenship, they tended to do so through their exhibits and structures of control, rather than automatically endowing their visitors with such qualities. National identity and citizenship was something which could be achieved with the resource of the museum but visitors did not perform such identity purely by entering the museum space. Visitors could produce or enhance alternative identities by enacting different performances in the same spaces; and women had a range of performances available to them. They could, and did, emphasise their class status and separateness from the working class, by enacting imaginative but well-informed reveries; or they might undertake the student role which gave legitimacy to their presence in the museum, until the 'lady-copyist' became a discredited museum type. They might also reject 'ladylike' and 'museum-appropriate' behaviour altogether (it is interesting how similar those two schema of behaviour are: ladylike behaviour is appropriate in museums and museum-visiting rules approximate to reasonably ladylike behaviour).

While working-class girls and women's misbehaviour caused minor annoyance to other museum goers, and women who experienced museums as tiring or boring completely internalised any resistance to such norms, suffragette attacks on museums and galleries shook the entire conceptualisation of women visitors. In a sea of women visitors who rarely caused problems, the respectable-looking suffragettes were completely invisible, and their actions were, in fact, far more damaging than that which had been envisaged from working-class woman visitors back around 1850 when mass public access was first experimented with.[83] Although commentators have rightly pointed out that the attacks were symbolic attacks on the masculine conception of the nation and of art, what is perhaps more striking is how rarely non-militant women visitors paid attention to or enacted the national identities immanent in the spaces. Such identities had become quite dormant in many museums as visitors used the spaces for other activities and concerns; the suffragettes re-politicised museum spaces and reinvigorated the idea that they could be an arena for debating concerns about the nation. As with shopping spaces, though, they were able to do this because of the fluid and ambiguous nature of urban identities and urban spaces by the early twentieth century.[84] Women went to museums because of the pleasures and possibilities they offered; these should not be divided into consumption and politics, but instead seen as deeply intertwined and mutually constituting.

Notes

1 Kenneth Hudson, *A Social History of Museums: What the Visitors Thought* (London: Macmillan 1975).

2 While Tony Bennett, for example, is not uninterested in actual visitors and their behaviour, he does bring very little historical evidence into play in his most relevant book, *The Birth of the Museum: History, Theory, Politics* (London: Routledge 1995). Meanwhile Eilean Hooper-Greenhill's *Museums and the Shaping of Knowledge* (London: Routledge 1992) saw active museum visitors as a phenomenon to be found only in the contemporary museum.

3 As Alberti says, 'in museum studies, visitor theory and contemporary surveys are replacing the passive audience with active participants in the construction of meaning, but seldom has the historical visitor been awarded the same courtesy.' Samuel J. M. M. Alberti, *Nature and Culture: Objects, Disciplines and the Manchester Museum* (Manchester: Manchester University Press 2009), p. 153.

4 Carol Duncan and Alan Wallach, 'The universal survey museum', *Art History* 3: 4 (1980), pp. 448–471.

5 Alberti, *Nature and Culture*, chapter 6; Kate Hill, *Culture and Class in English Public Museums* (Aldershot: Ashgate 2005), chapter 7.

6 Helen Rees Leahy, *Museum Bodies: The Politics and Practices of Visiting and Viewing* (Farnham: Ashgate 2012).

7 Rees Leahy, *Museum Bodies*, p. 153.

8 Rees Leahy discusses this in terms of Mary Poovey's concept of making a public body. *Museum Bodies*, pp. 21–22.

9 Jürgen Habermas, *The Structural Transformation of the Public Sphere*, trans. T. Burger (Cambridge, Mass.: MIT Press 1989). See also Geoff Eley, 'Nations, publics and political cultures: placing Habermas in the nineteenth century', in N. Dirks, G. Eley and S. Ortner (eds), *Culture/Power/History: A Reader in Contemporary Social Theory* (Princeton, NJ: Princeton University Press 1994); Craig Calhoun (ed.), *Habermas and the Public Sphere* (Cambridge, Mass.: MIT Press 1992); Mary Ryan, *Women in Public: Between Banners and Ballots, 1825–1880* (Baltimore, MD and London: Johns Hopkins University Press 1990).

10 By 'public sphere' I am not just referring to the distinct theory of Habermas, but also to the public half of the concept known as 'separate spheres', whose most well-known proponents (though they acknowledge its limitations much more than is often remembered) are L. Davidoff and C. Hall, *Family Fortunes: Men and Women of the English Middle Class, 1780–1850*, rev. edn (London: Routledge 2002). See particularly the 'Introduction' to the revised edition.

11 Particularly the blurring of boundaries between public and private, and the spectacular nature of museum visiting: Habermas, *Structural Transformation*, chapter 16; Douglas Kellner, 'Habermas, the Public Sphere and Democracy: A Critical Intervention', online, available at http://pages.gseis.ucla.edu/faculty/kellner/papers/habermas.htm, accessed 22 June 2014.

12 Simon Morgan, *A Victorian Woman's Place: Public Culture in the Nineteenth Century* (London: Tauris Academic 2007), p. 7.

13 Megan Smitley, *The Feminine Public Sphere: Middle-Class Women in Civic Life in Scotland, c.1870–1914* (Manchester: Manchester University Press 2009), p. 3.

14 Ruth Hoberman, 'Women in the British Museum Reading Room during the late-nineteenth and early-twentieth centuries: from quasi- to counterpublic', *Feminist Studies*, 28: 3 (2002), pp. 489–512.

15 See the discussion in Nick Merriman, *Beyond the Glass Case: The Past, Heritage and the Public* (Leicester: Leicester University Press 1991), p. 62.

16 Erika Rappaport, *Shopping for Pleasure: Women in the Making of London's West End* (Princeton and Oxford: Princeton University Press 2000). See also Judith Walkowitz, *City of Dreadful Delight: Narratives of Sexual Danger in Late-Victorian London* (London: Virago 1993).

17 Rappaport, *Shopping for Pleasure*, p. 5.

18 See, for example, A. R. Ellis (ed.), *The Early Diary of Frances Burney 1768–1778*, 2 Vols, vol. 2 (London: George Bell and Sons, 1889), p. 249.

19 Morgan, *Victorian Woman's Place*, pp. 66–68.

20 Arthur MacGregor (ed.), *Tradescent's Rarities: Essays on the Foundation of the Ashmolean Museum, 1683* (Oxford: Clarendon Press 1983), p. 62.

21 Ellis, *Early Diary of Frances Burney*, p. 249.

22 There was extensive discussion of an apparent problem of prostitution at St Paul's cathedral in 1841; the opinion was expressed that anywhere in central London which had free admission would suffer from a prostitution problem. *Report from the Select Committee on National Monuments and Works of Art (1841)*, Minutes of evidence p. 8 (Reverend Smith's evidence).

23 Colin Trodd, 'Culture, class, city: the National Gallery, London, and the spaces of education, 1822–57', in M. Pointon (ed.), *Art Apart: Art Institutions and Ideology Across England and North America* (Manchester: Manchester University Press 1994), p. 42.

24 Trodd, 'Culture, class, city', p. 44.

25 Quoted in Trodd, 'Culture, class, city', p. 42.

26 In the *Report from the Select Committee on National Monuments and Works of Art (1841)*, there is discussion of the problem of people relieving themselves in St Paul's cathedral; contradictory evidence was presented suggesting both that the canons

were responsible for this, and that women visitors were. Minutes of evidence pp. 4, 29 (Reverend Smith's evidence, Mr Sykes' evidence).

27 Uwins, assistant keeper at the National Gallery, said 'it must be a very dangerous thing to admit children; they do mischief in various ways'; *Report from the Select Committee on the National Gallery (1850)*, Minutes of evidence, p. 6.

28 *Report from the Select Committee on the National Gallery (1850)*, Minutes of evidence p. 6.

29 *Report from the Select Committee on the National Gallery (1850)*, Minutes of evidence p. 6.

30 *Report from the Select Committee on National Monuments and Works of Art (1841)*, Minutes of evidence p. 16 (Reverend Packman's evidence).

31 Tony Bennett, *The Birth of the Museum: History, Politics, Theory* (London: Routledge 1995), pp. 70–71.

32 Though Hoberman suggests that in the Edwardian period, the bodies which were particularly troubling in the museum were 'young, old, poor or female'. Ruth Hoberman, *Museum Trouble: Edwardian Fiction and the Emergence of Modernism* (Charlottesville, VA and London: University of Virginia Press 2011), p. 109.

33 Rees Leahy, *Museum Bodies*, p. 164.

34 Bennett, *Birth of the Museum*, p. 29.

35 T. Greenwood, *Museums and Art Galleries* (London: Simpkin, Marshall & Co. 1888), p. 74.

36 See Hill, *Culture and Class*, p. 130; a commentator in 1887 suggested the worst visitors to the Mappin Art Gallery were 'youths and girls from 15 to 18 or 19 years of age'.

37 Corporation of Liverpool, Minutes of the Museum Sub-Committee 24 December 1868, Liverpool Museums archives MM; Preston Council Free Public Library Committee, minutes 17 October and 20 October 1893, Lancashire Archives CBP 29/2. However, it is worth noting that in 1900, Liverpool Museum refused permission to the Lord Mayor of the city to borrow objects for a soiree at St George's Hall; Corporation of Liverpool, Minutes of the Museum Sub-Committee 29 January 1900, Liverpool Museums archives MM.

38 Samuel J. M. M. Alberti, 'Conversaziones and the experience of science in Victorian England', *Journal of Victorian Culture* 8: 2 (2008), p. 222.

39 Quoted in Alberti, 'Conversaziones', p. 217.

40 Samuel J. M. M. Alberti, 'Field, lab and museum: the practice and place of life science in Yorkshire, 1870–1904' (unpublished PhD thesis, Sheffield University, 2000) p. 94.

41 *Report of the 57th Meeting of the British Association for the Advancement of Science (1887)* (London 1888), p. 94.

42 At the National Portrait Gallery after 1896, around half of student tickets went to women. Lara Perry, *History's Beauties: Women in the National Portrait Gallery 1856–1900* (Aldershot: Ashgate 2006), p. 128.

43 See Sara M. Dodd, 'Art education for women in the 1860s: a decade of debate', in Clarissa Campbell Orr (ed.), *Women in the Victorian Art World* (Manchester: Manchester University Press 1995).

44 *The Times*, 10 June 1873.

45 For example, when Milly Theale visits the National Gallery in *The Wings of the Dove*, she spends much time observing the 'lady-copyists'. Henry James, *The Wings of the Dove* (London: Bodley Head 1969 [orig. pub. 1902]), p. 235.

46 Leslie Linder (ed. and transcr.), *The Journal of Beatrix Potter from 1881 to 1897* (London and New York: Frederick Warne & Co. 1966), p. 117. See also Rees Leahy, *Museum Bodies*, p. 164.

47 Hoberman, *Museum Trouble*, p. 132.

48 *Horniman Free Museum First and Second Annual Reports, 1891–2* (London 1892).

49 For more on women and education in the late nineteenth and early twentieth centuries, see Sheila Fletcher, *Feminists and Bureaucrats: A Study in the Development of Girls' Education in the Nineteenth Century* (Cambridge: Cambridge University Press 1980); Anne Digby, 'New schools for the middle-class girl', in P. Searby (ed.), *Educating the Victorian Middle Class* (Proceedings of the 1981 Annual Conference of the History of Education Society) (Leicester: Leicester University Press 1982), pp. 1–25; J. Burstyn, *Victorian Education and the Ideal of Womanhood* (London: Croom Helm 1980); Carol Dyhouse, *No Distinction of Sex? Women in British Universities, 1870–1939* (London: UCL Press 1995).

50 Victoria Mills, 'The museum as "dream space": psychology and aesthetic response in George Eliot's Middlemarch', *19: Interdisciplinary Studies in the Long Nineteenth Century* 12 (2011), online, available at www.19.bbk.ac.uk/index.php/19/article/view/596/713, accessed 3 October 2014.

51 Rappaport, *Shopping for Pleasure*, p. 3.

52 Mills, 'The museum as "dream space"'.

53 Mills, 'The museum as "dream space"'.

54 Dorothy Wordsworth, letter to Thomas Monkhouse, 5 December 1820, in E. De Selincourt, A. G. Hill, and M. Moorman (eds), *The Letters of William and Dorothy Wordsworth*, 2nd Ed., vol. 3: *The Middle Years, Part 2: 1812–1820* (Oxford: Clarendon Press 1970), pp. 691; Jane Carlyle, letter to Thomas Carlyle 26 October 1835, in J. A Froude (ed.), *Letters and Memorials of Jane Welsh Carlyle*, vol. 1 (New York: Charles Scribner and Sons 1883), p. 445.

55 Frances Anne Kemble, letter, 9 December 1847, in F. Kemble, *Records of Later Life* (London: Richard Bentley and Son 1882); M. E. Squirrell, *The Autobiography of Elizabeth Squirrell of Shottishaur and Selections from her Writings* (London: Simpkin, Marshall & Co. 1853), p. 300.

56 Marchioness of Dufferin and Ava, *Our Viceregal Life in India: Selections from my Journal 1884–1888* (New York: Charles Scribner 1891), p. 47; Annie Brassey, *The Last Voyage* (London: Longman, Green and Co. 1889), p. 288.

57 Matilda B. Betham-Edwards, letter, 1871, in M. B. Betham-Edwards, *Holiday Letters from Athens, Cairo and Weimar* (London: Strahan & Co. 1873), p. 247. Betham-Edwards was the cousin of Amelia Edwards, the Egyptologist, considered in Chapter 6, and was a professional writer; the publication of her holiday letters so soon after her travels suggests they were written with an eye to publication which may have led her to emphasise the imaginative intensity of the experience more than otherwise; but it does not invalidate her point. Joan Thirsk, 'Edwards, Matilda Barbara Betham

(1836–1919)', *Oxford Dictionary of National Biography* (Oxford: Oxford University Press, 2004), online, available at www.oxforddnb.com.proxy.library.lincoln.ac.uk/view/article/32983, accessed 21 June 2014.

58 C. Edmund Maurice (ed.), *Life of Octavia Hill, As Told in Her Letters* (London: Macmillan 1913), p. 542.

59 Hoberman, *Museum Trouble*, pp. 110–111.

60 Cf. Bennett, *Birth of the Museum*, p. 35, who refers to 'those who possess the appropriate socially-coded ways of seeing ... which allow the objects on display to be not just *seen* but *seen through*'.

61 Linder, *Journal of Beatrix Potter*, pp. 38, 87, 89, 114, 117, 372, 396.

62 Linder, *Journal of Beatrix Potter*, pp. 401, 402.

63 See Kate Hill, ' "He knows me ... but not at the museum": Women, natural history collecting and museums, 1880–1914', in S. Dudley, A. Barnes, J. Binnie, J. Petrov and J. Walklate (eds), *Collecting Stories, Narrating Objects* (London: Routledge 2012).

64 'Art in Liverpool', *Saturday Review* 20 August 1887.

65 National Portrait Gallery Heinz Archive and Library, NPG82/2/2, Warding and Security Staff Duty Reports, letter from George Zabriskie, 12 August 1912.

66 They also contained lavatories, the importance of which is stressed by Rappaport, *Shopping for Pleasure*, pp. 79–85.

67 Rappaport, *Shopping for Pleasure*, p. 22.

68 Hill, *Culture and Class*, pp. 130, 134.

69 Mills, 'The Museum as "Dream Space" '; James, *Wings of the Dove*, p. 237; on paintings, see Rees Leahy, *Museum Bodies*, p. 167–168.

70 Allison Pease, *Modernism, Feminism and the Culture of Boredom* (Cambridge: Cambridge University Press 2012), p. 62.

71 See also Perry, *History's Beauties*.

72 Jordanna Bailkin, 'Picturing feminism, selling Liberalism: the case of the disappearing Holbein', *Gender and History* 11: 1 (1999), pp. 145–163, 158.

73 Perry, *History's Beauties*, p. 137; Suzanne MacLeod, 'Civil disobedience and political agitation: the art museum as a site of protest in the early twentieth century', *Museum and Society*, 5: 1 (2007), online, available at www2.le.ac.uk/departments/museumstudies/museumsociety/documents/volumes/macleod.pdf, accessed 31 October 2011.

74 Hoberman, *Museum Trouble*, p. 124.

75 MacLeod, 'Civil disobedience'. See NPG Press Cuttings vol. 49, 1914, *Pall Mall Gazette* 25 May 1914, 'Closed galleries'.

76 National Portrait Gallery Heinz Archive and Library, NPG Press Cuttings vol 49, 1914.

77 Perry, *History's Beauties*, p. 137.

78 National Portrait Gallery Heinz Archive and Library, NPG Press Cuttings vol. 49, 1914, *Morning Post,* 22 July 1914, 'The Militants – National Gallery Outrage'.

79 MacLeod, 'Civil disobedience'.

80 Overtly national spaces such as the National Portrait Gallery were not only targeted by feminists attacking the exclusively male nature of such a nation; they might also be targeted as spaces which 'belonged to no one in particular, but also to

everyone', as the case of the man who shot his wife and then himself in the National Portrait Gallery in 1909, discussed by Hoberman, indicates. Hoberman, *Museum Trouble*, pp. 1–2.

81 National Portrait Gallery Heinz Archive and Library, NPG Press Cuttings vol. 49, 1914, *Daily Sketch* 18 July 1914, 'Carlyle Portrait Slashed'.

82 Bennett, *Birth of the Museum*, p. 32.

83 The incongruity of the respectable lady as saboteur, and the inability to tell respectable shopper from suffragette, was also clear in relation to attacks on department stores and other shops: Rappaport, *Shopping for Pleasure*, p. 215.

84 Rappaport, *Shopping for Pleasure*, p. 218.

5

Women as patrons: the limits of agency?

Although women who engaged with museums as workers, donors and visitors clearly helped to shape those museums, this was not necessarily a conscious shaping, and it worked through accumulation rather than direct action. How far could women consciously and single-handedly influence or run museums? Where were the limits of women's agency? This chapter investigates women who acted as important patrons of museums in a number of ways, and shows that leadership was the one area where women really struggled to make any impact before the First World War. Women are shown as either hiding their ambitions and achievements, or using wealth to establish themselves in marginal arenas, or in other ways drawing back from mainstream arts patronage and museum leadership. Thus, this chapter establishes the limits of the agency emanating from the distributed museum, and the limits of women's ability to introduce their own vision of museums; such visions were usually toned down by the vicissitudes women faced in leading, creating or shaping museums.

Women who were major donors and benefactors to museums have been more fully studied than other museum women, and scholars have asserted their importance in developing a modern feminine and feminist identity. In this chapter, I do not disagree with that assertion, but emphasise instead the variety of identities developed by major donors and patrons, and examine the extent to which the financial muscle and cultural and social capital of such women allowed them to evade the restrictions imposed on those women who either worked within museums or were only minor donors or visitors. As this suggests, studying such women allows us to bring into focus museums which were exclusively envisaged and enacted by women, and thus to ask whether men and women envisioned museums differently. It is also, however, the case that women tended only to turn to the patronage of new institutions because they found that masculine institutions excluded or marginalised them.

This chapter demonstrates that women as patrons, while their particular projects varied considerably, were generally concerned to introduce aspects of the domestic into the public. They highlighted, as had women working in museums, that efforts should be made to interpret museum displays to the less educated, and that a homelike museum space would encourage the lower classes to visit museums. The chief points of conflict are female autonomy and leadership; these women sought the chance to develop their concerns without having to negotiate with men, unlike those women in other chapters. This brings us back to the museum as distributed institution. How much influence could women wield in networks of meaning-making? Even for important donors, if they were female, museums managed to exert some control over the production of meaning; and where (male) curatorial staff and boards of trustees had high levels of expertise, political and social power, and were acknowledged to embody the nation in various ways, women's ability to influence museums through donation, funding or otherwise was limited.[1] This chapter, in many ways, is about the limits of the distributed museum.

In this chapter, then, I am particularly concerned with evidence that women had specific ends which they were trying to achieve in their intervention in museums, that such ends were not valued by the men who controlled the most important museum institutions, that women were frustrated in attempts to form museum policy, and often turned instead to other ways in which they could achieve those ends. In this, I am following up Jordanna Bailkin's suggestion that, around 1900, women were attempting to develop a feminist museology. By this she 'allude[s] not only to debates on the inclusion of women into the professions of connoisseurship and curatorship, but also to efforts … to construct museum practices which would promote the political ideology of feminism'.[2] In other words, women were not just seeking to be included in the world of connoisseurs, collectors and curators on the same terms as men, but were also seeking to create a specific feminist-inflected vision in museums and their collections. Bailkin particularly focuses on feminist museum practices which undermined the discourse of liberal individualism embedded in museums at the time. Although not all the women examined in this chapter can be interpreted as seeking to implement a gender-specific museum practice, enough of them can be to make this an important argument. Alternatively, Ruth Hoberman suggests that the attempt to develop a distinct, separate museum space for women only really emerged after the First World War; before this period women were content to seek inclusion within masculine museum spaces.[3] A key question for this chapter will therefore be the extent to which women in

positions of relative power aligned themselves with or against the masculine museum world, paying particular attention to the period between
1900 and 1914.

This chapter is also close in subject to Diane Sachko Macleod's book
on US women collectors and the fate of their collections, *Enchanted
Lives, Enchanted Objects: American Women Collectors and the Making
of Culture, 1800–1940*, and I aim to explore similarities and differences
between the situation in the USA, and that in Britain, particularly
England. Although she does not use the term 'feminist museology', she
does outline a distinctively *feminine* approach to museology. Macleod
suggests that, especially during the period I am most interested in from
the mid-nineteenth century to the early twentieth century, art collecting
was initially a way of dealing with a domestically framed existence for
women; but that it produced a specifically female aesthetic which was in
tension with male ideals of taste. She sees this as the basis for women's
attempt to move their collecting into the public arena, which led to new
gendered cultural spaces in the museums of the early twentieth century.
These were, however, reclaimed by men as masculine spaces in fairly
short order.[4] So for Macleod, this is about how feminine and feminist
approaches to art and culture could find public space. Collecting brought
the psychological readiness, the confidence, to occupy public space; but
such confidence alone was not enough, because as a female approach to
art seemed to be successful at colonising the institutions and spaces of
culture, a male backlash occurred.

Macleod argues that respective 'male' and 'female' aesthetics are
born of the practices embodied and embedded in the lives of men and
women of the moneyed classes of the USA. So, broadly speaking, the
feminine aesthetic she identifies values those objects which spoke to and
gained value from a domestic setting; which stimulated individual creativity; and demonstrated 'psychological affinity'. Men, conversely (and
not exclusively; she shows some men endorsing a 'feminine' aesthetic)
preferred culture which had no links to the domestic, and which formed
an impersonal compendium of knowledge.[5]

Macleod also suggests, in less definite terms than Bailkin, that such a
feminine approach might develop into a feminist museology. She points
out that women such as Phoebe Hearst used their involvement in exhibitions to promote women and women's roles and products. The specific
ways in which her 'moderate feminists' used public exhibitionary spaces
was as 'an extension of their love of family, home and country'.[6] They
acknowledged women's strengths in domestic, decorative art, and saw
these as important ways for women to achieve economic independence

and a public, political presence. As Louisine Havemeyer, collector and suffrage agitator, said, 'It goes without saying that my art collection also had to take part in the suffrage campaign.'[7] It is not always possible to recover the political ideas of women patrons in detail, but Macleod's case studies, who focused on the vote and on employment opportunities for lower middle-class women, do not suggest a wholesale rejection of liberal individualism; they did tend to stress an essentialised feminine ability to remoralise public life.[8] This highlights the broad nature of the 'women's movement' in the late nineteenth and early twentieth centuries; although, at least in Britain, women became increasingly united in the campaign for suffrage, their reasons for this and tactics used were not homogeneous (and indeed led to significant internal tensions).[9] Although some suffrage campaigners did espouse more socialist or radical views, there were many liberals among the suffrage camp, and women of all political views (including conservative) were among museum patrons.

While earlier in the book I tried not to focus too much on elite, atypical collectors, patrons and art critics, here my focus is exclusively on them, and in this again I am following Macleod.[10] This is, of course, partly because the resources needed to amass a big enough, important enough collection to have real impact on cultural policy were substantial and beyond the reach of all but a tiny number. It is also because these collectors bring the issues of gender and cultural practice into particular focus.

The chapter, therefore, engages with gendered identities and practices. I suggest that three main sets of identities and practices can be distinguished among major women patrons. In the first place, a 'professional', and therefore quite masculinised, position; this is identified with authoritative art historical or critical discourses, with a rejection of 'feminine' traits of various sorts, and with an ability to follow the rules of connoisseurship. Secondly, a feminine position, akin to that of Macleod's women collectors, characterised by a relational, domestic and decorative approach to collecting and museum spaces, and which tended not to view collecting and display as universal, objective practices.[11] It should be noted that the separation between these two was blurred by the aesthetic movement, which was interested in the decorative effect of art objects and held domestic interiors up for public admiration.[12] Thirdly, there was an overtly feminist approach, characterised by a position of dissatisfaction with the current, masculine museum spaces, and an attempt to reform those spaces so as to make them more useful and appealing to women and others currently excluded.[13] These positions were, of course, not found in their 'pure' forms; rather, women espoused complex and inconsistent mixtures of the three, and moved between them over time.

Importantly, it was not the case that women moved to a particularly feminist position by the end of the period; rather most women showed a tendency to try to combine a professional and a feminine identity in their patronage and commentary on museums. Only when they found museums actively exclusionary did they move towards feminist approaches.

The chapter examines a number of different ways in which women shaped or attempted to shape museum policy and practice, including through criticism, patronage (understood as financial support or other significant support such as major donations), and the founding of their own museums. These differ from the roles examined hitherto in that women sought them as a means of asserting cultural autonomy or even leadership. Although it was relatively easy for women to find positions assisting in museums in various ways, asserting leadership was a much more transgressive act in terms of gender identities, and therefore various tactics were used to reconcile cultural assertiveness with a suitable feminine persona; women were often profoundly ambivalent about engaging with the masculine establishment and the tendency to retreat to a separate space, while not always present, was an important aspect of this.

I do not use the term 'matronage' because of some significant differences between my study and the objects of study of those who have successfully used the term, pre-eminently Deborah Cherry. She suggests that such a coinage is needed to describe 'women [who] supported art by women'.[14] I do not examine only those women who helped women artists, and anyway by the time most of my women patrons were active, patronage had been changed by new commercial frameworks and public funding, making individual financial support of artists less important than setting the agendas of the organisations in various ways.[15] Besides, given women's ambiguity about feminine and feminist identities, and not infrequent alignment with professional masculine approaches, the term 'matronage' seems inappropriate.

Women as museum critics

Bailkin suggests that women critics in the mid-nineteenth century form a pre-history of feminist museologies.[16] Both Anna Jameson and Lady Elizabeth Eastlake wrote extensively about art for the periodical press, as well as authoring books on art history. Both were also critical in their writing on existing public museums and galleries. Lady Eastlake, of course, was the wife of the first director of the National Gallery, so one would certainly not look to her for criticism of that institution. She was extremely loyal to and supportive of Sir Charles Eastlake and his stewardship of the gallery, although she tended to give the impression, especially after his death, that she had been at least an equal partner in many of his decisions. She was certainly critical of subsequent directors, particularly Sir Frederic William Burton, who was 'totally unfit for it, & has introduced most inferior things'.[17] Despite her reluctance to criticise the National Gallery, she had no scruples about other institutions; with her friend Harriet Grote she wrote a critique of the BM for the *Quarterly Review*. In many ways, this critique followed the widespread view that the museum was extremely overcrowded, and that the natural history collections should be separated out and established in a new museum, preferably on government-owned South Kensington land. Similarly, there is nothing particularly new about her assertion that the problems facing national museum collections stemmed mainly from the ignorant actions (or lack of actions) of Parliament, whom she accused of 'ignorance, caprice, inconsistency and even niggardliness'; she consistently blamed Parliament, rather than the staff of the museum.[18]

Lady Eastlake did show, however, a consistent concern with making the collections accessible and comprehensible; she wanted to privilege arrangement, which helped the non-expert to understand the objects, over what she felt had been a tendency either to emphasise the monumental and prestigious aspects of the collection, or just to cram everything in without any regard for arrangement and order at all. Thus, of the coins, to all intents and purposes so hidden were they, she thought, that 'they might as well ... be in a private house'.[19] In discussing the natural history displays, she accused the policy makers of seeing their popularity with the ordinary visitor as proof of the lack of intelligence of the ordinary visitor; natural history was not worth bothering about for the reason that the 'lower classes' were interested in it. On the contrary, Eastlake thought that museums were duty-bound to exhibit the most striking (and largest) specimens of natural history precisely because they could exert a powerful effect on anyone; even, as she put it in a characteristically forthright way, 'the dormant brain of the veriest Hodge that ever stumped into the Museum on hobnails'.[20] She was certainly not suggesting, then, that all museum visitors were equal, but she was suggesting that museum policy was impacting particularly negatively on the least experienced visitors. She praised the curators and staff at the museum, as well as the Trustees; but saved her ire for Parliament and its inaction over the museum, despite several select committees on the issue.

Eastlake and Grote's article on the BM, then, does not express a specifically or exclusively feminine or feminist view of the museum;

the criticisms were the same as many men's, and indeed, the article cites both curators and others in support of its argument. The museological approaches of keepers such as Richard Owen are expressly favoured.[21] Yet it is noticeable that Eastlake is consistently in favour of free and meaningful public access to museums, and that she puts the blame for lack of such access in the hands of the all-male legislature. In this sense, she expresses a critique of the connoisseurial approach to museums. Public institutions should be open and accessible to all; she foregrounded a 'feminine' concern with the disadvantaged and childlike, quite possibly in a strategic way. She did not, however, call for any specific measures to 'feminise' museums. Her co-author, Harriet Grote, showed an explicit concern for women artists, through her role in the foundation of the Society of Female Artists in 1856; this concern with creating voluntary organisations to enhance women's ability to support themselves was a widespread concern among feminists and women in the art world.[22]

Anna Jameson, another friend of Lady Eastlake, with strong interests in feminist issues, wrote popular gallery guides which included frank views on the National Gallery. Bailkin suggests that she saw museums as a 'laboratory or potential haven of sexual equality and independent feminine judgement', and this can, to an extent, be discerned in Jameson's guides. However, her claims that Jameson 'attacked the Gallery's corrupted vision of Femininity', and opposed 'its masculinised 'lies' of taste … to a future Gallery of feminist truth, justice, and faith' are less sustainable; Jameson praised the National Gallery for promoting positive images of women.[23] It was not, thus, the National Gallery which Jameson felt distorted women's taste by showing them poor images of femininity, it was rather 'Books of Beauty, Flowers of Loveliness, and such trivialities'. The gallery itself provided the solution to this problem through its display of properly noble femininity in Raphael's St Catherine of Alexandria, which it had already bought in 1839.[24] And the gallery which 'lied' to its audience was not the National Gallery, but Hampton Court, which she criticised very harshly because of the lack of any connoisseurial input at all, male or female.[25] The all-male National Gallery was praised while the equally male Hampton Court was critiqued; of course feminism is not just about personnel but it is hard to see this as particularly feminist. It rested mainly on issues of competence and incompetence and supported, rather than criticising, the professional development of curatorial expertise. Unlike Eastlake, Jameson prioritised expert knowledge as highly as accessibility in a gallery.

Jameson was, nevertheless, clearly interested in highlighting both women artists and women patrons in positive terms whenever she could, for example praising the 'curiosity and intelligence' of Queen Caroline, as well as welcoming exemplary women subjects such as the noble St Catherine.[26] Jameson's focus, then, is on improving women artists' access to the art market and in encouraging women patrons. Despite Jameson's explicit feminism in other writing, in her work on galleries, overt feminism was fairly limited.[27]

Women as art critics and writers espoused a position which, though not always explicitly feminist, was critical of some (but not all) all-male institutions and their workings; and which endeavoured to foreground the needs of women and other less expert visitors, and to highlight the existing contributions and needs of women as artists. They were critical, not so much of new, professional, male curators, as of penny-pinching Parliament, and of civil servants in charge of collections which they did not understand. They were writing in a period when their ability to influence museums more directly was very limited, and the frustration they felt is clear.

By the 1880s, though, a few women were increasingly in a position where they could command the resources and status to become major collectors and patrons. In doing so, their patronage, while varied, tended to introduce feminine practices alongside masculine ones, as the chapter will now explore.

Women as major art donors

Donating a large and valuable collection was one of the most straightforward ways to exert the role of a patron, as Macleod shows. Art, both fine and decorative, was, of course, the most valuable type of collection in the second half of the nineteenth century, and a type of object which even national museums were struggling to afford and to outbid private collectors for; thus, large art donations created a different kind of donor–museum relationship. Museums were notably deferential to substantial art donors and often allowed them privileges with their collections which were not afforded to more ordinary donors; substantial art donors were also more likely to change the overall shape and direction of a museum's collection, as well as to influence the way it was displayed and used.

Lady Charlotte Schreiber was by far the most significant female donor to the BM and the SKM in this period. She was from a well-born family, and following an early marriage to a South Wales ironmaster, enjoyed a wealthy widowhood, marrying the young tutor of her son in 1855. She made two major donations: the first, of ceramics, which went to the SKM, was assembled together with her husband and donated after his death, in 1884. At this point, she stopped collecting ceramics but built another significant collection consisting mainly of fans and playing cards, which was donated in a more piecemeal fashion to the BM. Lady Charlotte is a well-known figure who was clearly exceptional in her possession of the money and leisure to pursue the collecting of ceramics and other applied arts; she can, then, help us to understand whether exceptional, wealthy women had different patterns of collecting and patronage to men.[28]

The extent to which the collection can be viewed as Lady Charlotte's sole creation is blurred by various commentators. Lady Charlotte herself framed the ceramics collecting as a joint undertaking with her second husband, Charles Schreiber; they 'hunted down' china in extended trips to Europe, and it all stopped upon his death.[29] Yet the initiative seems to have come from her; the collecting urge stemmed from the decorative china pieces she had in her previous home, and her appreciation of their aesthetic effect.[30] Her son, meanwhile, maintained that it was his own example and that of his brother which started her off, although also suggesting that she 'always had with her the spirit of the collector and connoisseur'; he downplayed the role of her husband (who was of course his stepfather, and not much older than him) in the collecting.[31] She asserted that she was looking for a project to undertake with her husband, to give him some purpose; there is a clear sense that she deflected any potential questioning of her femininity by giving the credit to her husband and framing her own role as merely supporting him. It seems unavoidable that she would be the dominant partner in any joint undertaking, considering that she was the social and financial superior of her husband as well as being considerably older than him.[32]

The ceramics donation consisted of English porcelain, mainly from the eighteenth century, and some enamels, also English; the continental acquisitions were not included. She explicitly said that she wished to make the donation 'as a tribute to my dear husband's memory',[33] and protested her unworthiness to complete the catalogue of the English ceramics, asserting that Charles Schreiber would have done it better than she could (he dictating, she taking down his words). She sought advice from A. W. Franks of the BM on the compilation of the ceramics catalogue; he recommended she seek professional assistance from a gentleman, Mr Harding, whom he had himself employed.[34] Harding and Lady Charlotte worked together on the catalogue in the evenings. Meanwhile she had been visited at home by Sir Philip Cunliffe-Owen, the Director of the SKM, to discuss the arrangements for the donation; this included a sum of £1000 to be made available to her by the museum for her cataloguing costs.[35] Indeed, Franks, together with others such as Robert Soden Smith of the SKM's Art Library, also devoted considerable time to helping her with the catalogue and with the terms of the donation agreement; sometimes at her house there were four men, from both the BM and the SKM, who were simultaneously helping her to prepare the collection.[36] It is unclear how much of the cataloguing was actually done by Harding, and how far he was working from her notes on account of her poor eyesight, though she wrote the preface entirely herself.[37] Thus, the nature and even authorship of the ceramics collection throughout its creation and during its transformation into a museum collection was contested and ambiguous. Although there is plenty of evidence that Schreiber approached it in a scholarly and connoisseurial way, she was also interested in ceramics' decorative function within the home, and the way it marked and memorialised a relationship; the scholarly apparatus of the collection was at least partly created by professional men.[38] How far she hid 'masculine' traits behind the performance of a more feminine collecting style is unclear.

Her donations to the BM began in 1887 and continued until her death in 1895, after which some further bequests were made.[39] The BM donations, made on twenty-three separate occasions, focused on fans and playing cards, but also included games, medals and seals, watches, ceramic, glass, horn and ivory artefacts, and watercolours.[40] This collection was very fully documented by Schreiber and indeed she wrote a detailed and scholarly catalogue for it herself. It seems that she had learnt much from the experience of the cataloguing of the ceramics collection by experts, and she started the catalogue almost as soon as the ceramics catalogue was finished.[41] While in some ways this signifies a 'masculine' collecting model – as, too, does her good relationship with curators such as A. W. Franks – there are also ways in which Schreiber can be read as resisting or subverting masculine norms of collecting, and asserting a different, feminine scheme of value. She made collections of lace and buttons which she did not offer to institutions but kept private (although well ordered).[42] Additionally, the strong motive of memorialising through collecting, noted in Chapter 2, emerges in this collection.[43] It has been suggested that rather than simply drawing on the expertise of the curators she knew, she could be seen as outmanoeuvring them in museological terms, thus ensuring that her collections were conceived of and displayed in ways controlled by her.[44]

Although she was always an exemplary wife and mother, Lady Charlotte would try to prove herself the equal of men, and her collecting and donating brought her adventure, competition, intellectual challenge

and the opportunity to adopt or play with aspects of a masculine identity. It is suggestive to quote here from her journal; she wrote both 'how
deeply I have felt this inferiority of sex', and 'I have given myself almost
a man's education from the age of twelve … but … toil as I may, I can
never succeed beyond a certain point and … my acquirements and
judgements must always be looked upon as those of a mere woman'.[45]
She was described by a contemporary as representing 'the union of feminine and masculine qualities'.[46] Thus Schreiber actively sought to master
practices which were seen as both masculine and feminine; she acquired
both manly and womanly ways of collecting, uniting scholarly and relational or affective modes of collecting, and played with significations of
gender.

When women expressed clear views on how their collections should
be used in significant public spaces, they might struggle to achieve them.
Gwendoline and Margaret Davies, who inherited great wealth from their
grandfather, a coal, railway and shipping magnate, also inherited his
Liberalism, Methodism and Welsh nationalism.[47] This combined with
their gender to produce a very distinctive pattern of arts patronage; they
have been described as liminal figures, inhabiting 'the space between',
neither insiders nor definitively outsiders to the art world, and in the light
of their difficulties with the national art establishment, this is of interest.[48]
They were well educated in Britain and abroad, and travelled frequently.
As Stephenson says, they 'embody and epitomise an expansive cosmo-
politanism associated with a growing sense of female confidence', but this
confidence could not necessarily give them access to the most prestigious
public cultural institutions.[49]

Their collecting took place at a point when modernist developments
were becoming important, bringing a more elitist attitude to aesthetic
sensibilities. The Davies sisters, though, continued to espouse a late
Victorian philanthropic ideal of social regeneration, and felt the purpose
of art was to inspire, though the art they collected was modernist; they
were thus at odds with both the avant-garde and the establishment.[50]
Additionally, they were keen to use art patronage to encourage the arts in
Wales as a means of economic regeneration.

Thus, in the years before the First World War, the Davies sisters
bought a number of French works of art; they also embarked upon
a career of arts patronage, making a large cash donation along with
their brother to the National Museum of Wales fund.[51] The collection
the sisters amassed between 1908 and the early 1920s contained over
200 works. Aspects of it were particularly important – it included
the largest collection of works by Daumier outside France, and the

largest private collection of Rodin sculpture in Britain, as well as work by Corot, Millet, Cézanne and Manet. While they collected British, especially Welsh, art, the French art was recognised as the most important aspects of the collection. There were nine important paintings by Monet and Renoir, which were exhibited in Cardiff and Bath, attracting large audiences; they especially sought a 'popular' working-class audience.[52]

This was art which few others were collecting in Britain at the time. However, it was not necessarily radical enough to explain their inability to give it away, to act as patrons to public art institutions, especially as institutions such as the National Gallery were coming under considerable pressure to display modern art. Just after our period, in 1921, the sisters offered to lend two paintings by Cézanne to the Tate Gallery, but the offer was turned down on the grounds of lack of space and the low quality of the works of art. An outcry in the press and considerable appreciation of the Cézannes by critics like Roger Fry led to capitulation on the part of the Tate in 1922.[53] It was in the aftermath of this incident, that the sisters stopped buying art and focused instead on their patronage of craft in a Welsh national, rather than British, context. In the end, they were also unable to donate their collection to the National Gallery in the 1950s and bequeathed it to the National Museum of Wales.[54] They later endowed an Arts and Crafts Museum at the University of Wales Aberystwyth, and gave etchings and engravings to the National Library of Wales.[55]

Major female art donors to museums, then, needed to ensure that their donations were taken seriously and that these donations were used as they wished, and achieving both aims was difficult. Such donors might use the apparatus of scholarly collecting, writing catalogues, for example, and forming respectful relationships with male professional connoisseurs, as Schreiber did. However, her career also shows that women still highlighted the aesthetic properties of their collections, as well as their relational and affective aspects, or ability to benefit the poor; this did not preclude the simultaneous appreciation of their role in a classificatory history of design, or as connoisseurial objects. They might also frame their collecting in such a way as to downplay their own role and highlight the work of men in it; and rarely expressed a view that women's objects or modes of display, or women themselves, needed to find public space. As the Davies sisters show, such self-deprecating strategies still might not be successful, and women donors might need to seek a separate space, or arguably a less prestigious space such as that offered by nascent Welsh institutions, in order to succeed.

Women founding museums

Women were also important in creating brand-new museums, though when they did, their specific roles and motivations were not usually explicit. Women museum founders in the arts commanded less expertise in the tropes of professional, 'masculine' museological discourse than the major donors discussed above but seemed rather to inhabit a feminine, 'outsider' position in museum terms. Two sets of couples were responsible for two of the most valuable and well-received collections, which moved from private, domestic settings to form new public museums during the period: the Bowes Museum and the Wallace Collection. It is interesting to note that both John Bowes and Sir Richard Wallace were illegitimate, though wealthy; and both married their Parisian mistresses, who were from humble, though not disreputable, backgrounds, and who exercised different amounts of control over the new museums.

Julie-Amélie-Charlotte, Lady Wallace, bequeathed the Wallace Collection to the nation in 1897, with strict conditions about how the collection was to be displayed. The collection had been accumulated by Lady Wallace's husband, father-in-law and grandfather-in-law, and there does not seem to be much evidence of her direct involvement in any collecting activity at all; her husband, Sir Richard Wallace, was first the agent for Lord Hertford (presumed to be Sir Richard's father, though he never acknowledged him as his son), and then a collector himself, though on a smaller scale. In the end, the collection was displayed in what had been the couple's London house, Hertford House, where it had already been accessible to suitably elite visitors, such as Disraeli, the Prince and Princess of Wales, Leopold II, and Lady Charlotte Schreiber, displayed in room settings as befitted a home, albeit an adapted one.[56] It had additionally been displayed on loan at the Bethnal Green museum in a highly classificatory way.[57]

While it is undoubtedly the case that the collection and the idea to leave it to the nation were Sir Richard's, Lady Wallace did play some role in the founding of the collection as a public museum.[58] It was she who actually made the bequest, though her husband's wish to present it to the nation was known; a 1913 guidebook refers to her 'splendid generosity'.[59] Lasic suggests the Wallace bequest arose from Sir Richard's concern to cement his legacy, given the apparent failure of his dynastic line; it also helped, she suggests, to give him a place in British society following his life in France.[60] In this, Lasic is in agreement with the Wallace Collection's own reading of its own history: its website states 'It was almost certainly the loyal desire to fulfil her husband's wishes that led her [Lady Wallace] to leave the collection at Hertford House to the nation on her death.'[61] At the time, however, the inevitability of Lady Wallace's bequest was not clear.[62] *The Times* reported that Sir Richard 'left everything to Lady Wallace without binding her in the slightest degree as to the ultimate disposition of the property, and from that time forward great was the curiosity on both sides of the Channel as to what Lady Wallace would do with it'.[63]

It is difficult, therefore, to pin down precisely what role Lady Wallace played in the establishment of the Wallace Collection as a public museum; she certainly was not an active participant in the formation of the collection, but her part in establishing the museum may have been underestimated. Probably the most anticipated alternative was that she might donate it to other museums, perhaps in France, either in parts or as a whole.[64] Her bequest can be read, then, as an active decision to commemorate her husband, not least because this was a typical feminine tactic, as shown by Lady Charlotte Schreiber and in Chapter 2.[65] However, once the bequest was made the collection passed under the control of an all-male committee; Lady Wallace's instructions in her will that the collection was to be displayed in a new purpose-built institution were over-ridden.[66]

Josephine Bowes, on the other hand, was clearly a substantial driving and directing force in the growth and establishment of the Bowes collection as a museum. The collection was composed of a similar mixture of fine and decorative art to that of the Wallace Collection, mainly from France. Kane's assessment is that the Bowes Museum shows how 'a French woman of dubious social standing used the wealth of her aristocratic English husband ... to finance a 12-year-long collecting spree ... Her determination to distinguish herself from other women of her background ... led her to the very unusual decision of marking this collection out not for display in the domestic sphere but for exhibition in the public domain'.[67] Such an assessment suggests that the default feminine approach was to collect for the home, with collecting for public display conversely masculine; but Kane asserts that Mrs Bowes was not attempting to assert a masculine approach, but rather to open up distance between herself and women of a particular social group. In fact, as we shall see, the gendering of the Bowes Museum was even more complex than this suggests.

The Bowes, who met and lived in Paris, accumulated large quantities of paintings and decorative art, especially ceramics, glass, enamels and silver. After 1860, when they sold their chateau, purchases accelerated. From 1863, some of these purchases were on display in a temporary

gallery which they had set up in Paris; from 1864, the Bowes were buying land back in England near John's birthplace; and in 1869 construction of the Bowes Museum in Barnard Castle, County Durham, began.[68]
John Bowes's role in the development of the museum is hard to separate from Josephine's, and in many ways it can be viewed as a genuinely
joint project. This complicates the gendering of the collection and subsequent museum considerably. He and others referred to it as 'Mrs Bowes'
Museum', and pointed out that her money had been used to purchase
the land, though the money came from the sale of a chateau which he
had bought and given to her.[69] Amassing the collection was achieved
in a number of ways. John made a number of purchases himself. These
were often of paintings, which he had started to collect before meeting
Josephine. John was not interested in paintings for the usual aesthetic or
art historical reasons, it has been claimed; rather, he chose them on the
basis of subject matter, collecting mostly historical scenes. This marked
him out from most art collectors of the period; and indeed, he has been
explicitly contrasted with Lord Hertford, Richard Wallace's presumed
father, whose purchasing activities were those of a 'proper' collector and
connoisseur.[70] Josephine, on the other hand, seems to have been responsible for most of the purchases of decorative art, curiosities, and antiquities; while the couple made purchases from the International Expositions
together.

The collecting was intended to form the basis of a public museum
from the outset; and as Kane points out, this was unusual.[71] She suggests that for Mrs Bowes, merely collecting for the home was unable
to distinguish her sufficiently from either bourgeois French ladies, or
indeed wealthy Parisian courtesans. This is, then, in Kane's reading, a
matter of particular female collectors asserting their superiority over
others through their mode of collecting. Such a reading suggests a different female collecting 'economy' to that of the US women collectors of
Macleod's study, who embraced a domestic approach to collecting, even
at the highest social ranks, and only thereafter moved into public display. In mid-nineteenth-century Paris, women's collecting was regarded
as 'pure' consumption, driven by fashion and frivolity, while men's was
purposive, with a vision, designed to illustrate principles and to follow
clear patterns (as we have seen, though, John Bowes' collecting fitted only
shakily into this model, and indeed the distinction was often made as an
assertion of gendered characteristics rather than an observation of actual
practice). Kane finds in Josephine's purchasing patterns, 'logical patterns
begin[ning] to emerge out of this seemingly chaotic assemblage'.[72] In particular, Josephine's purchases show an interest in collecting complete sets.

This is certainly in line with the ideas of Cole and the SKM about how decorative art could be rendered useful for display.[73]

Yet Kane does not think Mrs Bowes was entirely successful in building a systematic collection: she bought trivial items, such as buttons and a mantrap; she often bought in bulk; and she focused on domestic items, such as combs and cups.[74] The gendering of these practices is worth examining further. Buying in bulk may not be the mark of the most discerning of collectors but it was certainly relatively common among those with the means to do so, male or female.[75] It seems unlikely that anyone collecting ceramics would neglect 'domestic' items such as cups, saucers and teapots. The designation of other items as 'trivial' is telling; triviality, of course, is in the eye of the beholder. As I have suggested in Chapter 3, British women were often particularly important as donors of 'social history' objects, which had little prestige and were hard to make into a 'scientific' series, but could convey historical atmospheres well. The collection, then, may have distinguished Josephine from other Parisian women of middle-class status (though it is not that different from the donations of British women examined in Chapters 2 and 3), but it cannot be characterised as wholly 'masculine'.

Once the couple decided to open a museum in England, detailed plans were drawn up. Mrs Bowes intended to oversee the museum very closely, living on site (because of their ages, the couple assumed she would have a reasonably lengthy widowhood). Her aim was to orient it to the working classes of the area; again, a philanthropic motivation was asserted, although the museum as it came into existence does not seem particularly well suited to visitors without an art background.[76] The actual museum itself is of secondary interest to this book, as Josephine died before it had progressed very far.

The overall impression of the Bowes and their collection and museum is that they were both in many ways outsiders to the art world, concentrating on their museum in a small, awkwardly situated town. It is hard to believe that either of them was primarily motivated by museological practice of any sort; they collected to please themselves, with the formation of a museum designed to validate that pleasure. A major feature of the collection is its size, which suggests that the act of collecting may have preceded any rational sense of a plan, in the way that Larson has shown for Henry Wellcome.[77] The Bowes, then, were not like Macleod's women forming museums, despite some similarities in subject matter. There was little sense that Josephine wished to bring specifically feminine concerns into public, or to offer particular benefits to women. Nor can the museum be seen as offering an explicitly feminist vision. On the other hand, this was not a collection which followed mainstream masculine norms either. Significantly, because much of Josephine's collection remained in France on her death, and because her husband then died leaving considerable debts or at least an estate incapable of covering his bequests, her own property which she had left to the museum was seized by French authorities, as under French law it belonged to John Bowes.[78] The lack of protection for the property of married French women, as opposed, by this point, to married British women, could hinder their patronage efforts.

The difficulty of assigning 'masculine' or 'feminine' qualities to museums is sharply revealed by both the Wallace Collection and the Bowes Museum. Partly, of course, this is because these institutions were the product of husband and wife partnerships; but for many people, both men and women, their museums emerged as a result of interactions with other people and were distributed rather than individual. Beyond this, though, we can see the husbands in the partnership demonstrating 'feminine' collecting practices as well as the wives espousing 'masculine' practices. This reminds us that ideas about the gendering of collecting and museology were discursively constructed; and this discourse may not have circulated particularly widely in popular culture, being most closely associated with a connoisseurial, 'art establishment' audience.[79] Outsiders were less constrained by ideas about 'appropriate' collecting.

Outside the fine and decorative arts women also set up their own museums, but their motivations arose more clearly from explicit dissatisfaction with existing museums and their exclusionary practices, either for such women themselves, or for popular audiences. In areas like natural history, independent wealth did not necessarily bring women the advantages it did within the arts; though women built up both significant collections, and good relationships with leading curators, this did not create for them the influence that it did for someone like Lady Charlotte Schreiber. It was harder to make natural historical specimens tell a feminine or feminist narrative, though critiques of perceived misogyny at the BM(NH) did, as we have seen, exist. Women were less successful in combining masculine, professional museum practices with female concerns in existing natural history museums than in the decorative arts, and thus resorted to museums of their own because such institutions, though marginal and marginalised, allowed them to include other approaches, more feminine or even feminist in their focus on popular accessibility and enjoyment.

Two examples of women museum founders and patrons in natural history show the significant feminine emphases of their museology, but also their capacity to build bridges, to an extent, with masculine scientific institutions. Caroline Birley (1851–1907), a keen and highly scientific geological collector, kept her collection in her own private museum in a building in her garden, opened to the public in 1888. It had mostly been amassed through her own field collecting, which was highly scientific; she corresponded with Henry Woodward, the keeper of geology at the BM(NH), who wrote articles based on her fieldwork and named species after her;[80] she was, therefore, well connected with the 'official' museum world, but would have been unable to work at the museum in anything other than a very subordinate role (see Chapter 1), which would not have been an attractive proposition for her.[81] Given her independent means, therefore, she bypassed the problems of engaging with existing public museums by just making her own private space public. This was less prestigious than a publicly supported museum, and was only made possible by her wealth, but it was a very effective way of bypassing the masculine culture of such museums and keeping control of her objects, and may be read as an attempt to create a less masculine natural history space. In her own museum she could arrange her collection as she saw fit; she did not have to submit to the authority of either curator or museum committee, and she could retain characteristics of the domestic collection at the same time.

Another gallery founder, Marianne North, straddled the fields of natural history and fine art, in a way which was both characteristically feminine, and increasingly hard to do. Moreover, she avoided the problem of irrelevance faced by Birley by linking her gallery to an existing institution. North was a traveller and amateur botanist who painted landscapes and plants all around the world; she was a close friend of Amelia Edwards, discussed in Chapter 6. She funded the building of a gallery at Kew Gardens specifically to hold her botanical paintings, which she arranged and hung in the gallery herself, also supervising the addition of a dado created from wood from around the world; the gallery opened in 1882. She stipulated that the paintings should be arranged in perpetuity as she had left them, thus indicating that she had an extremely supportive relationship with the Royal Botanical Gardens at Kew.[82] This was an institution which Beatrix Potter later found to be very unwelcoming to women, describing its then Director, William Thiselton-Dyer, as a 'misogynist'.[83] North, whose father had known the two Hookers, Sir William and Sir Joseph, who directed the Gardens between 1841 and 1885, assumed a very masculine persona at times, describing, for example, wives as being like cats (and firmly aligning herself with their long-suffering husbands).[84] However, she was at other times much more positive about femininity and feminine pursuits, and championed the work of a number of women

Figure 9 The 'Marianne North' Gallery in the Royal Gardens, Kew, 1894.

artists.[85] The very genre of botanical painting, of course, was highly feminised. North therefore echoes Lady Charlotte Schreiber in her ability to play with both masculine and feminine personae and styles.

In setting up the gallery at Kew, she was motivated by a mixture of goals. The gallery would form a permanent home for all her work, which had been on temporary display in a number of galleries; it would also fulfil a strongly educational function, remedying what she saw as shocking ignorance of botany among the general public; and it would also provide 'a rest-house and a place where refreshments could be had'.[86] She thus encompassed a 'masculine' concern with public recognition and posterity and a more 'feminine' philanthropic orientation, especially in her desire to make the gallery a 'home from home'.[87] If one examines the North Gallery (see Figure 9), it becomes clear that, like its founder, it is not easily categorised: it draws heavily on tropes of domestic architecture, while sitting within a specialist research organisation. This suggests, moreover, that for wealthy, high status women who chose to travel extensively, conventions of any sort might not be very binding. Again like Schreiber, North enjoyed friendships on equal and respectful terms with the male experts in her area, and was able to play by the masculine rules of the game. However, like Schreiber, she did not consider herself bound by those rules and made feminine interventions when she wanted.

In natural history, then, patronage or foundation of their own museum was undertaken by women who did not want to occupy a subordinate position in a museum run by a man. This was not, in general, because they wanted to create a museum which was radically different from men's museums, but because they saw themselves as equal to men. These museums show a mastery of the 'masculine' approach of classification and scientific display. There were, however, certain differences in emphasis in such women's museums, most notably a commitment to access, to making the museum a welcoming, not intimidating place, and partly stemming from this, a rooting of the style or location of the museum in the domestic.

Women, funding and governance: taking on the art establishment?

Finally, I examine women's dealings with what might be called the 'establishment', and particularly the art establishment; art museums and galleries were institutions in need of large amounts of money which increasingly could only be accessed through bodies dominated by male elites. Looking at the small number of women among the group of people with the power to make big decisions for art collecting and art institutions, and controlling the purse strings in various ways, we can see an initial intention to contribute to national life in art, and a subsequent disillusionment with and disengagement from such centres of power, leading to the development of alternatives. Again, women espoused a feminine approach, believing that their femaleness gave them some unique qualities to bring to public life; however, by and large the discouraging experiences they encountered as public patrons of various sorts led them to withdraw and move towards separate, less influential organisations, and to articulate more clearly feminist positions.

Christiana Herringham was a founder of the National Art Collections Fund (NACF). The impact her actions had on art galleries such as the National Gallery and the Tate Gallery was profound. Yet gender was both a motivational and a limiting factor in her involvement with the Fund. Herringham, though married, had independent wealth from her father, was well connected and had wide-ranging interests in art. She was, though, outside the most central circles of the art establishment, with somewhat left-field interests such as tempera painting, which was ignored by Royal Academicians, though 'popular among followers of the arts and crafts movement and … with the Birmingham group of painters and craftsmen'.[88] The setting up of the NACF is an instructive example of the way gender, class and established power interacted in the art world. D. S. MacColl, the art critic, was the first to call for such a fund along the lines of *Les Amis du Louvre*, specifically to evade the deadening hand of the existing committee system for purchasing works for the National Gallery. Yet Lady Herringham was the prime mover in getting the Fund off the ground by contributing actual money, as MacColl readily acknowledged.[89] She and MacColl, along with Roger Fry and Sir Claude Phillips, raised support for the embryonic Fund, and by the time the first recorded meeting to organise the Fund took place, attendees included Lord Balcarres, a Conservative Member of Parliament, who had been invited as a possible chair or president, and Christiana's cousin, Robert Witt.

As the group expanded, two sets of tensions came to the fore. On the one hand, Christiana was unwilling to continue as the only woman involved in the Fund. She repeatedly suggested that either she should withdraw, or other women should be invited to join, giving several suggestions. Indeed, she maintained that 'I think it is a thing on which women could be decidedly useful.' The rest of the organising group were not keen to involve more women (though two women were later included in the NACF's council) and as a result her involvement became intermittent.[90] On the other hand, the Fund apparently became embroiled in disagreements over how far it should be dominated by the existing art establishment, and how far it should seek more wide-ranging membership and exercise more adventurous patronage. The Fund was an organisation poised between aiming to transform art patronage in Britain, and reinforcing the existing approach; Herringham's quandary was political as well as gendered.

By this point, women had made inroads into other all-male governing groups, albeit only those with local, not national responsibilities, like Boards of Education and the Poor Law; they were frequently in quite uncomfortable positions but found their best strategy was to keep quiet and be efficient, rather than exercise overt leadership.[91] The NACF contained a large proportion of high-status, powerful men and was thus unlike such local committees. Women were unlikely to be able to effect radical change on such a committee, and Herringham must have realised this. The case of Christiana Herringham, then, can be seen as an exploration of the role that women might attempt to play in the control of national art institutions. She found the 'art establishment' to be obstructive and unhelpful, and withdrew from it, and this sort of experience for women is confirmed also by the case of the Davies sisters considered above. The NACF was not open to ideas from 'outsider' men, either, but Herringham's focus was explicitly on women.

For women wishing to act as patrons in the fine and decorative arts, there was a substantial sense that leading, powerful institutions were not willing to grant them this role. As Perry has shown for the National Portrait Gallery, 'the privileged masculinity of nineteenth-century Britain was largely reproduced in the internal structures of the gallery'.[92] Not only were all the trustees of the national institutions male, but their recruitment and activities were based on elite masculine social networks, which were invisible and closed to women. These men did constitute an establishment, all the harder for women to engage with because of its very nebulousness.[93] Wives of trustees and leading curators, such as Lady Eastlake, were probably in the best position to influence the major institutions, though such a contribution would be hard to find in the records, leading to the ambiguity which has been recorded over Eastlake's role.[94]

Women's inability to access the most important, national levels of the art establishment is only highlighted by their occasional presence on the boards of small museums and galleries aimed exclusively at the working class, such as Henrietta Barnett at the Whitechapel Art Gallery, and Lady Burne-Jones at the South London Gallery, which will be examined in Chapter 7. This sense of exclusion from the top level of museum and gallery decision-making is illuminated by Bailkin's discussion of the campaign to save Holbein's 'Duchess' ('Christiana of Denmark, Duchess of Milan', from 1538) for the nation. Women did take a leading role in this campaign; of small donors, around half were women, while the outstanding sum of £40,000 needed to save the painting from sale to the USA, was supplied by 'A lady', identified by Bailkin as possibly Lady Rosalind Carlisle.[95] The significance of Lady Carlisle lay in her feminism which was noted in the cases of her other, not anonymous, donations to the National Gallery, portrayed as extremely radical by the press; several publications suggested that her aim was to stimulate discussion of feminism.[96] It is also notable that she attempted to intervene in curatorial decisions about her donations when they were with the National Gallery.[97] In other words, both frustrated patronage and frustrated feminism were expressed in Carlisle's interventions; but for many women, frustrated patronage was the fuel which drove their feminism further.

Conclusion

It seems clear, then, that some women saw museums as spaces dominated by men, which neglected and belittled women; and argued for the reshaping of museums to include women, women's concerns, and women's work, on equal terms with men. Women who had the means to form large collections, to set up their own museums, or to exercise significant patronage in national cultural life in other ways, often used this opportunity to put forward a vision which was broadly 'feminine' – that is, demonstrated distinctively female concerns with access for the working classes, with a different range of objects, with museums as 'home-like' spaces, and with collecting as simultaneously aesthetic or decorative and scholarly. There were also, however, a considerable number of instances where men's and women's practices were not distinct, and women, especially in natural history museum patronage and foundation, kept to a 'masculine' scientific norm in order to retain credibility.

Women clearly attempted to lead, influence and define museums on both a national and a local scale, but their attempts were not always successful. Women's collecting and patronage sometimes met with a very hostile reaction from the male press and art establishment, leading to a number of defensive strategies. Thus, both Christiana Herringham and the Davies sisters withdrew from their attempts at a feminist museology, and undertook different sorts of artistic endeavours; the Davies espoused an anti-English Welsh nationalism which benefited the National Museum of Wales after being snubbed by the London-based institutions. Josephine Bowes and Julie-Amélie-Charlotte Wallace do not seem to have been motivated by overtly feminist beliefs but rather deployed a number of feminine strategies; these would have been difficult to put into practice if they had given their collections to an already existing museum.

Women thus aimed at autonomy and leadership in cultural institutions as well as taking on the variously subordinate roles examined in previous chapters. The image of Lady Charlotte Schreiber with important male figures from both the BM and the SKM paying court to her is very powerful; though it should be remembered that in important ways she hid or downplayed her own leadership. Yet autonomy was so important to some women that they withdrew from national institutions when they found them unwelcoming, in favour of their own small and marginal organisations – which nevertheless offered them the opportunity to lead. The distributed networks of nineteenth-century museums were formed with a centre and a periphery, and women were to be found on the periphery.

Although women were significant agents in the formation and development of museums up to the First World War, there were limits to what they could achieve. Women's agency was most often cumulative and unconscious, and worked most successfully in the marginal areas of museology; individual women who wanted to change or lead large, national institutions were very constrained in this attempt, or found, like Macleod's US women and Bailkin's fundraisers for the Duchess, that there was a backlash. Lianne McTavish suggests that leading a museum was seen as masculine because of the kind of specialist intellectual qualities it was felt to require, as well as reflecting a strictly hierarchical (male) view of culture; men could be relied on to embed and defend elite cultural practices, while women, associated with practical skills, domesticity and 'all-round' knowledge, could not.[98] This needs to be added to Macleod and Bailkin's assertion that it was the increasing feminism of women museum patrons that created the backlash – even when women were not promoting feminism in their museology, they were contained and removed from the centre ground of public museums.

Notes

1 The identification of the main national museums, especially the BM, with the nation in the nineteenth century has been shown by, among others, Shawn Malley, *From Archaeology to Spectacle in Victorian Britain: The Case of Assyria, 1845–1854* (Aldershot: Ashgate 2013); see esp. p. 203. Such an idea of nationhood as immanent in the national museum can also be seen earlier in debates over the acquisition of what were referred to as the Elgin marbles: see Jonah Siegel, *The Emergence of the Modern Museum* (Oxford: Oxford University Press 2008), p. 50.

2 Jordanna Bailkin, 'Picturing feminism, selling Liberalism: the case of the disappearing Holbein', *Gender and History* 11: 1 (1999), pp. 145–163, 147.

3 Ruth Hoberman, 'Women in the British Museum Reading Room during the late-nineteenth and early-twentieth centuries: from quasi- to counterpublic', *Feminist Studies* 28: 3 (2002), pp. 489–512.

4 Dianne Sachko Macleod, *Enchanted Lives, Enchanted Objects: American Women Collectors and the Making of Culture, 1800–1940* (Berkeley, CA: University of California Press 2008), pp. 1–19.

5 Macleod, *Enchanted Lives*, pp. 9–11.

6 Macleod, *Enchanted Lives*, p. 104.

7 Quoted in Macleod, *Enchanted Lives*, p. 128.

8 Cf. in a British context, Lucy Bland, *Banishing the Beast: Feminism, Sex and Morality* (Harmondsworth: Penguin 1995).

9 Philippa Levine, *Victorian Feminism 1850–1900* (Tallahassee, FL: Florida State University Press 1989); Maroula Joannou and June Purvis (eds), *The Women's Suffrage Movement: New Feminist Perspectives* (Manchester: Manchester University Press 1998).

10 Macleod, *Enchanted Lives*, pp. 2–3.

11 As Macleod does, though, I argue that gendering such as 'the feminine' is a process varying both from person to person and even over the course of one individual's life,

socially constructed but producing myriad individual identities. Macleod, *Enchanted Lives*, pp. 4–5.

12 Charlotte Gere, *The House Beautiful: Oscar Wilde and the Aesthetic Interior* (Aldershot: Lund Humphries 2000).

13 On the complex relationship between femininity and feminism in the Victorian period, see, for example, Eileen Yeo (ed.), *Radical Femininity: Women's Self-Presentation in the Public Sphere* (Manchester: Manchester University Press 1998).

14 Deborah Cherry, *Painting Women: Victorian Women Artists* (London: Routledge 1993), p. 102.

15 The innovative and divergent ways in which patronage was being exercised by the early Victorian period is shown in Dianne Sachko Macleod, 'Homosociality and middle-class identity in early Victorian patronage of the arts', in Alan Kidd and David Nicholls (eds), *Gender, Civic Culture and Consumerism* (Manchester: Manchester University Press 1999). This also reveals the complex new ways in which new gender and class identities were inscribed in and shaped by new forms of patronage.

16 Bailkin, 'Picturing feminism', p. 148.

17 Quoted in Julie Sheldon, ' "His best successor": Lady Eastlake and the National Gallery', in Kate Hill (ed.), *Museums and Biographies: Stories, Objects, Identities* (Woodbridge: Boydell and Brewer 2012), p. 61.

18 Elizabeth Eastlake and Harriet Grote, 'The British Museum', *Quarterly Review*, 124 (1868), pp. 147–179, 148.

19 Eastlake and Grote, 'British Museum', p. 153.

20 Eastlake and Grote, 'British Museum', pp. 174–175.

21 Eastlake and Grote, 'British Museum', p. 164.

22 Deborah Cherry, 'Women artists and the politics of feminism 1850–1900', in Clarissa Campbell Orr (ed.), *Women in the Victorian Art World* (Manchester: Manchester University Press 1995).

23 Bailkin, 'Picturing feminism', pp. 148–149.

24 Anna Jameson, *A Handbook to the Public Galleries of Art in and near London* (London: John Murray 1842), p. 156; Bailkin, 'Picturing feminism', p. 149.

25 Jameson, *Handbook to the Public Galleries*, p. 286.

26 Jameson, *Handbook to the Public Galleries*, p. 172.

27 Judith Johnston, *Anna Jameson: Victorian, Feminist, Woman of Letters* (Aldershot: Scolar 1997), pp. 212–213; 226.

28 Ann Eatwell, 'Private pleasure, public beneficence: Lady Charlotte Schreiber and ceramics collecting', in C. C. Orr (ed.), *Women in the Victorian Art World* (Manchester: Manchester University Press 1995), pp. 126, 129.

29 Eatwell argues that in fact purchase through dealers and in England were more important than the Continental trips. Lady Charlotte clearly found them very exciting though. Eatwell, 'Private pleasure, public beneficence', p. 137.

30 The Earl of Bessborough (ed.), *Lady Charlotte Schreiber, Extracts from her Journal 1853–1891* (London: John Murray 1952), p. 51: 'I shall take a good deal of my much valued china, for besides that I am fond of seeing it and having it with me, there is nothing that sets off a house to so much advantage.'

31 Montague Guest, 'Introduction', in Montague Guest (ed.), *Lady Charlotte Schreiber's Journals; Confidences of a Collector of Ceramics and Antiquities Throughout Britain, France, Holland, Belgium, Spain, Portugal, Turkey, Austria and Germany from the year 1869 to 1885*, vol. 1 (London: John Lane 1911), pp. xxv, xxix.

32 Angela V. John, 'Schreiber, Lady Charlotte Elizabeth (1812–1895)', *Oxford Dictionary of National Biography* (Oxford: Oxford University Press, 2004) online, available at www. oxforddnb.com.proxy.library.lincoln.ac.uk/view/article/24832, accessed 8 July 2014.

33 Guest, *Lady Charlotte Schreiber's Journals*, vol. 2, p. 422.

34 Guest, *Lady Charlotte Schreiber's Journals*, vol. 2, p. 427.

35 Guest, *Lady Charlotte Schreiber's Journals*, vol. 2, pp. 428–429.

36 Guest, *Lady Charlotte Schreiber's Journals*, vol. 2, pp. 431, 432.

37 The diary entries slip from 'we are to begin tomorrow' to 'Mr Harding has been cataloguing the Tassies'; Guest, *Lady Charlotte Schreiber's Journals*, vol. 2, pp. 428, 438.

38 Macleod points out that the person herself was a contradiction, even before the layers of interpretation added by her family and associates. Dianne Sachko Macleod, 'Art collecting as play: Lady Charlotte Schreiber (1812–1895)', *Visual Resources* 27: 1 (2011), p. 18.

39 The Earl of Bessborough, 'Introduction', in Bessborough (ed.), *Lady Charlotte Schreiber*, p. xiv.

40 British Museum Book of Presents, 1887–1895.

41 Guest, *Lady Charlotte Schreiber's Journals*, vol. 2, p. 458.

42 Guest, *Lady Charlotte Schreiber's Journals*, vol. 2, p. 432.

43 Macleod, 'Art collecting as play', p. 26.

44 Macleod, 'Art collecting as play', p. 28. I am not entirely convinced by this argument given the extent to which, as shown above, Schreiber and a significant number of curators, art librarians and others worked together on the cataloguing of, at least, her ceramics collecting. But it is certainly true to say that she was keen to master the professional standards of museum work and that her collection be taken seriously.

45 Quoted in Macleod, 'Art collecting as play', p. 21.

46 Quoted in Macleod, 'Art collecting as play', pp. 19, 21.

47 Ceridwen Lloyd-Morgan, 'Davies, Gwendoline Elizabeth (1882–1951)', *Oxford Dictionary of National Biography* (Oxford: Oxford University Press 2004), online, available at www.oxforddnb.com/view/article/39573, accessed 19 May 2012.

48 Bryony Dawkes, 'A taste for modernity: the Davies sisters as art collectors', *Becoming Modern* (Oriel Davies 2008), online, available at www.orieldavies.org/en/resources/ taste-modernity-davies-sisters-art-collectors, accessed 2 June 2012.

49 Andrew Stephenson, ' "Feminine" anatomies of taste and cultures of collecting in early twentieth-century Britain: Gwendoline and Margaret Davies as women art patrons', *Aurora* 4 (2003), pp. 174–185.

50 Dawkes, 'A taste for modernity'. See Chapter 7 for an indication that a philanthropic orientation to art was strongly associated with women. On the radical nature of their art collecting, see Madeleine Korn, 'Exhibitions of modern French art and their influence on collectors in Britain 1870–1918: the Davies sisters in context', *Journal of the History of Collections*, 16: 2 (2004), pp. 191–218.

51 Oliver Fairclough, '"Knocked to pieces": The impact of the Great War', in Oliver Fairclough (ed.), *Things of Beauty': What Two Sisters Did for Wales* (Cardiff: National Museum Wales Books 2007), p. 62. Margaret continued collecting, especially after the Second World War; but Gwendoline felt disillusioned with art as a means of helping people after the First World War. Louisa Briggs, 'An "all-consuming drive": Margaret's later collecting', in O. Fairclough, *'Things of Beauty'*, pp. 149–163.

52 Stephenson, '"Feminine" anatomies of taste', p. 179.

53 Stephenson, '"Feminine" anatomies of taste', pp. 182–184.

54 This was at least as much to improve the cultural life of Wales as it was because of rebuff from the National Gallery, however. Mark Evans, 'The Davies sisters of Llandinam and Impressionism for Wales, 1908–1923', *Journal of the History of Collections* 16: 2 (2004), p. 233.

55 Stephenson, '"Feminine" anatomies of taste', p. 177; Lloyd-Morgan, 'Davies, Gwendoline Elizabeth'.

56 Barbara Lasic, '"Splendid patriotism": Richard Wallace and the construction of the Wallace Collection', *Journal of the History of Collections* 21: 2 (2009), p. 176.

57 Barbara Lasic, 'Going east: the Wallace Collection at Bethnal Green, 1872–1875', *Journal of the History of Collections* 26: 2 (2014), p. 255.

58 Henry C. Shelley, *The Art of the Wallace Collection* (Boston, MA: L. C. Page, 1913), pp. 22–23.

59 Shelley, *Art of the Wallace Collection*, p. v.

60 Lasic, '"Splendid patriotism"', p. 177.

61 The Wallace Collection, 'Lady Wallace', online, available at www.wallacecollection. org/thecollection/historyofthecollection/thecollectors/ladywallace, accessed 10 May 2012.

62 Shelley, *Art of the Wallace Collection*, p. 25.

63 *The Times* 23 June 1900.

64 Shelley, *Art of the Wallace Collection*, p. 23.

65 Wallace Collection, 'Lady Wallace'; Shelley, *Art of the Wallace Collection*, p. 32.

66 Lasic, '"Splendid patriotism"', p. 181 n. 33; Shelley, *Art of the Wallace Collection*, p. 28.

67 Sarah Kane, 'Turning bibelots into museum pieces: Josephine Coffin-Chevallier and the creation of the Bowes Museum, Barnard Castle', *Journal of Design History* 9: 1 (1996), p. 1.

68 Kane, 'Bibelots', p. 11.

69 Charles E. Hardy, *John Bowes and the Bowes Museum* (Bishop Auckland: The Friends of Bowes Museum 1989), pp. 144, 162, 192.

70 Hardy, *John Bowes*, pp. 139, 158.

71 See Owen Stanley Scott, *Handbook to the Bowes Museum, Barnard Castle* (Barnard Castle: W. R. Atkinson, 1893), p. 1.

72 Kane, 'Bibelots', p. 12.

73 Bruce Robertson, 'The South Kensington Museum in context: an alternative history', *Museum and Society*, 2: 1 (2004), online, available at www2.le.ac.uk/departments/ museumstudies/museumsociety/volumes/volume2, accessed 3 November 2014, p. 8.

74 Kane, 'Bibelots', pp. 10–11.

75 See, for example, Henry Wellcome, as discussed in Frances Larson, *An Infinity of Things: How Sir Henry Wellcome Collected the World* (Oxford: Oxford University Press 2009).

76 The Bowes Museum at the end of the nineteenth century consisted mainly of ceramics rooms and paintings rooms; only a very small number of other objets d'art seem to have been displayed and display methods, as far as can be ascertained, were of the classificatory 'glass case' method by manufactory and/or school; see Scott, *Handbook*. The increasing value of French fine and decorative art by this point is suggested by Shelley, *Art of the Wallace Collection*, pp. 27–28. However, Lasic reminds us that not much earlier than this, at the time when the Wallace Collection was on display at the Bethnal Green Museum, French art of the eighteenth century was seen as the product of a depraved society: 'Going east', p. 259.

77 Larson, *Infinity of Things*.

78 Scott, *Handbook*, p. 7.

79 The ability of Schreiber to understand and play with these discourses of gendering suggests that those who mixed with art professionals like Franks did understand and subvert the ideas of feminine and masculine collecting.

80 Potter, by contrast, was friendly with Woodward's daughter. Linder, Leslie (ed. and transcr.) *The Journal of Beatrix Potter from 1881 to 1897* (London and New York: Frederick Warne & Co. 1966), p. 355.

81 Bolton Museum and Archive Service, 'Caroline Birley', online, available at www.bolton-museums.org.uk/collections/geology/collectorscollections/aroline-francis-birley/, accessed 28 November 2007.

82 North was also a donor to the BM although not on such a large scale; she gave a number of ethnographic items to the museum in 1889. British Museum Book of Presents, 1889.

83 Linder, *Journal of Beatrix Potter*, p. 430.

84 Susan Morgan, 'Introduction', in Marianne North, *Recollections of a Happy Life: Being the Autobiography of Marianne North*, vol. 1 (Charlottesville, VA: University of Virginia Press 1993)[1892], p. xxxii.

85 Suzanne Le-May Sheffield, *Revealing New Worlds: Three Victorian Women Naturalists* (London: Routledge 2001), p. 88.

86 Sheffield, *Revealing New Worlds*, p. 87.

87 Eatwell, 'Private pleasure, public beneficence', p. 135; Sheffield, *Revealing New Worlds*, p. 87.

88 Mary Lago, 'Herringham, Christiana Jane, Lady Herringham (1852–1929)', *Oxford Dictionary of National Biography* (Oxford: Oxford University Press 2004), online, available at www.oxforddnb.com/view/article/64758, accessed 5 March 2012.

89 Mary Lago, 'Christiana Herringham and the National Art Collections Fund', *The Burlington Magazine* 135: 1080 (1993), p. 202.

90 Lago, 'Christiana Herringham', p. 206.

91 Patricia Hollis, *Ladies Elect: Women in English Local Government 1865–1914* (Oxford: Oxford University Press 1987).

92 Lara Perry, *History's Beauties: Women and the National Portrait Gallery, 1856–1900* (Aldershot: Ashgate 2006), p. 26.

93 Perry, *History's Beauties*, p. 28.

94 Perry, *History's Beauties*, p. 29.

95 Jordanna Bailkin, *The Culture of Property: The Crisis of Liberalism in Modern Britain* (Chicago, IL and London: University of Chicago Press 2004), pp. 149, 153.

96 Bailkin, *Culture of Property*, p. 155.

97 Bailkin, *Culture of Property*, p. 154.

98 Lianne McTavish, *Defining the Modern Museum* (Toronto: University of Toronto Press 2013), p. 151.

6

New disciplines: archaeology, anthropology and women in museums

The new human science disciplines of archaeology and anthropology expanded significantly in museum contexts during the second half of the nineteenth century and in the early twentieth century. Women were particularly prominent within these new areas; the conjunction of museum and new discipline seemed to offer specific opportunities to, and be attractive to, women at the *fin de siècle*. Museums offered women ways to be part of disciplines which complemented men's roles outside museums, but confined women to roles which ostensibly consisted of assisting and supporting men. Women's contributions to these disciplines, thus, tended to be distinct from men's. This chapter examines women's roles and routes in to these disciplines, and suggests that they characteristically mediated between the field, the museum and the public. Women who engaged in museum archaeology and anthropology came both from newly accessible higher education institutions and through amateur and family connections.

Women were also part of what we might see as distributed disciplines; the subjects of archaeology and anthropology themselves emerged from particular interactions of things and people. Gosden and Larson characterised anthropology as 'participatory', produced by a large network of 'ordinary' people, up to the interwar period and the same is undoubtedly true of archaeology; similarly they highlighted the extent to which disciplinary knowledge emerged from particular material practices: 'hands on' study.[1] These emergent properties of archaeology and anthropology allowed women to take part on their own merit or through family connections, and to develop expertise in certain ways of handling objects; but women also found certain other social and material networks emerging in their disciplines hard, or impossible, to access.

A key aim of this chapter is to understand how museums and disciplines co-evolved and how this affected and was affected by the gendering of spaces, practices and roles. From the earlier example of natural history, we can take the idea that within a discipline there might be different sorts of practice, structured partly by gender in terms of what was viewed as masculine or feminine, and in terms of practical access; but also, in overlapping ways, by other types of identity such as amateur/professional, and status or class, and that these might be in quite rapid flux at times.[2]

Moreover, museums and more particularly their objects might be active agents in the fluid entities that were developing disciplines and developing gender roles.[3] The particular ways that women engaged with museum objects defined and opened up the feminine contribution to archaeology and anthropology, but also positioned women's contributions as subordinate to, and less important than, men's. This requires us to engage with the peculiarly circular idea of the feminine and the subordinate – were women's roles subordinate because women were doing them, or were women doing them because they were subordinate? Or indeed were both true to some extent? It seems that women undertook tasks that men did not want to do; such tasks were often inherently less exciting and, moreover, generally poorly remunerated. However, the natural history comparison suggests that jobs already viewed as womanly were devalued, and the differences between archaeology and anthropology indicate that the gendering and valuing of similar activities could vary. In these disciplines, women's identification with family networks brought them good opportunities, and their association with home (here understood both to mean related to the domestic, and related to the home country) allowed them to dominate museum practices associated with cleaning, ordering and interpreting objects. Men, for their part, came to rely upon the silent support of wives, daughters and assistants to undertake work on museum objects and disciplines at home, in the sense of away from the field.

In this chapter, I examine the impact of the growth of archaeology and anthropology on women in museums; in many ways, what attracted women to the human sciences was the prospect of freedom in the field, together with the pleasure of encountering and trying to understand people who were distant, culturally, temporally or spatially. Although they had some scope to enjoy the latter, the freedom and prestige of the field was harder to experience, and they not infrequently had to settle for the museum as a second best, rather than as their intended outcome.

Women, fieldwork and museums: the social organisation of archaeology

Women's roles within archaeology and anthropology in the nineteenth century were not static, of course, but developed in response to the emerging disciplines themselves, as well as other sociocultural factors. Compared to natural history and science, any professionalisation drive was much less explicitly geared to defeminising the disciplines, but the distinct development of fieldwork in the human sciences affected women's participation in different and important ways. For subjects like botany, women's strength had been their ability to take part in fieldwork, the gathering of specimens, on an equal basis; in the project of identifying, classifying and ordering the natural world they played a significant role, and seemed positively to relish the field experience. Women natural historians were able to occupy the field in feminine, domestic ways; Margaret Gatty, the marine biologist, wrote extensively about what to wear when collecting seaweed, and also advised sorting one's seaweed into different soup plates.[4] Beatrix Potter stuck doggedly to field collecting as her key research method when experimental and laboratory-based methods had overtaken this.[5] This was fieldwork as compatible with a domestic existence, using equipment from the home and storing specimens at home. For the human sciences, the development of the field as the critical location for research and knowledge formation came later; indeed, while archaeological fieldwork had developed significantly by 1914, anthropological fieldwork still remained rather ad hoc at this point.[6] In both disciplines, though, the field was becoming more divorced from the home and harder to access with the tools and practices of domestic life, more theorised as a particular set of technical practices, and increasingly envisaged as an individual, heroic and masculine locale, and this had implications for women's involvement. Up to a point, early field practices could be undertaken by anyone, with no rules or standards or authority other than, often, social authority.[7] As it developed, fieldwork became more rule-bound and controlled by those with professional authority; however, more developed archaeological and anthropological fieldwork also created new roles, not least in 'museumifying' and interpreting growing volumes of finds whose meaning might be much more obscure than earlier monumental or exotic objects. This is exemplified in archaeology, where William Matthew Flinders Petrie was a key figure in the development, or even mystification of fieldwork and excavation, popularising the idea of the heroic male excavator. Yet he also encouraged a large number of women into Egyptology, in the roles of teaching and lecturing, recording, documenting, fundraising and museum work.[8] His prolific excavation of archaeological artefacts from digs allowed a number of women to take up roles 'museumifying' these artefacts in various ways, as I will explore in this chapter.

Women had experience of fieldwork in British archaeology. This goes back to the eighteenth century; a small number of women corresponded with the Society of Antiquaries about buildings, burials and objects discovered or at least most fully investigated by them.[9] The social organisation of archaeology, in amateur societies, increasingly included women. Women were active in the milieu of the county archaeological societies – the Yorkshire Antiquarian Club undertook a dig which had been begun by the landowner, a woman, in 1855; while Kent Archaeological Society, at its inaugural meeting in 1858, noted the presence of a significant number of ladies. However, the wording concerning the ladies is itself noteworthy: 'It is also a matter of congratulation that there should be so many ladies present today, and that there are such a large number of them among the Members of the Society, because I am sure that they will be instrumental in promoting its welfare, and many of them will assist it by recording with their pencils the features of old buildings and other objects of interest.'[10] By the 1890s, around 6 per cent of members of the East Riding Antiquarian Society were female, though this society did not appear to be engaged in much actual digging.[11] But through this and other routes, women did dig, and even, by the early 1900s, direct excavations themselves. Nina Layard, a cousin of Austin Layard and Lady Charlotte Schreiber, undertook some large-scale excavations in and around Ipswich from 1898 through to the First World War (see below and Chapter 1).

British archaeology was marked from at least the 1870s by its relationship with museums; those most focused on archaeology were private museums such as John Mortimer's in Driffield, and Pitt Rivers' at Cranborne Chase. These two demonstrate the continuing openness of archaeology to the interested amateur, as well as the fact that disciplinary specialisation could actually be led by amateurs; Mortimer, a corn merchant of limited means and only elementary education, collected ancient artefacts and undertook a substantial number of barrow excavations; he opened his self-financed museum in 1878 but went bankrupt in the 1880s.[12] Pitt Rivers, meanwhile, was a wealthy collector; sometimes characterised as the epitome of the 'armchair anthropologist', his archaeological fieldwork was, it is increasingly clear, extensive and systematic and certainly not 'armchair' based.[13] His Cranborne Chase museum was not exclusively an archaeological museum, however; aimed at the poor and ill-educated of the locality, it included a number of primarily educational rooms, including some on anthropology. The two disciplines were still quite ill-defined and overlapped in several ways.

Curators of general provincial museums increasingly undertook digs to supplement their collections.[14] But archaeological objects were more widely distributed through the general population than this might suggest; museum accession books show that quite a number of women donated archaeological objects, usually British and/or Roman, to museums.[15] In notable cases, such women were the daughters of local historians and antiquarians.[16] So even while archaeology was professionalising, the antiquarian approach remained strong, partly because it could produce a flow of materiality into the discipline; and at the same time archaeology and anthropology retained a great deal of common ground.

Accidental anthropologists?

Within anthropology, fieldwork initially involved the collection of objects by almost any means, including by casual travellers, through commercial sources, and by people travelling on specific business, often military, colonial or missionary. Contextual material was considered useful but could be supplied by almost anyone. Those who contributed anthropological objects to museums were either not anthropologists at all, or only hobbyists with intermittent interest in such collecting. While men were often in a more favourable position to collect in the field, for example if they were part of military or diplomatic missions, the expansion in women travelling, exploring and undertaking missionary work also put them in a strong position to contribute to anthropological field collecting.[17] Those women who became recognised anthropologists often began in such an 'accidental' way, such as Mary Edith Durham, who drifted into collecting anthropological material; she developed a high level of expertise in the languages and culture of the Balkans.[18] Durham had a close relationship with the University of Cambridge and contributed quite a number of objects to its Museum of Archaeology and Anthropology, corresponding at length with William Ridgeway, Disney professor of archaeology at the University. For her, though, fieldwork was far preferable to working back in the museum, because of the freedom from conventional restraints it brought; she could 'slop about when and where I like'.[19]

Women missionaries also collected; they directly serviced museums and anthropologists in Britain, but also had quite different motivations and agendas. Women were prominent as missionaries in the late nineteenth and early twentieth centuries.[20] There were areas where it was not thought suitable to send women, of course, but in other areas, such as China and Africa, both married and single women worked in Christian missions, in large numbers.[21] Inbal Livne's study of Annie Taylor, a missionary who worked in and around China, Tibet and India, demonstrates that 'whilst the growing professionalism of the discipline [anthropology] altered the role of non-professionals within the field, in the 1890s Taylor still had the opportunity of significantly adding to the imperial knowledge producing mechanisms of the British Empire'.[22] Taylor sold objects to the Edinburgh Museum of Science and Art and to museums in Glasgow, as missionaries often did, and made reasonable sums which she used to fund more missionary activity. While women's involvement in anthropology through missionary work was substantial, it can be hard to discern and to unpick different elements of agency within it; as Livne shows, Taylor's servant Pontso clearly assembled some of the objects she sold, while Taylor's own expertise was not highly rated in Britain because of her gender and religious zeal.[23]

Additionally, women who were half of a husband and wife missionary team could easily disappear as objects were collected in the field and then made their way back to the museum. Jeanne Cannizzo's account of the collections made by missionaries in Africa tantalisingly suggests the possible role of the wife of one of the missionaries considered, Walter Currie. Mrs Currie wrote in her diary in 1903 that 'we have succeeded in buying a couple [of pipes] for curios, not for smoking', leaving it unclear just what her involvement in this acquisition was.[24] The under-recording of missionary wives' contribution is confirmed by the case of Mr and Mrs Davidson, missionaries in China, who sold a large quantity of ethnographic objects to the Horniman Museum in 1895.[25] Levell argues convincingly that Mary Davidson had a distinctive input into this collection, which is recorded at the Horniman only as coming from Mr Davidson; and it was Mary's access to and interest in the lives of women and children which allowed her to contribute to museum anthropology.[26] However, single women missionaries did not necessarily fare better, as the example of Mary Slessor reveals. Slessor was a lone female missionary in West Africa from 1876 to 1915, who knew Mary Kingsley well. She did not, as far as can be ascertained, set out to collect or document ethnographic material, though she understood the area rather better, in her view, than some of the colonial officials.[27] Some material associated with her has ended up in Dundee's museum, but this seems to have been given on her behalf or after her death by colonial administrators and other, male, missionaries.[28] There are, therefore, a range of stages of collecting and producing anthropological knowledge associated with women missionaries; they were generally 'accidental' anthropologists to some extent, and not infrequently presented themselves or were presented in this way; but the motivation of being able to produce new knowledge and assert expertise, independently, was certainly present among them.

Both women missionaries and female independent travellers like Durham were 'accidental' anthropologists, but they valued the extended action and authority they could accrue by moving from more accidental to more purposive collecting.[29] While women were not always successful in rebranding themselves as anthropologists and/or collectors (and some conversely refused to present themselves this way because of a reluctance to threaten male authority), there were distinct advantages, especially for single women, in aiming at this goal. Durham sometimes disavowed any deep interest in her collections ('I collect the stuff from a sort of sporting instinct and when I've got it don't know properly how to use it'), yet in other writing an awareness of the potential value of her purposive collecting is apparent ('the contents of a second grave I am keeping in case I get the chance later of visiting Sarajevo and comparing them with the things in the museum there').[30] Such women, away from the museum and in the field, were in a position of relative authority in relation to the museum.

They resembled the collectors and donors examined in Chapter 2, however, in that the anthropological material they collected was used to build relationships as well as to build scholarly identities. Accidental anthropologist women such as Durham, and also Charlotte Wheeler Cuffe, demonstrate this. Durham divided her objects among museums, scholars, and friends; along with the material she sent to Professor Ridgeway for the Cambridge museum, she also gave textiles to Mrs Ridgeway as a gesture of friendship.[31] Charlotte Wheeler Cuffe's donations to the Cambridge museum similarly seem designed both to contribute to the scholarly project of museum anthropology, and to affirm and enhance a set of more personal relationships; she sent Ridgeway photographs illustrating ethnographic themes from a range of people in Burma, including missionaries and colonial officials. One of those who gave her photographs said in his letter, 'I heard from Mrs McNab in Rangoon that you were collecting photos ... I shall be very glad to do anything I can to help', highlighting the extent to which, while serious, Wheeler Cuffe's collecting was also embedded in a set of social relationships.[32] Thus in anthropology, collecting in the field was the main way in which women interacted with, and accrued authority in museums; they were suppliers. In archaeology, by contrast, increasingly men supplied objects and women worked on them in museums.

Single women and wives in archaeology

A fundamental fact of women's social existence shaped their engagement with these disciplines and with museums, and this is particularly clear in archaeology: whether they were married or single. Both states offered opportunities and constraints, which can be illustrated by case studies from early twentieth-century archaeology. Nina Layard, a single woman, undertook a number of archaeological excavations in Ipswich, including one which produced a large number of Anglo-Saxon artefacts which she donated to the municipal museum in Ipswich on terms which are striking. They were to be housed in a separate room which she was to have sole responsibility for arranging and displaying; she was to have the key to the room, and to the cases themselves, with the curator only allowed in with permission; and she was free to remove any of the objects whenever she wanted in order to use them to illustrate lectures she was giving.[33] As this indicates, she was keen to gain public recognition as an archaeologist who was making important contributions to knowledge, and her position of control at Ipswich Museum was instrumental to this aim. She was aided significantly in her goal by Sir John Evans and his third wife, Maria Evans nee Lathbury; Evans, Boyd Dawkins (of Manchester Museum) and E. Ray Lankester of the BM(NH) supported her in her negotiations with Ipswich Museum, and also tried to help her access the Society of Antiquaries, where she had hoped to present a paper based on her excavation. In the event none of these luminaries could persuade the Society of Antiquaries to let her read her paper.[34]

Lady Evans had had similar experiences with the Society of Antiquaries before her marriage, as a single woman, attempting to attend a lecture there to which the lecturer had invited her despite not being authorised to do so; it was while standing outside that she had met Sir John Evans, who, as the president of the Society, was able to facilitate her entry. Not long after this, the Society of Antiquaries explicitly banned her attendance, apparently because she was not quiet and decorative enough.[35] As a young woman she had studied classics at Somerville College, Oxford, and delivered a course of lectures in London on classical archaeology.[36] Six months after she met Evans, they married. On their honeymoon, they travelled in England and France, looking for flint implements, visiting dealers and museums, going to gravel pits, and touring old buildings and monuments (in fact all three of Evans's wives had quite archaeological honeymoons, whether they wanted to or not; but Maria seems to have been a willing partner here, according to her diary at least).[37] From the evidence of correspondence between Layard and John Evans, Maria Evans and Nina Layard appear to have been reasonably close.

Yet their experiences in archaeology were significantly different. Layard directed several large-scale excavations, lectured widely and occupied a position of power in Ipswich Museum. Evans had a much less active role in archaeology after her marriage (though she did publish on aspects of Classical archaeology), probably because she was always travelling with a retired husband who was substantially older than her. However, she became part of her husband's network of connections. She laid the foundation stone of Hertfordshire County Museum but seems not to have been involved in any other way.[38] Evans's daughter, Joan Evans, went on to become the first female President of the Society of Antiquaries, showing the very different environment of the post-Second World War period; but it is noticeable that she remained unmarried. Marriage to an archaeologist fundamentally affected women's involvement with archaeology; it brought significant opportunities for women to have contact with the discipline, but it also tended to constrain them to act behind the scenes. Unmarried women might struggle to find a way in to archaeology but if they did, they could act independently and make their own contribution clear. The changing nature of archaeological fieldwork meant women could now only rarely be 'accidental' field archaeologists in the way they had previously.

However, in one growing area of archaeology, wives and single women, though entering through different routes, had experiences which were relatively similar. In Egyptology, they found themselves being pushed towards the museum and away from active fieldwork. Hilda Petrie, the wife of Flinders Petrie, demonstrates this. As Hilda Urlin, she had already shown a talent for drawing, which had led to her introduction to Petrie, as someone who could illustrate his book.[39] She left for Egypt with Flinders Petrie on the day of their marriage, and thereafter always accompanied him on excavations, staying at home in Britain only when pregnant and while the children were small.[40] Moreover, other family members were also sometimes present on the excavations, including Hilda's sister Amy Urlin; their presence is not always clear in documents and histories.[41] There was no expectation that women would undertake anything particularly domestic on such excavations; the camps were extremely Spartan, everyone did their own washing, and the limited cooking was undertaken by native Egyptians. This is one of the reasons why women such as Hilda Petrie found it so liberating, along with the opportunity it gave to discard European norms of dress.[42]

Hilda Petrie's tasks were described thus: 'all the plan-drawing, some sorting and piecing of carved slate, copying of inscriptions, arranging of stores and antikas, keeping the courtyard in order, and the drawing of all the 1st dynasty hieroglyphics'.[43] She also undertook a number of other activities including a single instance of excavation; in 1902 Hilda Petrie, along with Margaret Murray and Miss Hansard, an artist, took charge of an excavation at Abydos.[44] Hilda Petrie was also involved in the writing of the reports for the Committee and with cataloguing and arranging displays of finds for the summer exhibition at UCL. Much of her work, therefore, in Egypt and Britain, was about working with the objects, 'museumifying' them, and introducing them to popular and scientific audiences. She organised lectures (she lectured herself as well, especially to women's groups), wrote letters to solicit support for Egyptian archae-ology, and worked on Petrie's publications, proofreading and illustrat-ing.[45] She had a close relationship with the excavated artefacts, formed by washing, drawing, sorting, cataloguing and interpreting them to a British audience, rather than by digging them up. Her opportunities in Britain were partly caused by the fact that Petrie himself was not there, but absent in Egypt excavating. Although this did create opportunities for her, which she would not otherwise have had, she most certainly did not experience the enforced stays in Britain as particularly empowering; she hated being at home with the children by herself, and her letters and diaries suggest that being in Egypt was the truly liberating experience for her.[46]

In this, she was similar to Margaret Murray, a single female archaeologist who was a subordinate of Petrie at UCL; Petrie's absence in Egypt meant that she could not go out to the excavations there but was employed in fact to do his teaching at the college along with museum work.[47] Again, this could be construed as offering opportuni-ties for her to develop a university teaching and museum role, and to do it well, which she might not otherwise have had, but it is clear that she also would have focused on fieldwork in Egypt if she could have done. In this case, both a wife and a single woman (a protégée of the heroic male Egyptologist) were able to become much more involved in Egyptological work through Petrie's patronage and because of his prolific digging; however, their opportunities in field excavation were thereby limited. Instead, they occupied and developed roles back in Britain, in teaching, museum and exhibition work. It would not be satisfactory to say that they seized these roles as a way of developing a specifically female vision of archaeology, though they deployed 'feminine' expertise to successfully mediate scholarly knowledge for a popular audience. Rather, they experienced them as less exciting, liberating and desirable than the field roles which continued to be dominated by men.

Fundraising, museums and the female community of the Egypt Exploration Fund

For other women, Egyptian fieldwork was not possible at all, and here it may be more accurate to say that museum work offered a real, new opportunity for access to Egyptology by proxy. The role of the Egypt Exploration Fund (EEF), later Society, in developing Egyptology in a museum setting has recently been demonstrated, and the roles and practices of women within the Fund are of particular interest.[48] The Fund was set up by Amelia Edwards, following her absorption by Egyptology in the wake of her travels in Egypt; although she collected plenty of Egyptian objects, which were later donated to UCL, and arguably even did some excavating on her Nile trip, she preferred to occupy a primarily fundraising role, endowing a chair in Egyptology at UCL, setting up the Fund and undertaking lecture tours to raise money.[49] Her relationship with the man who occupied her new chair, Flinders Petrie, could be characterised as a respectful partnership based on an understanding of gender roles as being distinct; they appear to have seen their involvements as complementary and certainly both were crucial to the development of Egyptology.[50]

However, the structure which she set up in the EEF gave a key role to women in mediating between museums and Egyptological finds. Edwards's friend, Kate Bradbury, who had come with her on lecturing tours in the USA, and helped establish her legacy at UCL, sat on the board of the EEF along with Francis Griffith, an Egyptologist who she later married; her money allowed him to devote himself to Egyptology.[51] A number of other women were also involved in the organisation as secretaries, subscribers and committee members. Miss Emily Paterson acted as secretary for many years; she had been a friend of and secretary to Amelia Edwards and took on the secretaryship of the EEF after Edwards's death.[52] Of the central committee of the Fund, four out of twenty were women in 1890; these were Edwards, Kate Bradbury, Mrs McClure and Mrs Tirard.[53]

In the regions, there were also some very active secretaries: Miss H. M. Adair in north London, Miss Bradbury in Manchester (this was presumably Kate Bradbury), Mrs Jesse Haworth later in Manchester, Miss Booth in Macclesfield, Miss Brodrick in Salisbury, Miss Crosfield in Liverpool, Miss Ferguson in Carlisle, Mrs Goodison in Ambleside, Miss Lister in north-west London, Mrs McClure in south-west London, Mrs Tirard in west London, Miss J. Williams in Bristol, and Miss Annie Barlow in Bolton.[54] Such a large number of women was noted by the Fund; its Report for 1887 states the following: 'It is with particular gratification that we count the names of several ladies on this special staff of officers.'[55] Although the absolute number of local secretaries, as well as the number of women secretaries, varied considerably from year to year, women seem to have generally formed around one third of the total. The main role of the local secretaries was to raise money and solicit subscriptions from their locality. When subscribers to the Fund are considered, the role of women becomes even more prominent. Women rarely, but occasionally, outnumbered men as contributors in Britain, particularly among the relatively small numbers contributing to some of the regional funds. In 1889–90, four women, one man, and one married couple contributed to the £6 6s collected by Miss Brodrick in Salisbury, for example.[56]

Among US subscribers to the Fund, the prominence of women was even more marked, and noted by Edwards, who in discussing the US local secretaries, said of them, 'the majority of whom are, I am happy to say, ladies. It is my belief that this is especially a field in which woman's work is calculated to be eminently successful. I hold that ladies make the best beggars in the world, and that their begging is always likely to be more fruitful than that of gentlemen, because the gentlemen do not like to refuse them.'[57] For Edwards, women's talents were distinct and separate from men's; women could bring skills to Egyptology which men could not. She did not seek to emulate men but to complement them. Women's substantial but unacknowledged involvement in fundraising for museums has been noted by Whitelaw who suggests women are ill-served by our focus on male roles in museums, and there is a very real sense in which Egyptology, more than any other museum discipline, was created by women.[58] Egyptology exerted a strong attraction on women which may have come partly from its prominence in popular culture.[59] However, while acknowledging women's fundraising contribution, it is also clear that they had few other avenues open to them.

The secretaries of the EEF were, additionally, the main go-betweens between the field and the museum; the local secretaries essentially ensured that a large number of provincial museums filled up with

Egyptological finds. The Bolton secretary, Annie Barlow, daughter of a prominent mill owner, was clearly a devotee of ancient Egypt; a lengthy report on her visit to Egypt in 1887–88 with her brother was included in the Fund's Report from that year.[60] As a result of Barlow's dedication, Bolton Museum amassed a large and significant Egyptological collection (it is worth noting, however, that the majority of the items in the collection are actually rather small; this is a result of both Petrie's approach to excavating, and to distributing finds, as Stevenson shows).[61] From the centre, both Emily Paterson and Margaret Murray dealt with the various tasks involved in distributing objects to a large number of museums and educational institutions, and although Flinders Petrie decided the destinations of major finds, Murray certainly assigned some of the material. Her copious notes on the topic show her both attempting to carry out Petrie's wishes but also dealing with the large number of requests and material on an ad hoc basis.[62] Moreover, Stevenson argues convincingly that distribution was not simply decided by central figures such as Petrie and the EEF, but was heavily influenced by some of the funders in the regions, creating a 'tangle of objects, places and people.' It is particularly significant that major fundraisers, many of whom we know to be women, would intervene to secure particular objects for their location, as in the example Stevenson gives of Mrs Pilkington, who secured Egyptian material for St Helens.[63]

From an examination of the EEF, the organisation probably responsible for the largest number of archaeological accessions in British museums, certainly of non-British archaeology, during this period, it is thus clear that women played a significant role. This was, in many ways, both 'outside' archaeological fieldwork, and 'outside' the museum; nevertheless it helped to form museum archaeology and to link museum and field. The success of the EEF is partly because women themselves also put so much effort into the popular communication of Egyptian archaeology; Edwards's lecturing tours and books were enormously popular, while Hilda Petrie lectured particularly to women's groups.[64] It is particularly important to acknowledge and understand how women acted between museums and academic archaeology in order to understand how both developed; as Stevenson argues, a general impression has been established that archaeology at this period was not a museum-based discipline, but certainly museums were essential to Egyptology, at least, and this centrality was partly caused by a funding and distribution mechanism which was substantially operated by women.[65] Not only this, but the distributed and 'entangled' system by which objects travelled from Egypt to, say, Bolton's museum, created particular skills and knowledge among women which secured them more official positions within the archaeological and museological worlds. Something emerges which might be described as a female network of interest in Egyptology, and although most of this network was technically amateur, such an ascription is not entirely useful, because as Chapter 1 showed, individual women moved between what might be considered 'amateur' and 'professional' roles and often carried out the most apparently professional work in their capacity as wives or friends of professional men.

Women, archaeology, anthropology and the academy

In addition, both archaeology and anthropology grew within the academy, and women were involved within the academy in specific ways, which also had clear implications for museums. Although postgraduate, and even more so undergraduate, teaching of these new disciplines was slow to develop, it was present by the start of the First World War. The University of Oxford allowed research degrees in anthropology from 1899, with a diploma in anthropology from 1907. At Cambridge University, the first diploma by thesis in anthropology was offered in 1908 and from 1913 anthropology was allowed as part of the examination tripos, while at the University of London bachelor degrees in anthropology were offered from 1912.[66] Chairs in archaeology were appearing throughout the country in the second half of the nineteenth century; the Disney chair of archaeology at the University of Cambridge was endowed in 1851, while Liverpool University had chairs in classical archaeology and Egyptology by 1906, as well as a reader in ethnography (who was also the director of the Liverpool Museum) by the 1890s.[67]

All this disciplinary growth, therefore, happened at the time when women were beginning to access higher education in very much the same piecemeal and uneven way. As Carol Dyhouse has shown, despite the promise of provincial universities in particular that there was 'no distinction of sex', there were some ways in which women's experience at such institutions was second-rate compared to men's.[68] Different approaches were taken to the provision of higher education for women, largely as a result of different ideas about how to counter the strong opposition such provision provoked. It has been asserted, for example, that Girton College at Cambridge, founded in 1869, attempted to provide an education which was as close as possible to that open to male students at Cambridge, while Newnham College founded a few years later provided a syllabus more tailored to women's perceived needs and skills.[69]

There was considerable concern about the potentially dangerous environment of the university and how to balance the life of the mind with domesticity; young women might ideally, especially in London, live at home and merely attend lectures and classes. If a collegiate environment was to be created for women, it might resemble a home as much as a community of scholars. However, in Manchester, accommodation of any sort for women was an inadequate afterthought. For reasons such as these, and the still-patchy school education of girls, only a small number of women gained official qualifications in these subjects or became part of the academy during our period. But it is notable how far women sought out the opportunity to study these new disciplines, though it was not easy. Before there were specific programmes of study in the new disciplines, they crept into other subjects, and could also come to the attention of students through university museums. Thus Thornton shows how at least one history student at Newnham College, Cambridge, Agnes Conway, was inspired by a lecture given to first-year students by Jane Harrison, who had been appointed as the lecturer in classical archaeology at Newnham in 1899.[70]

At Oxford, the acquisition of the Pitt Rivers Museum in 1884 was intended to lead to the establishment of anthropology at the University but the diploma did not start for over 20 years. Barbara Freire Marreco, who was one of the first students on the diploma course, attended lectures by Henry Balfour while studying for her first degree, also in Classics.[71] For such students as Conway and Freire Marreco, the presence of women's colleges at Oxford and Cambridge was essential; Freire Marreco's college was Lady Margaret Hall, but she later had a fellowship from Somerville.[72] Of the students on the Oxford Diploma between 1907 and 1912 (enrolment jumped sharply in 1913 which distorts the figures somewhat), nine out of thirty-four, or just over a quarter, were women, all except Freire Marreco from Somerville.[73]

Both Newnham and Girton colleges at Cambridge produced relatively large numbers of archaeologists, as Gill has shown in his study of the British School at Athens (BSA). Of the fourteen women admitted to the BSA between 1890 and 1914, six were from Newnham, five from Girton, two from London University and one from St Andrews.[74] Thornton asserts that the female colleges of Oxford and Cambridge were very important in allowing women to encourage and mentor other women, and for normalising the idea of women intellectuals, and this was undoubtedly the case.[75]

However, other higher education institutions which followed a different model produced as many or more women, in archaeology at least, and significant examples here come from the University of London and its constituent colleges. At UCL, of course, Flinders Petrie had been appointed to the first chair in Egyptology in the country, and most of his first students were women; a few years later, in 1896, Jane Harrison came close to being appointed to the Yates chair of classical archaeology at London.[76] UCL was apparently known for being supportive of women; this was why Amelia Edwards had established her chair of Egyptology here, and Margaret Murray recounts the campaign to get a larger common room for women staff during her stay there.[77] So women took advantage of different models of university; the ability to live at home in the London suburbs, and the availability of willing male mentors made up for the benefits offered by the women's residential colleges at Oxford and Cambridge. The situation in Manchester, where women were to an extent segregated in separate buildings, while attending some mixed lectures, also showed that women could flourish outside the college environment created at Oxford and Cambridge.[78]

What all the women who took advantage of the growth of archaeology and anthropology in the academy found was that museums, and the material practices they created and encouraged, were often the best way of finding a role. In all settings, the new disciplines were gendered, shaping the precise ways in which women could engage with them in overt and subtle ways. While women seemed to have relatively free access to anthropology, Margaret Murray related how at the BAAS meeting in 1913, when she prevailed upon Alfred Haddon to speak in favour of women being trained in anthropology, he suggested that it was necessary to have women anthropologists in order to find out about 'the women of these primitive people'. After Haddon's speech, Edward Sidney Hartland of the Folklore Society said that he felt women should not be involved in anthropology because there were 'many things a woman ought not to know'.[79] Women tended to have worse Latin and Greek than men as a result of their schooling, so 'pure' Classics was harder for them than archaeology; but the BSA also forbade women to take part in actual excavation, at least organised by them, until 1911.[80] While outright bans on women excavating do not seem to have been common and women were certainly involved in excavation elsewhere, a gendered division of labour tended to see the actual excavating as predominantly a task for male archaeologists; in 1910 a former director of the BSA suggested that archaeology was 'not too nice a trade, you see, dear lady'. Moreover, the perceived drama and heroism of dirty fieldwork was contrasted with the 'humdrum' nature of sorting, cataloguing and other 'feminine' activities, despite the fact that the second might actually contribute more knowledge than the first.[81]

Under these circumstances, women found, as with natural science, that the museum might be the most welcoming part of a university. Freire Marreco, for example, stayed on at the Pitt Rivers Museum as a volunteer after gaining her diploma, cataloguing the amulets; she also did some cataloguing work at Liverpool Museum.[82] Museum cataloguing repeatedly comes up as work which university-educated women did, not just because of its mundanity, but because it was extremely badly paid, echoing the findings of Chapter 1 on women's cheapness as employees. Freire Marreco also undertook fieldwork, but this served largely to allow her to donate to museums and thus build relationships with the leading (male) scholars; she gave 845 artefacts to the Pitt Rivers Museum between 1905 and 1962.[83] Balfour, at the Pitt Rivers Museum, in particular had reason to be particularly grateful to her. He wrote the following in a letter to her: 'I should very much like to have the specimens you offer as I think that they would all fit into series here … I wonder if your friend in Paraguay could secure some examples of a musical instrument which I have been long wanting.'[84] She also donated to the Horniman Museum.[85]

We have seen how Margaret Murray was unable to undertake much archaeological fieldwork.[86] However, she did find time to work at a number of museums beyond UCL; most famously at Manchester Museum where she carried out a ground-breaking mummy unwrapping; she also catalogued at the National Museum of Antiquities in Edinburgh, the National Museum in Dublin, and the Ashmolean Museum.[87] Some of this work was, again, motivated by the need to supplement an extremely small income, rather than by a commitment to museum archaeology, and the difficulty which women within archaeology faced in trying to earn a living wage was clearly significant.

Within museums, women had opportunities to develop and innovate in the material practices of the museum.[88] Sheppard argues that Margaret Murray's unwrapping of one of the Two Brothers' mummies at Manchester Museum in 1907 was not only a major part of Murray's career, but shows distinctive material practices – Murray drew on the spectacular mummy unwrappings of the nineteenth century but combined these with new, scientific practices to set the standard for mummy investigation.[89] Thus again, Murray's archaeology was fundamentally linked to the distinctive material practices of museums (see Figure 3).

Kathleen Sheppard seeks to reclaim the work of women archaeologists as representing a contribution different in kind, but not in value, from men's. She says, 'The field was not the only place archaeology was done ... the heroic excavator was not the only person working long hours.'[90] This is true; however, it is also the case that women worked long hours at tasks which they would not necessarily have chosen. They were reliant on offering help of various sorts to male mentors and patrons who offered them, in return, some professional work but not a career path, or security, or a life anywhere near as comfortable as their own. Women took up university study of archaeology and anthropology in unusually large numbers; they took advantage of the opening up of higher education. But the opportunities did not go much further than postgraduate study; and those women who built careers from the academy were disproportionately focused on cataloguing and other lowly but crucial tasks in museums.

This section once more confirms how unsatisfactory the categories of amateur and professional were, in significantly different ways for men and women, in these developing disciplines. The benefits of professionalisation accrued to men, and women were generally unable to access them even if they obtained a paid position; in many ways they gained more benefit from professionalisation by marrying a professional scholar or curator. Men could move between the domestic and the academic easily and frequently without any effect on their status as professionals or at least as scholars, and used both a household model of knowledge production where their wives and daughters helped them, and a model of knowledge production based in academic institutions. For women, the household model of production offered them opportunities but general meant their contribution would be hidden and seen as 'amateur'; while in a professional mode of production, they were hampered by low wages and lack of the household support men enjoyed. Museums, as spaces which were suffused with both academic and more domestic practices and networks, and which were distanced from fieldwork, allowed women more chance than other spaces to move between amateur and professional practices, and to deploy the materiality of the new disciplines to their own advantage.

Conclusion

Within the new human sciences, associated closely with museums at this stage, a number of spaces, practices and roles emerge as gendered male or female. Women can be seen making small-scale donations encompassing personal connections; as curators' and others' wives both working with their husbands and assuming responsibility for the transferral of their husbands' collections to public museums; as independent archaeologists, anthropologists and folklorists in the 'field'; as museum 'assistants' who catalogued, documented and displayed material supplied by fieldworkers to the museum; and as fundraisers, organisers, illustrators and popular authors. This multiplicity of ways to contribute explains why these disciplines seem to have been particularly popular with and populated by women. While in many ways archaeology and anthropology were distinctive in allowing women access to museums as university-trained professionals, women's access to museums because of domestically formed skills, amateur status and tendency to perform caring roles within and beyond their family remained very prominent.

Within disciplines, women were distinctive in both mediating between the field and the museum, and between the discipline and the wider audience, in important ways, and their development of museum material practices was significant. Their roles and practices can be easily overlooked if we use the categories which apply to male involvement in disciplines and museums. In fact, labels are often unhelpful here, as much of women's contribution was framed as 'assisting' men in some way; and the 'wife' label has even more actively rendered women invisible. But clearly as suppliers and transferrers of data, and as interpreters and recorders, they did shape the disciplines in ways that the 'assisting' label does not acknowledge, as Sheppard has argued.

Thus far, there are distinct similarities with the findings that women in natural history museums in the USA occupied the education and interpretation roles which men did not want to take on, and used them as a base to change museums and embed women's position within them further.[91] However, in addition to the problems women were shown in Chapter 1 to have encountered within the MA, the argument does not work fully in archaeology and anthropology for additional reasons; most clearly the sense of longing women demonstrated to be able to work in the field, and disappointment they sometimes expressed at having to undertake teaching and museum roles away from the 'real' sites of discovery. Moreover, interpretive and educational roles including those in museums were not revalued in the way they were in US natural history museums; indeed in both archaeology and anthropology, the valuation of masculine fieldwork at the expense of processing and interpreting work only intensified after the First World War. The development of Malinowskian immersion fieldwork was in part a reaction against many of these female incursions into the new disciplines, and the same is true of the development of archaeology in the interwar period.[92]

In these disciplines, men tended to monopolise whichever area was perceived as the most heroic, serious and requiring expertise, but this varied; the field was seen as suitable for inexpert amateurs in anthropology, while it was widely (but not universally) seen as too physical, intellectually demanding and requiring too much leadership for women in archaeology. Similarly, the practices of classifying objects and data might be seen as the key intellectual process and suitable for men, as with Pitt Rivers, or as a secondary, assisting role, and therefore most suitable for women. Although women were active in both archaeology and anthropology, household divisions of labour can therefore be traced in these disciplines. Interpreting this as either women playing to their strengths and knowledge, as Amelia Edwards saw it, or as women's exclusion from 'official' practices and roles, is to an extent equally valid. Women did what they were good at and had some advantage in pursuing, but their roles were often ignored, or conceptualised only in relation to men's (apparently more valuable) activities. Once women began filling such roles in the human sciences, the roles and practices themselves became identified as feminine, and therefore to a certain extent 'non-scientific', and thus gendered divisions of labour within the discipline became harder, not easier, to dismantle. While women did move into the disciplines of archaeology and anthropology in greater numbers in the inter-war period, there is some indication that their association with museums rather than the field persisted or even strengthened.[93]

This may be because the 'field' could be metaphorically in opposition to 'home'; though home in this sense often meant 'Britain' rather than specifically a domestic dwelling, the fact that wives were sometimes left at home to look after children suggests there was some overlap between the meanings of 'home'. Fieldwork was starting to be asserted as a technically specialised activity which was less compatible with involvement in the daily processes of domestic life than it had seemed to the early Victorians; women were less likely to be able to combine fieldwork with running a home and be taken seriously as scholars than Margaret Gatty had. Those women who did undertake fieldwork, such as missionaries, were not seen as scholars and their contribution to the disciplines, though significant, was hidden. Although in other areas of museum activity, women were able to mobilise understandings of domesticity, and the attributes of domestic femininity, to make space for themselves, in the emerging disciplines of archaeology and anthropology such understandings served more to constrain women's roles than to enable.

Distinct, complexly gendered material practices and disciplines emerged from dense networks of people and things. Women had experience of particular ways of interacting with the material world, but the influx of new things from different cultures and different times, in giving rise to new ways of knowing, produced particular opportunities for women, as well as new hierarchies of value between different material practices. As a result, women were key figures in the shaping of museum archaeology and anthropology up to 1914.

Notes

1 Chris Gosden and Frances Larson, *Knowing Things: Exploring the Collections at the Pitt Rivers Museum 1884–1945* (Oxford: Oxford University Press 2007), pp. 39, 122.

2 See, for example, Ann B. Shteir, *Cultivating Women, Cultivating Science* (Baltimore, MD and London: Johns Hopkins Press 1996) and Martin Willis, 'Unmasking immorality: popular opposition to laboratory science in late Victorian Britain', in D. Clifford, E. Wadge, A. Warwick and M. Willis (eds), *Repositioning Victorian Sciences: Shifting Centres in Nineteenth-Century Scientific Thinking* (London: Anthem 2006). The analogies between the history of women in archaeology and the history of women in science are also considered at some length by Kathleen Sheppard in her thesis on Margaret Murray. She makes some useful points about women's distinctive but different contribution to Egyptology, but tends to subscribe to a view of disciplinary formation as a process of linear progress whereby archaeology goes through the process of professionalisation at a later date, but in much the same way as, the natural sciences. However, I would argue that though the similarities between sciences and archaeology were there, the new human science disciplines and their gendered characteristics were most importantly formed by the relationships between different material practices, especially those distinguishing the field and the museum, which were less similar, and more open to women, than the natural science model suggests. Kathleen Sheppard, 'The lady and the looking glass: Margaret Murray's life in archaeology' (unpublished PhD thesis, University of Oklahoma 2010).

3 Samuel J. M. M. Alberti, *Nature and Culture: Objects, Disciplines and the Manchester Museum* (Manchester and New York: Manchester University Press 2009), chapter 4.

4 Note by Margaret Gatty, n.d., Gatty/Eden correspondence, Museums Sheffield archive.

5 Kate Hill, ' "He knows me … but not at the museum": women, natural history collecting and museums, 1880–1914', in S. Dudley, A. Barnes, J. Binnie, J. Petrov and J. Walklate (eds), *Narrating Stories, Collecting Stories* (Abingdon: Routledge 2012).

6 The 'museum period' in anthropology has been placed as the 1840s to 1890; Stocking notes that from the 1890s museums were important sponsors of anthropological fieldwork, though equally this is when universities started to emerge as institutions which would come to dominate anthropology; 'Essays on museums and material culture', in G. Stocking (ed.), *Objects and Others: Essays on Museums and Material Culture* (Madison, WI: University of Wisconsin Press 1985), pp. 7–8. On the other hand, although the epistemological change created by the Malinowskian fieldwork paradigm is made clear by Gosden and Larson, it is also clear that fieldwork perhaps more

resembling that of natural history, systematic specimen collecting, had been going on in varying ways since earlier in the nineteenth century; Chris Gosden and Frances Larson, *Knowing Things: Exploring the Collections at the Pitt Rivers Museum 1884–1945* (Oxford: Oxford University Press 2007).

7　The BM records the donation of terra cotta Roman objects from Smyrna, 'excavated by Mrs W. R. Paton', the donor (who was the wife of a classical scholar): British Museum Book of Presents, January 1895.

8　Margaret S. Drower, *Flinders Petrie, A Life in Archaeology* (Madison, WI: University of Wisconsin Press 1995 [1985]).

9　Anna Catalani and Susan Pearce, ' "Particular thanks and obligations": the communications made by women to the Society of Antiquaries between 1776 and 1837 and their significance', *The Antiquaries Journal* 86 (2006), pp. 254–278.

10　*Archaeologica Cantiana* 1 (1858), p. xxxvii.

11　East Riding Antiquarian Society, 'Third Annual Report', *Transactions of the East Riding Antiquarian Society*, vol. 3 (Hull: William Andrews and Co. 1895), pp. xv–xviii.

12　S. Harrison, 'A local hero: John Robert Mortimer and the birth of archaeology in East Yorkshire', *Bulletin of the History of Archaeology*, 19 (2009), online, available at www.archaeologybulletin.org/article/view/47, accessed 19 May 2014; M. Giles, 'Collecting the past, constructing identity: the antiquarian John Mortimer and the Driffield Museum of Antiquities and Geological Specimens', *The Antiquaries Journal* 86: 1 (2006), pp. 279–316.

13　Pitt Rivers' excavations, museums and archaeological collecting have recently been re-examined; see Dan Hicks, 'Excavating Pitt-Rivers: studying the archaeological collections made by Augustus Henry Lane Fox Pitt-Rivers', online, available at http://excavatingpittrivers.blogspot.co.uk/, accessed 19 May 2014; Jeremy Coote, 'Archaeology, anthropology and museums, 1851–2014: rethinking Pitt Rivers and his legacy – an introduction', and Peter Saunders, ' "The choicest, best arranged museums I have ever seen": the Pitt-Rivers Museum, Dorset, 1880s–1970s', both in *Museum History Journal* 7: 2 (2014), pp. 126–134 and 205–223.

14　For example, Montagu Browne at Leicester Museum; Kate Hill, 'Collecting authenticity: domestic, familial, and everyday "old things" in English museums, 1850–1939', *Museum History Journal* 4: 2 (2011), p. 207.

15　See Chapter 3.

16　Hill, 'Collecting authenticity', p. 209.

17　There is a substantial literature on women travellers in the nineteenth century. See for example, Sara Mills, *Discourses of Difference: An Analysis of Women's Travel Writing and Colonialism* (London: Routledge 1991); Jordana Pomeroy (ed.), *Intrepid Women: Victorian Artists Travel* (Aldershot: Ashgate 2005); Maria H. Frawley, *A Widening Sphere: Travel Writing by Women in Victorian England* (Rutherford: Fairleigh Dickinson University Press 1994); Dea Birkett, *Spinsters Abroad: Victorian Lady Explorers* (Oxford: Basil Blackwell 1989).

18　Harry Hodgkinson, 'Durham (Mary) Edith (1863–1944)', rev. *Oxford Dictionary of National Biography* (Oxford: Oxford University Press 2004); online edn, January 2011, available at www.oxforddnb.com.proxy.library.lincoln.ac.uk/view/article/37379, accessed 19 May 2014.

19 Letter from Mary Edith Durham to William Ridgeway (later Sir), Disney Professor of Archaeology at Cambridge University, 15th (no month given), 1911, archives of Museum of Archaeology and Anthropology, University of Cambridge, W10/3/4.

20 Claire Loughney, 'Colonialism and the development of the English provincial museum 1823–1914' (unpublished PhD thesis, University of Newcastle 2006), p. 329.

21 T. O. Beidelman, 'Altruism and domesticity: images of missionising women among the Church Missionary Society in nineteenth-century East Africa', in Mary Taylor Huber and Nancy C. Lutkehaus (eds), *Gendered Missions: Men and Women in Missionary Discourse and Practice* (Ann Arbor, MI: University of Michigan Press 1999); Delia Davin, 'British women missionaries in nineteenth-century China', *Women's History Review* 1: 2 (1992), pp. 257–271.

22 Inbal Livne, 'The many purposes of missionary work: Annie Royle Taylor as missionary, travel writer, collector and empire builder', in H. Nielssen and I. M. Okkenhaug (eds), *Protestant Missions and Local Encounters in the Nineteenth and Twentieth Centuries: Unto the Ends of the World* (Leiden: Brill 2011), p. 48.

23 Livne, 'Many purposes of missionary work', pp. 43, 52.

24 Jeanne Cannizzo, 'Gathering souls and objects: missionary collections', in Tim Barringer and Tom Flynn (eds), *Colonialism and the Object: Empire, Material Culture and the Museum* (London: Routledge 1998), p. 158.

25 Horniman Museum Accession Register March 1898; see also Nicky Levell, *Oriental Visions: Exhibitions, Travel and Collecting in the Victorian Age* (London: Horniman Museum and Gardens/Museu Antropológico da Universidade de Coimbra 2000), pp. 231–232.

26 Nicky Levell, 'The translation of objects: R. and M. Davidson and the Friends' Foreign Mission Association, China, 1890–1894', in A. Shelton (ed.), *Collectors: Individuals and Institutions* (London: Horniman Museum and Gardens/Museu Antropologico da Universidade de Coimbra 2001).

27 J. H. Proctor, 'Serving God and the Empire: Mary Slessor in South-Eastern Nigeria, 1876–1915', *Journal of Religion in Africa* 30: 1 (2000), pp. 45–61.

28 The McManus, 'Dundee and the world', n.d., online, available at www.themcmanus-dundee. gov.uk/sites/default/files/dworldp1.pdf, accessed 2 June 2012; Mundus (gateway to missionary collections in the United Kingdom), 'Slessor and Calabar collection', n.d., online, available at www.mundus.ac.uk/cats/57/1043.htm, accessed 2 June 2012.

29 Durham also donated to the BM and the Pitt Rivers Museum. British Museum Book of Presents, June 1914; Pitt Rivers Museum, The Other Within Project, Mary Edith Durham entry, online, available at http://england.prm.ox.ac.uk/ajax-individuals. html, accessed 4 November 2014.

30 Note from Durham to Ridgeway, 17 March 1908; letter from Durham to Ridgeway, 17 October 1910, archives of Museum of Archaeology and Anthropology, University of Cambridge, W10/3/4.

31 Letter from Durham to Ridgeway, 17 October 1910, archives of Museum of Archaeology and Anthropology, University of Cambridge, W10/3/4.

32 Letter from T. A. Stewart to Mrs Charlotte Wheeler Cuffe, 31 July 1914, archives of Museum of Archaeology and Anthropology, University of Cambridge, W10/3/26.

33 Letters between E. Ray Lankester and Nina Layard, September 1907–July 1908; in S. J. Plunkett, 'Correspondence of Nina Frances Layard (1853–1935) transcribed and collected by Steven J. Plunkett' 1992/3, Ipswich Museum.

34 Letter from Lady Evans to Nina Frances Layard, c. 1906/7; letters between E. Ray Lankester and Nina Layard, October 1907–July 1908; all in S. J. Plunkett, 'Correspondence of Nina Frances Layard (1853–1935) transcribed and collected by Steven J. Plunkett' 1992/3, Ipswich Museum.

35 L. C. Carr, *Tessa Verney Wheeler: Women and Archaeology before World War Two* (Oxford: Oxford University Press 2012), p. 126.

36 David Gill, ' "The passion of hazard": women at the British School at Athens before the First World War', *Annual of the British School at Athens* 97 (2002), p. 494.

37 Sir John Evans Centenary Project, Ashmolean Museum, 'Maria Millington Lathbury (1856–1944)', online, available at http://johnevans.ashmolean.org/evans/ maria-lathbury.html, accessed 14 May 2010.

38 'Maria Millington Lathbury'.

39 Margaret S. Drower, *Flinders Petrie: A Life in Archaeology* (Madison, WI: University of Wisconsin Press 1985), p. 233.

40 Petrie Museum, UCL, Archives PMA/WFP1 16/2/1, letter from Flinders Petrie to F. Spurrell, 22 September 1897.

41 See, for example, Hilda Petrie's journal entry for 4 February 1901: 'My sister Amy sorts out fragments of special bowls ... and spends days in her hut piecing them together ... She also marks the pottery etc outside with the letter of the tomb.' In the same entry, Hilda Petrie describes her friend, Beatrice Orme, contributing thus: she 'draws all the potmarks, inks in all Flinders' sealings and vase-drawings, develops all his photographs in the evening, sorts and pieces, and does a quantity of odd jobs, besides photographing and violin practising'. In Margaret S. Drower (ed.), *Letters from the Desert: The Correspondence of Flinders and Hilda Petrie* (Oxford: Oxbow Books 2004), p. 164.

42 Drower, *Flinders Petrie*, pp. 270–271; Drower, *Letters*, pp. 147, 188.

43 Hilda Petrie journal entry 4 February 1901, quoted in Drower (ed.), *Letters from the Desert*, p. 164.

44 Margaret S. Drower, 'Margaret Alice Murray (1863–1963)', in Getzel M. Cohen and Martha Sharp Jonkowsky (eds), *Breaking Ground: Pioneering Women Archaeologists* (Ann Arbor: University of Michigan Press 2004), pp. 113–114.

45 Drower, *Flinders Petrie*, pp. 248, 307.

46 Petrie Museum, UCL, Archives PMA/WFP1 16/2/2, letter from Hilda Petrie to William Flinders Petrie, n.d., annotated in pencil 'Jan? 1910'.

47 Margaret Murray, *My First Hundred Years* (London: William Kimber 1963), p. 103.

48 Alice Stevenson, 'Artefacts of excavation: the British collection and distribution of Egyptian finds to museums, 1880–1915', *Journal of the History of Collections* 26: 1 (2014), pp. 89–102.

49 Brenda Moon, *More Usefully Employed: Amelia B. Edwards, Writer, Traveller and Campaigner for Ancient Egypt* (London: Egypt Exploration Society 2004), pp. 185, 189, 194, 213.

50 See, for example, the way they are shown to have worked together in Debbie Challis, *The Archaeology of Race: The Eugenic Ideas of Francis Galton and Flinders Petrie* (London: Bloomsbury 2013), pp. 92–93.

51 *Egypt Exploration Fund, Report of the Fourth Ordinary General Meeting* (London 1890).

52 *Egypt Exploration Fund, Report of the Sixth Ordinary General Meeting* (London 1892).

53 *Egypt Exploration Fund, Report of the Fourth Ordinary General Meeting* (London 1890).

54 *Egypt Exploration Fund, Report of the Fourth Annual General Meeting* (London 1886); *EEF, Report of the Fifth Annual General Meeting* (London 1887); *EEF, Report of Second Ordinary General Meeting* (London 1888); *EEF, Report of the Fourth Ordinary General Meeting* (London 1890); *EEF, Report of Tenth Ordinary General Meeting* (London 1896).

55 *EEF, Report of the Fifth Annual General Meeting* (London 1887).

56 *EEF, Report of Fourth Ordinary General Meeting* (London 1890).

57 *EEF, Report of Fourth Ordinary General Meeting* (London 1890).

58 Anne Whitelaw, 'Women, museums and the problems of biography', in Kate Hill (ed.), *Museums and Biographies: Stories, Objects, Identities* (Woodbridge: Boydell and Brewer 2012); see also Lianne McTavish, *Defining the Modern Museum* (Toronto: University of Toronto Press 2013), esp. chapter 3.

59 Iman Hamam, ' "A race for incorporation": Ancient Egypt and its mummies in science and popular culture', in Richard Pearson (ed.), *The Victorians and the Ancient World: Archaeology and Classicism in Nineteenth-Century Culture* (Newcastle: Cambridge Scholars Press 2006), pp. 25–40; Nicholas Daly, 'That obscure object of desire: Victorian commodity culture and fictions of the mummy', *Novel: A Forum on Fiction* 28 (1994), pp. 24–51. See also Sara Brio, 'Unwrapping the self: Victorian mummy unwrappings and questions of mortality', blog post, The Victorianist, online, available at https://victorianist.wordpress.com/2015/04/20/unwrapping-the-self-victorian-mu mmy-unwrappings-and-questions-of-mortality/, accessed 9 June 2015.

60 *Egypt Exploration Fund, Report of the Second Ordinary General Meeting* (London 1888)

61 Bolton Museum and Archive Service, 'Egyptology: Provenance', online, available at www.boltonmuseums.org.uk/collections/egyptology/egyptology-collection/for-researchers/provenance/, accessed 7 August 2013; Stevenson, 'Artefacts'.

62 See Egypt Exploration Fund distribution lists, Lucy Gura Archive, Egypt Exploration Society.

63 Stevenson, 'Artefacts'.

64 Deborah Manley, 'Edwards, Amelia Ann Blanford (1831–1892)', *Oxford Dictionary of National Biography* (Oxford: Oxford University Press 2004), online, available at www.oxforddnb.com.proxy.library.lincoln.ac.uk/view/article/8529, accessed 7 Aug 2013; Margaret Drower, 'Hilda Petrie', Brown University Women in Old World Archaeology project, online, available at www.brown.edu/Research/Breaking_Ground/results.php ?d=1&first=Hilda&last=Petrie, accessed 7 August 2013.

65 Alice Stevenson, 'Between the field and the museum: archaeological context and finds distribution', unpublished conference paper, online, available at www.academia.edu/3807596/ Between_the_Field_and_the_Museum_archaeological_context_and_finds_distribution, accessed 7 August 2013.

66 Henrika Kucklick, *The Savage Within: The Social History of British Anthropology, 1885–1945* (Cambridge: Cambridge University Press 1991), p. 53.

67 Kate Hill, *Culture and Class in English Public Museums, 1850–1914* (Aldershot: Ashgate 2005), p. 63.

68 Carol Dyhouse, *No Distinction of Sex? Women in British Universities 1870–1939* (London: UCL Press 1995).

69 Amara Thornton, 'The allure of archaeology: Agnes Conway and Jane Harrison at Newnham College, 1903–1907', *Bulletin of the History of Archaeology*, 21: 1 (2011), online, available at www.archaeologybulletin.org/article/view/bha.2114/7, accessed 7 August 2013, p. 40.

70 Thornton, 'Allure of archaeology', p. 37.

71 Gosden and Larson, *Knowing Things*, p. 132.

72 Mary E. Blair, *A Life Well Led: The Biography of Barbara Freire-Marreco Aitken, British Anthropologist* (Santa Fe, NM: Sunstone Press 2008), p. 27.

73 Chris Wingfield and Alison Petch, 'Diploma students in anthropology, University of Oxford 1907–1945', *Relational Museum Project*, Pitt Rivers Museum, online, available at http://history.prm.ox.ac.uk/students.php?, accessed 14 July 2014.

74 Gill, '"The passion of hazard"'; Thornton, 'Allure of archaeology'.

75 Thornton, 'Allure of archaeology', p. 40.

76 Kathleen Sheppard, 'The lady and the looking glass: Margaret Murray's life in archaeology' (unpublished PhD thesis, University of Oklahoma 2010), p. 111–112; Gill, '"Passion of hazard"', p. 497.

77 Murray, *My First Hundred Years*, p. 159.

78 The Women's Department in Manchester even had its own newsletter from 1887–1894; here the students did compare their lot to those of women in residential colleges but it was apparently the lack of sporting facilities of which they were complaining. Mabel Tylecote, *The Education of Women at Manchester University 1883–1933* (Manchester: Manchester University Press 1941), p. 38.

79 Murray, *My First Hundred Years*; Sheppard, 'Lady and looking glass', pp. 166–168.

80 Kate Hall, considered in Chapter 1, did not take a degree at London University, apparently because of her poor Latin.

81 Sheppard, 'Lady and looking glass', p. 121.

82 Blair, *A Life Well Led*, chapter 2.

83 Alison Petch, 'Barbara Freire-Marreco (Mrs Robert Aitken)', The Other Within, online, available at http://england.prm.ox.ac.uk/englishness-Barbara-Freire-Marreco.html, accessed 18 March 2011.

84 Letter from Balfour to Barbara Freire-Marreco, quoted in Gosden and Larson, *Knowing Things*, pp. 132–133.

85 Horniman Museum Accession Registers, 1914.

86 Sheppard, 'Lady and looking glass', p. 118.

87 Sheppard, 'Lady and looking glass', p. 174.

88 Gosden and Larson, *Knowing Things*, pp. 125–132; Sheppard, 'Lady and looking glass', pp. 183, 186.

89 Sheppard, 'Lady and looking glass', p. 205.

90 Sheppard, 'Lady and looking glass', p. 9.

91 See Sally Gregory Kohlstedt, 'Innovative niche scientists: women's role in reframing North American museums, 1880–1930', *Centaurus* 55: 2 (2013), pp. 153–174, and Leslie Madsen-Brooks, 'Challenging science as usual: women's participation in American natural history museum work, 1870–1950', *Journal of Women's History* 21: 2 (2009), pp. 13–14. Their arguments are considered at greater length in Chapter 1.

92 On the development of anthropological fieldwork, see George Stocking, 'The ethnographer's magic: fieldwork in British anthropology from Tyler to Malinowski', in G. Stocking (ed.), *Observers Observed: Essays on Ethnographic Fieldwork* (Madison, WI: University of Wisconsin Press 1983). On archaeology, there seems to be less historical methodological reflection but there are some useful essays in Andrew L. Christenson (ed.), *Tracing Archaeology's Past: The Historiography of Archaeology* (Carbondale, IL: Southern Illinois University Press 1989).

93 At the Pitt Rivers Museum, women's donations start to become much more numerous in the 1930s, while David Gill's work on Winifred Lamb suggests the critical benefits of her honorary position at the Fitzwilliam Museum to her career. On the other hand, Dorothy Garrod does not support this theory very well, and more research is needed into the actual trajectories of women's involvement in this period.

7

Ruskin, women and museums: service and salvage

In the obituary of Henry Swan, curator of St George's Museum, Sheffield, in the *Sheffield Independent* in 1889, it was said that Mr Swan, 'in connection with Mrs Swan and the whole of his family, strove to bring home to Sheffield ... helpfulness, beauty, and joy in life, which are the great principles in Mr Ruskin's life and writings'.[1] The prominence of Mrs Emily Swan in the running of the museum was such that Ruskin himself described her as the 'Curatress'. She was not alone; women were particularly prominent around the *fin de siècle* in museums which were inspired by a Ruskinian ethos. This chapter investigates the Ruskinian approach to museology and asks why women particularly identified with it, suggesting that it allowed them to reshape museums along feminine lines, prefiguring twentieth-century museums. Women were prominent among those advocating and developing museums which were Ruskinian in two main respects; first of all by focusing on authentic modes of craft production, especially domestic crafts, and on the past as the locus of an authentic craft tradition, which might be revived or merely preserved in museums; and secondly by seeing museums as institutions which might help save or reform modern society by engaging women, children and working-class audiences, viewed as potentially pure but ignorant, in ways of looking and making which could harness their simplicity for the redemption of civilisation. Their involvement in Ruskinian museums, thus, can be seen as the culmination of trends visible elsewhere in late Victorian museums, where women attempted to orientate institutions, collections and audiences towards the domestic, the feminine and the excluded. However, women's involvement in Ruskinian museums may also be seen as developing previous trends in new ways, by making more overtly political statements about the shape of modern society and culture, and of women's roles within it.

Through such museums, we can see the ways in which women most successfully blended domestic and museum spaces, private and public. In Ruskinian museums, women particularly articulated and created a different way of dealing with the public/private divide which most clearly clashed with a masculine idea that museums should be public because the public was more rational and epistemologically sound than the private.[2] Women influenced by Ruskin, and by William Morris whose ideas were similar though distinct, articulated a different valuation of public and private, by making the household and the domestic, as the locus of craft traditions and unalienated labour, the object of study, by recreating the mode of arrangement of the domestic and creating an illusion of the home in public, and by attempting to create an economy of value which placed the child, the mother, and the ignorant at the centre of the endeavour rather than at the bottom of the hierarchy. Such a vision took issue with a masculine idea of disembodied knowledge and put forward instead a view of knowledge as embodied and embedded, affective and even sentimental, practical and predicated on both a different economy of value, and a different relationship with materiality. From the somewhat unlikely raw materials created by Ruskin, women forged a style of museology which critiqued mainstream museology and even took issue with the emerging underlying value system of modernity.

It has been suggested that modernism in art led to Ruskin's ideas falling out of favour with male curators, whose professional practice was increasingly aligned with an objective, disembodied art history and, with the encouragement of the avant-garde, set apart from the rest of society.[3] Modernity simultaneously privileged a masculine individuality over the social concerns of the Victorian museum. Ruskin was certainly an emblematically Victorian figure increasingly disdained by artists during the *fin de siècle*, but he offered considerable ambiguity over the nature and importance of the feminine in public life.[4] I argue that the appropriation and development of his ideas about art, craft and museums by women in the late nineteenth and early twentieth centuries allowed them to colonise public space and to counter the very masculine discourses of modernism and modernity with an argument for the continued relevance of the domestic for the public, and vice versa. Women, in espousing an apparently increasingly 'old-fashioned' approach, and one moreover which seemed to reaffirm the essentialist understanding of masculine and feminine characteristics, pioneered the idea of the socially engaged museum.

Modernity has often been read in connection with 'masculine' developments such as improved technology, and faster transport, while nostalgia and tradition have been coded as 'feminine'.[5] Yet the modernity of nostalgia itself is also clear, and we will see how women used their association with tradition and the primitive to expand their field of action in a modern world.[6] In this context, Mark Sandberg's study of changing material representational practices around 1900, *Living Pictures, Missing Persons*, which argues that modernity both separated the traditional from the new, and simultaneously came close to collapsing the two together, is highly relevant. In addition, I examine here the gendering of such practices. Women led a response to modernity and to modernism which promoted museums as welcoming, pseudo-domestic places of empathy, where tradition and pre-modernity could be preserved, emphasising the very elements which had been designated 'feminine' in discussions of collecting practices.[7] They highlighted the recreated historic domestic environment as a place which could engage the working classes and children, thus enabling a Ruskinian revitalisation of society. Although men as well as women engaged with the Ruskinian museum project, by 1900 those men who did so were increasingly 'outsiders' to the world of museums, and in some ways, therefore, equally excluded by the official masculine world of professional curatorship.

I focus on the museums which themselves explicitly or implicitly prioritised Ruskinian ideals, on museums which took the salvage or preservation function of museums as their prime goal, seeking to recover or prevent the decay of traces of the past which enshrined the superior nature of that past; which valorised craft and craftspeople; which put children, and simple childlike visitors, at the centre of their attention in various ways; and which developed ideas about display which echoed Ruskin's own in various ways. In these areas, I show that women significantly changed the focus from the ways in which men had explored these areas – starting with Ruskin and Morris themselves. Women drew on their acknowledged 'feminine' expertise in the domestic, in serving others, and in communicating with children and the less educated, and used it to redirect museums away from masculine museological approaches. What this chapter tells us is how women were inscribed, and inscribed themselves, within modernity; it reveals a tension between the tendency to align them with the traditional pre-modern, which might be understood as authentic and disappearing, and the role they played in facilitating the ultra-modern project of visiting the past. Similarly, at the point where many men came to understand museums as about pure art or knowledge without social purpose, the ways in which women developed the community service element of museums formed an important new aspect of modernity.

While in some formulations, the growth of modernity and, in particular, the growth of modernist cultural practices led to a growing disdain for tradition, nostalgia and the authentically old in favour of the brand new, others see the old and the new as more intertwined in modernity. As Outka suggests, 'the two camps of artifice and authenticity are usually considered in opposition, roughly mapping onto, on the one hand, a cutting-edge modernity, and, on the other, a more conservative impulse to preservation and stability'.[8] Instead, these 'camps' were deeply connected, and indeed, the very fusion of authentic oldness and artificial availability was, it seems, the distinguishing feature of a new, 'modern' relationship with the past. The appeal of this connectedness was its ability to 'weave temporal fragments together', but it also, more subtly, 'challenged the organising binary that divided the authentic from the mass market, or a pure art from a sullied materialism'.[9] For modern, open-air museums, it has been argued that an emphasis on the 'actual' object and original space was combined with increasingly elaborate, 'artificial' scene setting.[10] So the combination of authenticity and artifice was a particular characteristic of modern museums from around 1900.

If modernity itself promoted, or essentially was, a cross-fertilisation of new artificial mobility and traditional authenticity, what was the place or role of women within it? Women were often positioned as traditional and authentic, in opposition to the modern and artificial, and therefore had some incentive to bring the divisions together, and to produce more positive valuations of the traditional. Outka suggests that women, particularly the middle-class lady shopper, valued the hybrid modern because it could both stimulate and soothe anxiety about change, as they took on more visible public roles. A hybrid understanding of modernity allowed them to enjoy the pleasures and possibilities of newly enhanced mobility while also asserting identities which were still rooted in the 'feminine' home and authentic tradition.[11] Whether this is a strategy to comfort anxieties or a more combative response is a difficult question. At Selfridges, as Outka shows, it was a vision which was manufactured specifically for women in order to encourage them to consume more; but in the museum setting women themselves took the lead, and emphasised those aspects of domesticity which they themselves had exclusive access to, and could mediate to a wider public, such as feminine domestic crafts.[12]

Preservation and 'salvage' museology

The idea of preserving and saving the past was developing throughout the nineteenth century. It is, perhaps, most clearly associated with William

Morris; in founding the Society for the Protection of Ancient Buildings (SPAB), he endowed old things with both a new-found sense of authenticity, and with the potential to be radical reshapers of the future. In other words, for Morris preservation was not about nostalgia but had practical value; it was 'an act of defiance against capitalism', which also showed how a future without capitalism could be achieved.[13] Many of those who took a Morrisian approach to preserving certain objects in museums did so in order to help develop a new type of society; they focused on objects which showed unalienated labour, a people's art, as exemplars for how such art could be taken forward in future.

However, the ways in which concepts of authenticity underlaid Morrisian ideas about museums and preservation meant that nostalgia was always close to hand. As Miele shows, the idea of authenticity as lying in the continuity of materiality over time could be found from the mid-eighteenth century but Ruskin and Morris articulated it more clearly and to more people. This was why preservation rather than restoration was required; style was not as critical as substance. What an object looked like was not as important as its actually being old. Such a view of authenticity prioritised 'the mood and feel' of materiality and thus was an ideal vehicle for nostalgia and romantic longing.[14] While SPAB was founded in 1877 to prevent over-enthusiastic conservation measures being carried out on old buildings, Morris does not seem to have linked museums to the project of preservation, viewing them mainly as a source of examples for trainee craftspeople to use for instruction and inspiration (although his dislike of the SKM's Circulating Collection is possibly indicative of a preservationist view).[15]

The preservationist and salvage impulse was underpinned by a contradictory mixture of progress and nostalgia, in the same way as women's modernity.[16] This is made clear in Edwards's examination of how such impulses played out in photographic surveys of historic buildings and customs. Those who took part in the surveys simultaneously believed in progress and were nostalgic; they represented a 'complex intersection of poetics, salvage and science'. Nostalgia was a powerful presence but it was a dynamic, and potentially transformative, force; and one which mixed with ideas about progress.[17] However, initially there was little sign of the power it might offer women. Neither SPAB nor the photographic surveys were particularly feminised, and at times they were noticeably masculine environments. SPAB's origins and concerns with practical interventions and advice for specific historic properties meant that practising architects, artists and clergymen were its founding members.[18] Female membership thereafter hovered around 18 per cent, while among the committee members of SPAB up to 1896 there were just two women: Rhoda Garrett, the interior designer and women's suffrage campaigner, and Mrs Thackeray Ritchie, daughter of W. M. Thackeray and an author and Ruskinian.[19] Meanwhile, around 13 per cent of the photographers in the surveys studied by Edwards were women, although they could be both prominent within the structures of amateur and professional photography, and also form independent groups such as the Norwich Ladies' Camera Club.[20]

Women's involvement in the National Trust was more noticeable, however. This organisation, of course, combined a preservationist impulse with a strong element of service to the poor and disadvantaged of society, aiming initially to preserve access to public spaces, especially rural spaces, for the urban poor. Compared to preservationist movements in France and Germany, the National Trust had both more women members, and more of those were members in their own right as opposed to being wives and daughters of male members; by 1914, 20 per cent of National Trust members were women. Moreover, women held positions of responsibility in the National Trust, and it was heavily dependent on women for its committee and campaign work; they drove the philanthropic agenda of the organisation.[21]

Thus both the 'femininity' of the authentically material past and the impulse to put the past to work to benefit the disadvantaged of the present shaped the possibilities for women to work within the preservation movement. Although women were involved in preserving entire buildings, and recording this through photography, smaller physical objects were easier for them to engage with.

John Ruskin and Ruskinian museums

John Ruskin was an extremely influential cultural critic (and indeed critic of a good deal more than culture) in the second half of the nineteenth century. Although his ideas ranged very widely, at the heart of his critique was dissatisfaction with industrial, capitalist and urbanised Britain; with modernity, although his response to it encompassed both conservatism and 'radical invention'.[22] He argued that nature, beauty, and the autonomous craftsperson able to be inspired by both of these things were necessary both for a healthy society, and for individuals to be able to reach their full potential.

He also made significant interventions in debates about gender in the period, although these were not always marked by consistency, and shifted around during the course of his writing career. Ruskin outlined a vision of men and women as exhibiting very different gendered natures, competences and roles, though emphasising a common need for high-minded service to produce spiritual regeneration for society.[23] Such service would be built through an embodied engagement with art and craft workmanship; and Ruskin's appreciation of the nature and social role of women's traditional domestic crafts was significant for those who used his writings as a blueprint to produce a better society.[24] Ruskin also idealised the domestic as the main productive unit of past society, and one which, contrasted with his contemporary society characterised by merely commercial relationships, and a separation of domestic and public, produced a healthier, better society. The role which Ruskin envisaged for women, as guardians of the domestic as the moral centre of society, and therefore as the possible agents for a remoralisation of society, was one which chimed substantially with the campaigns women were waging for a role in governance based on their ability to bring higher moral standards into public life.[25]

Moreover, while he may have identified masculine and feminine qualities, he was happy for actual men and women to exhibit unique mixtures of these qualities, often writing himself in a feminised voice, and accepting 'masculine' traits in women.[26] His actions, especially after 1870, also show him to be in fact a strong advocate and supporter of women in a number of key areas: education, art and employment more generally. He supported girls' schools and women's colleges both through his writing and through practical steps like donating artworks and other objects, helping them financially, and giving lectures and lessons.[27] He championed a number of women artists, most notably Kate Greenaway; and was closely involved in initiatives to enable women to earn their own living, for example through the Langdale, later Ruskin, Linen Industry which sought to provide spinning and weaving work for poor women of the Lake District, while also employing a few middle-class women in managerial roles.[28] Thus there were good reasons why women in the later nineteenth and earlier twentieth centuries might be drawn to Ruskinian ideas, projects and programmes of reform; Ruskinian milieus were increasingly arenas where they would be taken seriously and seen as having an important role to play.[29]

In a number of ways, Ruskin exercised an important degree of influence on the period at least up to the First World War, and his views on the past and the future were particularly influential. Scholars have traced his influence on new fields such as social reform and labour politics, fields which arguably positioned themselves as forward-looking and rejecting the Victorian inheritance.[30] However, Ruskin's ideas did not always appeal to dominant masculine groups as he increasingly positioned himself on the side of the outsider or marginalised.[31] This further enhanced his appeal to women.

Museums, potentially, might be a means of reforming society along the lines Ruskin envisaged; but he himself was decidedly ambivalent on the subject of museums, and his views also changed markedly during his life. He did not wish art and craft to be sequestered in museums, but rather to form a living tradition which reflected a society in touch with its own past. Craft, particularly, was something to be done not looked at, a way in which every individual's inherent seeking after beauty and truth could be put into practice through making.[32] Yet given the absence or attenuation of living traditions of art and craft, the hand and the eye needed to be trained, and Ruskin came to see the role of museums in offering such training.

Equally, though, Ruskin stated that museums were not for everyone, and should be reserved to those with expert knowledge. Ruskin was associated with the development of the University Museum in Oxford in the 1850s. This was envisaged as a museum which would affirm the divine order in natural creation, while also acting as a building project which would restore autonomy to craftspeople and allow them scope for true creativity, in the spirit of great cathedral building; stonemasons working on the building were encouraged to develop decorative motifs themselves.[33] The museum was, of course, primarily intended for elite university students. Writing in 1875, Ruskin asserted that museums should be only for advanced students of a subject, not for the masses of untrained and uneducated people, with children and babies, who would gain nothing from the experience. A museum was 'not at all a place of entertainment, but a place of education', and, moreover, 'not a place of elementary education, but that of already far-advanced scholars'.[34] Thus he stressed museums' importance in the creation of advanced knowledge, and for specialised students in natural history and art; but also showed an interest in the ways in which museums as built institutions could function to revivify craft and empower craftspeople.

As women were not included in the category of specialised, advanced students, and were equally not included as practitioners in the crafts being revived at the Oxford Museum, it certainly seemed as if women were not particularly envisaged as part of Ruskin's museum vision. It has even been asserted that Ruskin saw museums, even those containing textiles or other examples of more female crafts, as offering a critique of feminism, and a blueprint for renewing or celebrating traditional female behaviour against new models of women's roles: 'a masculine institution

preserved and regenerated a pre-feminist culture'.[35] This needs to be analysed in a number of ways, though; female crafts, though traditional and
domestic, did not automatically support a pre- or anti-feminist view of
women's role in society as a whole, indeed feminists were keen to recuper-
ate and celebrate women's crafts as a way of debunking masculine ideas
about artistic prowess. In this sense, there is very little difference between
Ruskin and many feminists. It is also, as will become clear, not entirely
correct to suggest that masculine institutions were the ones which sought
to preserve female crafts.

Ruskin's views on museums developed as a result of his fuller
involvement with the creation of an actual museum. He came to see
them as potentially useful for broader audiences, especially for the group
he saw as at the heart of a reformed society and culture: craftspeople.
The Guild of St George, which he founded and under whose aegis he
formed a museum, had a number of wider social aims including bringing
together people from different classes and building settlements outside
the capitalist system. Its museum aimed specifically at the education of
the craftsperson, developing a distinctive approach which rejected what
Ruskin saw as the alienation inherent in capitalist-inspired programmes
of design education put forward by men such as Henry Cole.[36] Ruskin
wanted the museum to reconnect craftspeople with nature, to educate
their eye in observation, and thereby to encourage the production of
authentic beauty, of a sort which had been possible in societies less dam-
aged by the primacy of profit than that of Victorian Britain.[37]

The museum which he formed, in Walkley on the outskirts of
Sheffield, thus departed from the model of local museums which had
been emerging in municipally funded institutions.[38] It relied heavily on
copies, it mixed art with natural history, and it used unique display methods, both didactic and domestic. The museum was set up in a modestly
sized cottage, in a hilltop location with views out across the moors to the
west of Sheffield; it was referred to as being out of the smoky city, and
the considerable uphill walk required to reach it was felt to be beneficial
in symbolically indicating the discarding of industrial capitalist society.[39]
The exhibits were personally selected by Ruskin; they included a number
of studies of Venetian architectural detail, and copies of Ruskin's favour-
ite Venetian artists' work, by Ruskin and his favoured copyist Bunney.[40]
Additionally, there were studies from nature, geological and botanical,
some by Ruskin himself; and large numbers of specimens, particularly
geological, again mostly from Ruskin's own collections.

The rooms in which these objects were displayed were not adapted
in the same way that other domestic spaces were adapted when becoming

Figure 10 Interior of St George's Museum, Walkley, Sheffield. Unknown photographer, c. 1887.

a museum (the best example here is the Weston Park Museum, also in Sheffield, which was a large house received as a bequest by the city corporation, where new galleries were created and extensive built in cases made before it was opened to the public; the aim was to eradicate its origins as a domestic space).[41] It is clear that the Walkley Museum retained features like fireplaces, included chairs and other furniture for use as well as display, had unusual display cases designed by Ruskin himself, and had vases of flowers to create a homely feel (see Figure 10).[42] Moreover, all the objects, including the natural history specimens, were arranged to create an aesthetic whole in a room, rather than being classified and sorted into ceramics rooms, geology rooms and other such categories. Visitors should be able to compare objects and images as they saw fit; 'fluidity' was the watchword of the display.[43]

This innovative museum, therefore, was ostensibly focused on craftspeople, and on their ideal training and crucial role in helping to build a new society. The first curator of the museum, Henry Swan, was a craftsman (an engraver) whose life had been transformed by reading Ruskin.[44] Moreover, Ruskin's statement about museums being not for elementary education but for advanced scholars was posted on the door. This was, apparently, a masculine space and experience, which was not just for workers, but specifically for 'workers in iron'; and indeed Ruskin wrote as follows to a girl he knew: 'the St George's Museum is for working men, not little girls, and you must not waste Mr Swan's time'.[45]

The references to working men with a particular trade may have been owing at least partly to opportunism by Ruskin, as the chance to establish the museum in Sheffield arose. He also described the potential of the museum to offer education to all the poor of Sheffield, and planned to open similar museums elsewhere (though none were actually created).[46] Women and girls certainly visited the museum in substantial numbers; they came alone, in mixed family groups, and in all-female groups. Some of them identified themselves in the visitor book as 'students', which suggests that by the 1880s Ruskin's favoured category of 'advanced student' did not in itself exclude women.[47] Moreover, the museum was much less of a masculine creation than it may have appeared. The active role of Henry Swan's wife Emily has already been indicated; Ruskin recognised the significant contribution of both Swans to the museum. She particularly seems to have undertaken work unpacking, preparing and displaying objects in the museum.[48] Additionally, from the 1890s the museum had a woman assistant curator, Genevieve Pilley, a craftswoman herself: a highly skilled calligrapher who carried out a number of high-profile commissions.[49] Thus, as with many of Ruskin's projects, however exclusionary they may have appeared in conception, in practical terms and towards the end of the nineteenth century they actually created significant spaces and opportunities for women.

An additional feature of the museum is that Ruskin envisaged it as a place where aspects of Venice's architectural past could be preserved, through copying and photographing architectural details.[50] This was the most clearly articulated instance so far of the museum as a way of salvaging and preserving what was being destroyed by the forces of modernity. Although museums had sometimes been envisaged as places to keep and preserve the past, an alternative role driving and materialising knowledge had become increasingly prominent from the eighteenth century. For Ruskin, his museum in Walkley was partly a way of preserving records and fragments of a dead or dying Venice in order to mourn and elegise it, though not to save the original, an apparently impossible task. The museum might thus foster efforts to preserve traditions, including those which were still revivable and might form the basis of a new culture of manufacturing.

Ruskin, then, laid out some significant new directions for museums, though they were not always developed fully or consistently by him. These were often directions which were rather at odds with, or maybe on a divergent track from, mainstream museology; we know that he disliked the SKM for its size and incoherence, though Morris supported both this museum and Birmingham Museum and Art Gallery.[51] Women, in various ways, developed his museological examples and ideas from the 1880s.[52]

Ruskinians felt that museums might offer even greater possibilities than Ruskin had suggested to effect a rebirth of society and civilisation. Amy Woodson-Boulton has recently shown how deeply a Ruskinian ethos motivated the founders of art museums in northern industrial cities in England in the late nineteenth century. In Liverpool, Manchester and Birmingham, influential civic leaders argued that art and nature, or nature through art, would rehumanise and redeem industrial society by offering the poor and uneducated a better life through beauty.[53] It is notable that Ruskin himself was often only a lukewarm supporter of these initiatives, because while he believed in the transformative power of beauty, he thought that this was an inappropriate response to industrial cities where one should focus instead on the provision of basic necessities (arguing, for example, that 'children should have enough to eat, and their skins should be washed clean'[54]), or, for preference, get rid of industrial society completely.[55] However, for the Ruskinians within civic elites, amelioration was the goal and art museums were the means by which this would be achieved. The ideal approach was to offer art which was narrative, which was 'true' to nature, and morally beautiful, in settings which were as far as possible accessible and welcoming to the working classes, through opening hours or 'extras' offered like musical events, for example. This meant that contemporary British art dominated the exhibits, as it seemed to have the qualities that were needed to create a transformative experience, rather than an art history lesson, as well as being 'accessible', that is, perceived as being attractive to uneducated workers.[56]

In civic museums, though, Ruskinian ideals were forced to compromise with other groups, leading to watered down practices including, for example, quite restricted access; far from serving the people, the museum still appeared to be set aside to act as a forum for the display of middle-class cultural capital and as an assertion of civic pride.[57] This was one of the reasons for the establishment of a number of new museums, sometimes branch museums of the city centre museum, sometimes small independent museums, in working-class suburbs in the 1880s and 1890s. In particular, Thomas Coglan Horsfall, who had been a leading figure in the campaign to set up the Manchester City Art Gallery, next turned his attention to the setting up of an art museum in the deprived area of Ancoats in Manchester, partly because he felt that the City Art Gallery had failed to deliver the type of approach he was seeking.[58] The Manchester Art Museum he founded, opening in 1886, was possibly the most explicitly Ruskinian of the Ruskin-inspired museums; it was, he said, 'formed for the purpose of giving effect to Ruskin's teaching'.[59]

Such a development was not just produced by explicitly Ruskinian reformers from northern English cities; similar initiatives were also developed in London by those also indebted to Ruskin. The exhibitions which were held in Whitechapel, followed by the foundation of the Whitechapel Art Gallery, all the work of Canon Samuel and Henrietta Barnett, were also based on the conviction that the beauty of art could redeem the working class and cancel out the deleterious effects of living in an impoverished urban industrial environment upon them.[60] Both exhibitions and gallery were situated in the heart of East End London, designed to act as 'lamps in a dark place', and were open till 10 p.m., even on Sundays.[61] The South London Art Gallery, founded in 1878–79, had slightly more complex motivations and aims, but shared the common aim of accessibility, with Sunday and evening opening, and a concern to welcome children.[62]

Thus a heavily Ruskin-inspired movement was one of the most dynamic elements of museum development in the last 20 years of the nineteenth century. It privileged displays and objects which offered spiritual transformation, and took these enclaves of beauty directly to the working classes, with evening opening and special events designed to entice children, particularly, into the institution, in the hope that thus society and the environment would gradually be reformed. But how was gender figured in this movement? In many ways, the Ruskinian museums were both actually dominated by men, and used gendered discourse to position the masculine as the provider of the beautiful to an often feminised or infantilised audience.[63] The prominence of the idea of 'brotherhood' in the university settlement movement and in organisations like the Guild of St George, as well as the control of cultural policy by exclusively male local government bodies, meant that men made most of the running in campaigning for and setting up such museums.[64] The sense that such museums might be envisaged as offering the perspective of the middle-class educated male to the working class, women and children, all groups deficient in properly masculine qualities, can also be discerned in museum attempts to improve society.[65] *Punch* sardonically suggested that working-class women would, either ignorantly or knowingly, fail to appreciate the moral refinement emanating from beautiful paintings such as those by Lord Leighton (see Figure 11).

ART IN WHITECHAPEL.

"Well, that's what I calls a himpossible Persition to get yerself into!"

Figure 11 'Art in Whitechapel'.
(*Punch*, 1897)

The gendering of Ruskinian museums was, however, much more complex than that. In particular, I want to show how a Ruskin-inspired programme for museums actually created significant spaces for women, and was enthusiastically taken up by them. This includes not just the provision of spaces containing beauty and nature, sited in places where the urban poor could access them and made further accessible through opening hours and activities, but also the 'salvage' museology which Ruskin had inaugurated: using museums as places in which to preserve the disappearing material culture of the pre-modern period, not so much to keep it alive as to keep it safe. It also includes the emphasis on craft and making, changed from the more exclusively male reference to 'workers in iron' to include dressmaking and other female domestic productions for the household, not the market.

Women and the feminine philanthropic: domestic expertise

Women, as has been widely noted, asserted their apparently caring nature in order to extend their involvement in philanthropic activity, and thence to parlay this activity into a generalised stance of service to society, conceived in terms of maternal care of the vulnerable.[66] In this, the increasing focus on the family as the locus of social problems around 1900 allowed women's domestic expertise to be brought into public play even more fully. Middle-class women had undertaken charitable visiting to the homes of the poor from at least the late eighteenth century, but as the end of the nineteenth century approached, this concern to intervene in family life took different forms and became more systematised.[67] One of the key figures in this development, Octavia Hill, was herself close to Ruskin, sharing ideals about working-class education, and was advised and supported by him financially.[68] One prong of her work was to develop and systematise home visiting, but another was to change the working-class home through external means, including through public education and publicly disseminated models of a better kind of domesticity, as well as providing public spaces for family life such as playgrounds and concert halls. She was also prominent in campaigns to preserve both public land and public access to particular places, again largely because of the benefit such spaces might offer to working-class family life, and particularly to children.[69] Her aims were thus both to transform domestic spaces, and to improve access to public space for excluded groups.

Although the university settlement movement, and Ruskin's own Guild of St George, appeared to improve the lives of the poor in the late nineteenth century through a chivalric model of masculine service and protection, the gendering of these initiatives was not always so straightforward.[70] University settlements were composed of graduates, and in cases such as Toynbee Hall these were men; but following the foundation of women's colleges, and women's expanded access to higher education generally, women's settlements were also created, such as the Women's University Settlement in Southwark with which Octavia Hill was associated; and mixed settlements existed such as the Manchester University settlement, where men's and women's sections were separate, but the women's section was arguably the most energetic.[71] At Toynbee Hall, of course, the settlement was run by a husband and wife team, Samuel and Henrietta Barnett, and Mrs Barnett's influence and role was significant. It was largely thanks to Henrietta that the settlement focused attention on poor children, and on the public and private spaces and aesthetic pleasures open to them.[72] Moreover, the Barnetts formed the centre of a circle in which women were prominent; Beatrice Potter (later Webb) apparently 'enjoyed evenings in the Barnetts' drawing room discussing problems with other social workers'.[73]

Meanwhile, Ruskin's Guild of St George was formed in an attempt to realise a pre-capitalist form of society, with a hierarchical structure that it was hoped would at its highest level be composed of 'men of independent means'; Ruskin's own description of his ideal mentioned only men and masculine ideals.[74] Yet here as well, women were prominent. Its strong philanthropic orientation – Ruskin himself said 'you are to give your time, and thoughts, your labour, and the reward of your labour as far as you can spare it, for the help of the poor and needy' – appealed strongly to women such as Marian Twelves, who ran the Ruskin Linen Industry in Keswick and was described as 'self-sacrificing'.[75] Women's wider involvement in increasingly ambitious, Ruskinian-influenced forms of philanthropy from the 1870s and 1880s meant that they were suitably positioned to take up the challenges and possibilities offered by Ruskinian museums and galleries thereafter.[76]

Women and Ruskinian museums

Women were, in fact, particularly strongly represented in Ruskinian museums, especially in later periods after about 1890 when a Ruskinian approach may have been falling out of favour among both male curators and male philanthropists.[77] Moreover, in such museums they might take on roles which were inaccessible to them in other museums. The first women on the committee or board of governors of a museum or art gallery were Georgiana Burne-Jones and Mary Watts at the South London Art Gallery, and apparently 'much of the practical work of fund-raising and administration' was undertaken by Mrs Burne-Jones.[78] In 1890, around 25 per cent of committee members at the Gallery were female, as well as a good proportion of donors. Although both Burne-Jones and Watts became involved in the Gallery because of their marriages to artists, the very fact that they were not generally trying to sustain an artistic practice meant they had much more time to devote to the enterprise than their husbands; and what the gallery needed was time, not least for fund-raising which was urgently needed.[79] Mary Watts had actually met her husband while teaching art and craft in Whitechapel; he was a mainstay of the Whitechapel exhibitions and then Gallery, so both husband and wife were immersed in the idea of the Ruskinian museum. Ormond suggests that though both Mrs Watts and Lady Burne-Jones were key members of the Board, Georgiana Burne-Jones was second only to Lord Leighton in keeping the gallery going. He himself suggested that she had 'gone into these matters more than anyone', and it seems that she almost single-handedly put on some of the exhibitions.[80]

In Manchester, Horsfall's commitment to a Ruskinian vision of art as offering redemption and social reform at the Ancoats Museum was particularly appealing to middle-class women, who were initially important volunteer helpers there.[81] Horsfall himself had, to an extent, envisaged this, suggesting that 'assistant curators, who may well be women', work in galleries to help visitors appreciate art.[82] Such women brought enormous energy to the task of attracting working-class women and children into the museum. Once the Manchester University Settlement started to use space in Ancoats Hall, and more particularly when women Settlers were allocated rooms there in 1898, their initiatives developed the museum as a social hub for the community. Among other things, the museum became the base for classes and social events for disabled people, debating societies – both a general one and the Fawcett Debating Society exclusively for women – a field club, a variety of girls' clubs to cater for different age groups (boys' clubs were held elsewhere), lectures, an 'Elizabethan Society' run by Eva Gore-Booth and Miss Pankhurst, a choral society, Mothers' Meetings, 'at homes', a children's entertainment every Friday evening, and excursions of varying lengths and aims.[83] Nearly all of these initiatives were created and run by women, and, it can be seen, brought a specifically feminine and in many cases feminist sensibility to the museum and its relationship with its local community.

Moreover, the museum itself had been run on and off by a succession of volunteers, mostly female. Alice Crompton, the head of the Women's House from 1898, was also co-secretary of the museum, and in 1900 Miss Beatrice V. Vernon was described as the assistant curator.[84] By 1907, Vernon was the 'curator', although in the 1901 census, her title was rather more ambiguously given as 'curator and secretary'.[85] In fact, over the years Vernon was responsible not just for the museum, but for the elementary school classes, the Art and Education Committee, and anything else which needed doing. Both Crompton and Vernon resided at Ancoats Hall at least part of the time, which may have helped them to overcome the kind of domestic issues which seemed to have blighted the career of Kathleen Dearden, discussed in Chapter 1. Equally, though, this residence tended to mitigate against a compartmentalised view of their roles and duties, and any development of a more 'professional' approach to curating.

By 1912, however, the Museum Committee decided they needed a paid curator. However, because of their straitened funds, they determined that they would need to hire a woman, 'since it was impossible to get such a [refined and educated] man at the salary the settlement could offer'. Bertha Hindshaw was appointed at the undoubtedly extremely low salary of £50 a year in 1912 (this was for a part-time position; but it was hardly practicable to make up the income by combining it with another position).[86] Miss Hindshaw, described as a 'single-minded enthusiast', rearranged the rooms, tirelessly raised the profile of the organisation, and continued the practice of offering a very wide range of activities such as 'informal conversations' on Sundays.[87] Again, her duties (or rather, the things she did) went well beyond 'normal' curatorial duties.

Meanwhile in philanthropically oriented institutions in Whitechapel, women were also prominent. Kate Hall, the curator of the Whitechapel Museum, considered in Chapter 1, was part of a local grouping including the Whitechapel art exhibitions and later Art Gallery created by the Barnetts. Henrietta Barnett often presented herself as merely the supporter of her husband, but she was a Trustee of the Whitechapel Art Gallery, and the extent of her influence is suggested by C. R. Ashbee's comment that she was 'the Prior and Prioress of this place – the worthy head'.[88] As the Whitechapel Art Gallery developed, it has been suggested that it was characterised by competing discourses of philanthropy against professionalism, and Mrs Barnett was firmly on the side of philanthropy. This was most clearly shown in the Twentieth-Century Art exhibition, held in 1914, after the death of Samuel Barnett. The exhibition, planned by the director, Gilbert Ramsay (the Gallery had employed a director from its opening in 1901, in contrast to the temporary art exhibitions held before that date), aimed to show the recent progress of art and to showcase young British artists. Its subject matter was thought by the Trustees, particularly Mrs Barnett, to be in conflict with the gallery's purpose of bringing beauty to the deprived; her view was that residents of the East End of London could not understand Cubist and other works, and anyway, such works could not strengthen the moral character of the poor (or the rich for that matter).[89] Mrs Barnett was, in other words, defending the Ruskinian approach to museology against a modernist one which saw art as a realm apart, and one which moreover required increasing amounts of expert knowledge to appreciate. The Twentieth-Century Art exhibition went ahead, with the grudging and apprehensive consent of the Trustees.

In Surrey, there was another enclave of feminine-inflected Ruskinian museums, although these were, by reason of their location, much less focused on philanthropic engagement with the social problems of the urban slums. They nevertheless showed a focus on preserving tradition, emphasising the process of handcrafting, and helping the poor and children. In Haslemere, there were two museums, Sir Jonathan Hutchinson's 'educational' museum, largely natural history, and the Peasant Handicrafts Museum; while in Godalming Gertrude Jekyll was collecting material which was later donated to Godalming Museum.[90] Additionally, the Watts, so closely involved with the South London Art Gallery, lived just outside Godalming and close to Haslemere; and Mary Watts created what could be seen as a suite of cultural institutions to further Ruskinian-derived ideas. She opened the Watts Gallery in 1905, which while mainly set up to display works by Watts, showed its indebtedness to a Ruskinian museology through its use by craftspeople, especially potters. She had also previously set up handicraft guilds, both in pottery and in general craft, in 1899, and museum and guilds worked together.[91] Much of her focus was on offering training to local women which would allow them to make their own living and work in harmony with nature. The Watts' establishment at Compton resembled other enclaves of arts and crafts endeavour, such as C. R. Ashbee's Guild of Handicraft, itself allied with Toynbee Hall until its move to the Cotswolds. However, Ashbee's Guild did not consider museums and collections to be as central to its purpose as the various feminine-inflected Surrey initiatives did.[92]

The Haslemere Peasant Handicrafts Museum, set up in Surrey in 1905, opened in 1910. Inspired by folk museum collections in Scandinavia, its collection was based on work made by peasants 'for their own use and not for sale'; it explicitly rejected the idea of the industrial commodity, and of 'art' as a category removed from everyday life.[93] The museum founders argued that none of this type of material could be found in Britain, because of the extent of capitalisation there; objects came instead from the 'pristine' peasant cultures of Scandinavia, the Baltic countries, and the Balkans.[94] None of its founders were museum professionals or academics; rather, they were two married couples, Godfrey and Ethel Blount, who were both artists, and Joseph and Maude King, one a Member of Parliament and the other a writer.[95] The Handicraft Museum was associated with their Peasant Arts Society, which among other things set up craft production and sale opportunities for local women, following the Arts and Crafts Movement ethos. They closely followed the vision of craft revival as a way of ameliorating or even holding back capitalism, and are known to have had connections with George Bernard Shaw, among others (though their political position was more mainstream than his). Although the official positions of the museum were filled by the men of the group, it is noticeable that the museum was transferred to the nearby Educational Museum when Maude King became too ill to contribute; this apparently made the museum too much for the remaining group, suggesting her involvement was substantial.[96]

There is, therefore, a definite clustering of women in Ruskinian and Morrisian inspired museums from the end of the nineteenth century; while men may have made the running earlier, there are signs that they (or at least those men with the most professional masculine identities) were moving out of what was seen as an old-fashioned model at this time. Women and to some extent outsider men not only continued with this 'old-fashioned' museology but developed it in important new directions, as the following sections will explore.

Craft and making

The act of making by hand was crucially important for both Ruskin and Morris, and was, for them, a key goal of museums. While museums did not in themselves produce handiwork, they could encourage it in various ways. The capacity of museums to encourage all their visitors to make a wide variety of goods, often domestic and for use by the family, was developed in a number of ways; Ruskinian women involved in museums were attracted to craft production and attempted to encourage its domestic adoption, to use it as a way to revalue feminine labour and feminine skills, and to enable women to earn their own living. The Ancoats Museum was particularly keen on this approach because it was concerned about the domestic environment experienced by many of the inhabitants of Ancoats, both in emotional and material terms. Experiencing handcrafting, whether dressmaking for women or wood working for men, would enhance the moral fibre and self-reliance of visitors, and would allow them to improve their domestic environment cheaply, replacing the tawdry products of commercialised productions with low-cost but high-quality goods of various sorts. Courses in wood-carving, for example, were introduced from an early stage, while girls were endlessly encouraged to sew.[97] Moreover, the disabled group, the Santa Fina Society, were offered classes in sewing, leatherwork and woodcarving, as useful ways to fill their time, and which offered them the chance to sell the things they had made and thus contribute usefully to society and the economy.[98] Using the museum to reintroduce habits of handcrafting would therefore perform a practical and moral intervention in the lives of the poor and disadvantaged, focusing primarily on their homes.

The Haslemere Peasant Handicrafts Museum was marked by a very sustained and integrated emphasis on making by hand as the solution to a wide variety of problems. For the group at the heart of the enterprise, making things by hand could connect society to its historical roots, could solve the problems of poverty and under- or unemployment, would be empowering for women in particular, and could heal the sickness of modern capitalist society by replacing alienated labour and inauthentic art with a truthfulness at the heart of all things. The link between the museum and the various handiwork classes and studios is not always clear; in some ways this was a continuation of the idea of Henry Cole that workers would learn by having examples of various techniques and design principles to look at, but in other ways it was more radical. This was to be not just teaching, but the conscious revival of a mode of art which could create a new way of living which also drew on the past. The vitality of the link between the collected historic objects and the process of making things by hand was something which the group attempted to emphasise across a number of sites including not just the museum but the workshops and outlets selling handicraft products. Myzelev suggests that this is where Maude King and Ethel Blount made their strongest contribution to the Haslemere enterprise: 'numerous textiles, clothing, embroidery, toys, jewelry and other objects were produced by and for women', and this meant that 'women ... tied Haslemere to the present'.[99]

One woman who particularly championed 'bygone' or 'folk' objects in museums for their ability to train the hand-maker was the garden designer Gertrude Jekyll. She was, like the Haslemere Peasant Handicrafts group (who were only ten miles away from Jekyll's home in Godalming), interested in traditional craft as a nobler form of labour which could bring about national renewal; and she was also interested in the embodied practice of craft, trying her hand at many techniques before her eyesight became too bad. She amassed a sizeable collection of 'bygones', mostly domestic and everyday items, from the area around Godalming in Surrey. These were partly gathered as research for her book, *Old West Surrey*, published in 1904.[100] The donation she made to the Godalming Museum consisted of nearly 200 items such as mousetraps, fire dogs, cooking pots, reaping hooks, a spinning wheel and several examples of that social history staple, the flat iron. What was most obvious in their selection was a sense of peasant workmanship, and she evinced a Morrisian belief that truth in relation to function and material constituted their value: 'they are not only adapted by centuries of experience to their practical uses, but are also beautifully expressive of the native materials from which they are fashioned'.[101]

Although the Whitechapel Art Gallery focused on paintings and was therefore not so concerned with the process of handcrafting artefacts, there is evidence that when it did intervene to encourage a particular approach to domestic production among its visitors, Henrietta Barnett was in the forefront of the attempt. A notable newspaper report on the Whitechapel Art Gallery which specifically names Mrs Barnett is a *Times* article from 1908 covering the opening of an exhibition entitled 'Country in Town'. The aim of the exhibition was to show 'what can be done to cultivate flowers in town gardens, particularly those of the East-end'. Mrs Barnett presided over the opening, and thus aligned herself with direct attempts to use museums and galleries to bring Ruskinian values into the homes of the poor by encouraging them to make, or in this case grow, things themselves.[102]

Women in Ruskinian museums, then, were concerned to put the museum to direct use in the homes and lives of the poor. Museums were not just to be a passive resource holding historic examples of handcrafting; they were to be animated by the concomitant provision of classes and workshops in craft techniques, and would not just instruct but inspire with a holistic vision of a better way of life.

Preservation and tradition

For these people who created a museum as part of a wider interest in traditional crafts, part of the aim seems to have been to revive, preserve or mourn 'bygones', and a domestic mode of production. Museums were to be a place to preserve the almost-vanished objects, skills and traditions of the past which were envisaged as being swept away by a tide of modernity. This was not, of course, a purely feminine view, but the prominence of the female voice in articulating a relatively new view of the museum as a preservationist institution is notable. Partly, this is because many of the things that needed to be preserved came from a domestic or at least household setting, encompassing 'everyday' items of agricultural or domestic use. Women were drawn to the preservation of the domestic and handmade, not just in a connoisseurial way, but because they could revalue feminine expertise, and could promote a different way of relating to the past, emotional and affective, and drawing on the different material qualities of the handmade.

In Haslemere, the sense of museums as a bulwark against the disappearance of traditions was clear, and owed much to the influence of the Scandinavian 'salvage' approach, where peasant culture was seen as being endangered by industrialisation, swiftly disappearing, and in need of 'saving' in purpose-made institutions.[103] It seems that although such a sense responded to actual changes in some ways, it was also heavily influenced by evolutionary thinking at the end of the nineteenth century, which suggested more strongly than hitherto that ways of life which had been superseded by progress would inevitably become extinct.[104] Moreover, as the photographic preservation movement shows, such an impulse was poised between a scientific recording motive, and a nostalgic desire to mark the ravages of time.[105] Such an interpretation was strongly inscribed in the Haslemere museum because of the stated 'fact' that peasant crafts had already died in Britain, and were in decline in the rest of Europe; only insofar as true peasants still existed in regions untouched by progress, such as Russia and the Balkans, could peasant culture be found. Nevertheless, in preserving these artefacts, they could serve to inspire the creation of a new authentic tradition of peasant craft.

Gertrude Jekyll was also strongly motivated to record and preserve traditional objects and skills before they vanished. Unlike the Haslemere group, Jekyll did not think craft traditions could be revived, and thought attempts to do so were 'in the nature of exotic or hothouse plants'.[106] But she did think that collecting such objects for preservation in museums could help encourage the 'natural' English tendency to seek out the simple life of the countryside. It was critical for a sense of national identity to preserve lost craft traditions; she shared the Ruskinian view that modern productions were tawdry and debased, but hoped that the English could be encouraged at least to seek out a simple rural life.

Women therefore developed the idea of museums as repositories of vanished or vanishing craft traditions, to validate their own domestic craft expertise, for the aesthetic pleasures of such objects, and, as Edwards has shown for photographic survey movement, because nostalgia allowed them to link tradition and progress.

Children and toys

The idea of attracting children to museums emerges strongly in Ruskinian museums, and shows how women altered Ruskin's own focus as they developed his ideas. Toys as a focus of museum collecting were not obvious until after the First World War (although it is not necessarily axiomatic that toys in a museum equates to a focus on children as visitors); in the 1920s, Mary Greg gave the Bethnal Green branch museum of the V&A a significant number of dolls and toys, being therefore instrumental in orienting it as a Museum of Childhood (although it only officially became such a museum in 1974). The V&A itself was decidedly lukewarm, a curator saying of her proposed donation, 'In view of the ultimate destination intended for these interesting, but rather trivial, little toys, I recommend their acceptance'.[107] However, after 1930 Mary was joined by Queen Mary as a donor of toys and dolls, at which point they were accepted much more readily. Greg also gave a number of items to form a Children's Corner to Manchester Art Gallery. They were used to create an area specifically designed to appeal to children; Greg expressed her belief that museums should do more to attract and interest children.[108]

There were some important precedents before 1914 as well, with Victorian and Edwardian museums using various methods to attract children. As discussed in Chapter 1, Kate Hall, curator of the Stepney Borough Museum, and friend of the Barnetts of Toynbee Hall and Whitechapel Art Gallery, set up a small nature study museum aimed entirely at children, as a branch of the main museum, in the 1890s; she also spent a lot of time encouraging school groups and teachers to visit the museum, and conducted nature walks with children (see Figure 1).

Interest in promoting children's involvement with museums was less prominent, though not entirely absent, among men; back in the 1870s, the Reverend Henry Higgins, a volunteer at Liverpool Museum, had started creating circulating boxes to send out to schools.[109] Edward Lovett, a folklorist who tried to give his folk culture collection to the London County Council (LCC), had lots of material relating to childhood, mostly toys, which he envisaged as forming a display for children; however, his collection and planned children's display was not accepted.[110] Horsfall, in pursuit of his aim of including working-class children in the Manchester Art Museum, successfully lobbied for a change in the Education Code in 1895 so that schools could take children to museums and count it as an educational activity.[111] However, as noted above, it was under Bertha Hindshaw that the museum successfully positioned itself as a leisure venue for children. It was reported that after her appointment children of the area 'flocked' to the museum on Sundays, and there is some independent corroboration that children used and valued the museum into the 1920s.[112] Even the connoisseurly V&A, admittedly under wartime conditions, put on a Christmas exhibition of toys in 1915 to entertain children who were at a loose end because of wartime curtailment of other entertainment; this was, significantly, instigated by the volunteer Miss Spiller.[113]

At the South London Art Gallery, Mary Watts was a key figure in the debate over children in the gallery, arguing that they should be encouraged (and indeed her husband had earlier argued that he hoped 'the very youngest children would be admitted to the gallery'); Mr Rossiter, the founder, was in favour of children in the gallery but found it hard to deal with them 'on the ground'. Significantly, before the gallery came into public ownership, it was two women, his wife and the secretary, Mrs Olver, who took extremely practical steps to encourage child visitors (who were repeatedly referred to as 'monkeys'), including apparently physically pulling them in.[114]

Toys were more widely of interest at the time, not only as a way of interesting children in museums, but as craft products and as a way of providing wholesome employment for men and women, or of occupying children themselves. Explicitly 'old-fashioned', traditional toys were viewed as able to resist the meretricious commerciality of modernity, maintain knowledge of embodied craft skills, enable children to expand their capacity to experience beauty, and build character.[115] The first histories of toys and collections of toys in Britain were being written (significantly, by women) around 1900.[116] While the Haslemere Peasant Handicrafts Museum does not seem to have particularly collected toys and dolls, the quartet who ran the museum both published about and produced toys in their craft workshops. They suggested that 'primitive' toys which stimulated a child's imagination were better than fancy modern toys. Thus toys – historical, handmade toys – were increasingly positioned by Ruskinian women as helping with the problems of children, capitalist production and preserving craft tradition, and thus the groundwork was laid for the greater prominence of toys in museums after the First World War.

It is perhaps not surprising that women were particular advocates of children's use of museums and asserted expert knowledge of what would actually attract and retain children there. It has been shown that women in the USA based a great deal of their claim to be museum professionals on their expertise with children, and British women followed them to a certain extent in this.[117] However, women involved in Ruskinian museums placed a slightly different emphasis on their work with children; it was not about a narrowly defined educational programme, or just getting school groups into museums. It was more, in a suitably Ruskinian way, about a holistic approach to the development of the whole child, in a moral as well as an intellectual sense; it also involved a certain idealisation of the state of childhood, and its material culture, which aligned it with the simple and authentic characteristics of the ideal society. In this sense, Ruskinian women who encouraged children and toys into museums perhaps also hoped that they would teach adults about purity and wholeness.

Conclusion

It may well be the case that Ruskinian ideas were particularly Victorian and that by the end of the nineteenth century, interest in Ruskinian ideas was waning in some quarters, as Woodson-Boulton suggests; but it is equally true that ideas tend not to change uniformly overnight. The ongoing influence of Ruskin in the twentieth century is very clear, and this is as true for museums as it is for other fields.[118] Under the increasing scorn of avant-garde artists, and with the increasing specialisation and professionalisation of leading museums and their curators, the Ruskinian museum faded from prominence. The ideas of Ruskin lived on into the twentieth century, in small branch and private museums, as women developed the idea that museums should be 'domesticated' in their contents, atmosphere, activities and space; and that domestic objects contained the sedimented remains of an authentic craft tradition which could be actively engaged to remake society and revive true beauty. Their championing of traditional crafts showed up the masculine professional version of museums as partial and non-universal.

However, women could develop such a niche largely for the reason that it was not valued by the museum profession as a whole. All of the examples come from branch museums, small museums, museums in the slums and suburbs. Though women fought successfully to define their gendered competences in museum work as legitimate, such competences were not seen to give women roles at national and large museums. Women were enabled to take such a prominent role in small museums largely because men did not want to have much to do with them after 1900, seeking better paid and more specialist roles wherever possible. The feminising of Ruskinian approaches to museums rested on the gendering, and devaluing, of tradition, authenticity, childcare and service as feminine.

As scholars have noted, modernism marginalised women's cultural production which took place in the wrong spaces and drew on the wrong experiences; women did not seem modern enough. And it enshrined the idea of the masculinity of artistic endeavour, a so-called 'male mystique' opposed to the feminine impurity of hybridity and sentimentality.[119] While of course there were women in the avant-garde, Ruskinian museums, defiantly not avant-garde, involved a wide spectrum of mainly middle-class women, including both the radical and the highly respectable, the leisured and those seeking paid employment. All these women helped to make a public argument for the importance of women's 'impure' and even sentimental cultural production, for the possibility of re-interpreting the domestic and for considering how it might help to interpret the experiences of women in modern society.

This women-led attempt to develop Ruskinian-inspired museums from the late nineteenth century was also an attempt to remodel both public and private lives. The role of public institutions such as museums was envisaged as engaging citizens on a private as well as a public level and remodelling their intimate lives. Museums and other institutions, women suggested, should put children and the poor at the centre of their efforts, and for this reason should become more feminine places which were welcoming, and even felt like an extension of families' own spaces. They should be embedded in their neighbourhood and offer resources, such as dress patterns, craft co-operatives and children's clubs, to improve family life. What this amounted to was an attempt to use museums in order to put the authentic traditional to work in modern society. This mirrored similar attempts by, for example, the National Trust, but where the Trust tried to give people access to the traditional, these museums (and their women workers) attempted to formulate a space where people and tradition could encounter one another. In this sense, museums offered a more mobile incarnation of tradition.

Thus women shaped Ruskinian museums into places where time was hybrid, both modern and traditional. Equally, these museums created a new hybrid of public and private, mobility and stasis. These should be understood in the light of accelerating awareness of modernity around the *fin de siècle*; while in some ways the elite modernist response to modernity emphasised differently gendered responses to novelty, commercial forces were also packaging and selling hybrid modern–traditional experiences as part of a mass culture.[120] In museums, we see women using their 'natural' affinity with the authentic, traditional and childlike in order to put these qualities into service in the community. Thus, while many of the underlying qualities of Ruskinian museums rest on the same nostalgic aesthetic in housing, such as the Ideal Home Exhibition and E. M. Forster's *Howards End*, that Outka has examined, and the rationale and appeal is also akin to the Scandinavian exhibitions covered by Sandberg, in museums women possessed more control through their ideology of service.[121] The possibilities offered to women by modernity, as filtered through the ideas of John Ruskin, were wide-ranging; and the orientation of museums to community service was, far from being eradicated by the modern age, actually developed by it.

Notes

1 Quoted in Mark Frost, *Curator and Curatress: the Swans and St George's Museum, Sheffield* (York: Guild of St George Publications 2013), p. 35.

2 Amy Woodson-Boulton suggests that male museum founders influenced by Ruskin were aiming at a sort of public–domestic hybrid in their museums in the 1880s, but suggests that by the end of the nineteenth century men were starting to reject such a model. It is at this point, I suggest, that women took up the idea and developed it much further, working alongside men who might be considered 'outsiders'. Amy Woodson-Boulton, *Transformative Beauty: Art Museums in Industrial Britain* (Stanford, CA: Stanford University Press 2012).

3 However, as Chris Miele reminds us, in the 1870s the avant-garde was itself concerned with an affective engagement with the past. Chris Miele, 'Preface', in Chris Miele (ed.), *From William Morris: Building Conservation and the Arts and Crafts Cult of Authenticity, 1877–1939* (New Haven, CT and London: Yale University Press 2005), p. viii.

4 Modernism as a movement which dismissed all that came before it, including the aestheticism of Whistler, who himself was the main anti-Ruskinian of the *fin de siècle*, is usefully discussed by Elizabeth Prettejohn: 'From aestheticism to modernism and back again', *19: Interdisciplinary Studies in the Long Nineteenth Century* 2 (2006), online, available at www.19.bbk.ac.uk/index.php/19/issue/view/65, accessed 7 July 2014.

5 This way of gendering the modern is discussed by Rita Felski, in *The Gender of Modernity* (Cambridge, MA: Harvard University Press 1995), esp. chapter 2. However, she also makes clear that there were and have been other ways of gendering modernity.

6 Nostalgia as an element of modernity predicated on the sense of loss of the authentic, organic pre-modern is discussed by Felski, *Gender of Modernity*, chapter 2, and Susan Stewart, *On Longing: Narratives of the Miniature, the Gigantic, the Souvenir, the Collection* (Durham, NC and London: Duke University Press 1993).

7 Contemporary discussions of 'feminine' collecting practices are covered in Beverley Gordon, *The Saturated World: Aesthetic Meaning, Intimate Objects, Women's Lives 1890–1940* (Knoxville, TN: University of Tennessee Press 2006), chapter 6.

8 Elizabeth Outka, *Consuming Traditions: Modernity, Modernism and the Commodified Authentic* (Oxford: Oxford University Press 2009), p. 3.

9 Outka, *Consuming Tradition*, p. 7.

10 Mark Sandberg, *Living Pictures, Missing Persons: Mannequins, Museums and Modernity* (Princeton, NJ: Princeton University Press 2003), pp. 7–8.

11 Outka, *Consuming Traditions*, pp. 14–15.

12 Outka, *Consuming Traditions*, pp. 113–114.

13 Chris Miele, 'Conservation and the enemies of promise?' in Chris Miele (ed.), *From William Morris: Building Conservation and the Arts and Crafts Cult of Authenticity, 1877–1939* (New Haven, CT and London: Yale University Press 2005), p. 2.

14 Chris Miele, 'Morris and conservation', in Chris Miele, *From William Morris: Building Conservation and the Arts and Crafts Cult of Authenticity, 1877–1939* (New Haven, CT and London: Yale University Press 2005), p. 36. See also Elizabeth Edwards, *The Camera as Historian: Amateur Photographers and Historical Imagination, 1885–1918* (Durham, NC and London: Duke University Press 2012), p. 18.

15 Barbara Morris, 'William Morris and the South Kensington Museum', *Victorian Poetry* 13: 3 (1975), p. 175.

16 Charles Dellheim, *The Face of the Past: The Preservation of the Medieval Inheritance in Victorian England* (Cambridge: Cambridge University Press 1982), p. 26.

17 Edwards, *Camera as Historian*, pp. 163–165.

18 Miele, 'Morris', pp. 31–32.

19 Jenny West, 'Appendix 1: The Society for the Protection of Ancient Buildings 1877–1896: committee, membership and casework', in Miele, *From William Morris*, p. 310.

20 Edwards, *Camera as Historian*, p. 44.

21 Astrid Swenson, *The Rise of Heritage: Preserving the Past in France, Germany and England, 1789–1914* (Cambridge: Cambridge University Press 2013), p. 132.

22 Dinah Birch, 'Introduction', in Dinah Birch (ed.), *Ruskin and the Dawn of the Modern* (Oxford: Clarendon Press 1999), p. 2.

23 Rachel Dickinson, 'Of Ruskin, women and power', in Keith Hanley and Brian Maidment (eds), *Persistent Ruskin: Studies in Influence, Assimilation and Effect* (Aldershot: Ashgate 2013); Linda H. Peterson, 'The feminist origins of "Of Queens' Gardens"', in Dinah Birch and Francis O'Gorman (eds), *Ruskin and Gender* (Basingstoke: Palgrave 2002).

24 Stuart Eagles, *After Ruskin: The Social and Political Legacies of a Victorian Prophet, 1870–1920* (Oxford: Oxford University Press 2011), p. 53.

25 Peterson, 'Feminist origins'.

26 Dinah Birch, 'Ruskin's "womanly mind"', in D. Birch and F. O'Gorman (eds), *Ruskin and Gender*.

27 Dickinson, 'Of Ruskin'; Dinah Birch, ' "What teachers do you give your girls?" Ruskin and women's education', in D. Birch and F. O'Gorman (eds), *Ruskin and Gender*.

28 Eagles, *After Ruskin*, pp. 70–71, 73.

29 For example, in his Guild of St George; Eagles, *After Ruskin*, pp. 78–81.

30 See Eagles, *After Ruskin*, and essays in K. Hanley and B. Maidment (eds), *Persistent Ruskin*.

31 This is a point made particularly well by Birch, in 'Ruskin's "womanly mind"'.

32 Eagles stresses the significance of his mantra, 'to do and to act'; *After Ruskin*, p. 71.

33 Michael W. Brooks, *John Ruskin and Victorian Architecture* (London: Thames and Hudson 1989).

34 From Fors Clavigera letter 49, quoted in Hilary Edwards, 'Protecting life from language: John Ruskin's museum as autobiography', *Biography* 32: 2 (2009), p. 301.

35 Jordanna Bailkin, *The Culture of Property: The Crisis of Liberalism in Modern Britain* (Chicago, IL and London: University of Chicago Press 2004), p. 127.

36 Arguably, though, Cole and Ruskin had more in common than either of them would have recognised; Ezra Shales, 'Toying with design reform: Henry Cole and instructive play for children', *Journal of Design History* 22: 1 (2009), pp. 3–26.

37 Marcus Waithe, 'John Ruskin and the idea of a museum', in K. Hanley and B. Maidment (eds), *Persistent Ruskin*, p. 42.

38 This is particularly clear from the mutually unimpressed correspondence between Ruskin and representatives of Sheffield Corporation: Frost, *Curator and Curatress*, pp. 22–23.

39 Waithe, 'Idea of a museum', pp. 43–44.

40 Waithe, 'Idea of a museum', p. 46.

41 On the refurbishment of the Weston Park Museum, see Kate Hill, *Culture and Class in English Public Museums 1850–1914* (Aldershot: Ashgate 2005), p. 100.

42 Ruskin did design some display furniture but this was very different from standard museum display cases. Edwards, 'Protecting life from language', p. 302.

43 Edwards, 'Protecting life from language', p. 303.

44 Frost, *Curator and Curatress*, p. 11.

45 Edwards, 'Protecting life from language', p. 300.

46 Waithe, 'Idea of a museum', pp. 44–45.

47 Visitors' Book, St George's Museum, September 1880–September 1881, Museums Sheffield Archive.

48 Frost, *Curator and Curatress*, pp. 30–31.

49 Genevieve Pilley, full name Constance Genevieve Pilley, appears in the 1891 and 1901 census living in Sheffield and working as an 'assistant librarian'. Her father was an artist and illustrator. Census returns available at ancestry.com, accessed 6 July 2014; see also Marcus Waithe, 'Ruskin at Walkley: reconstructing the St George's museum', online, available at http://ruskinatwalkley.org, accessed 6 July 2014.

50 Waithe, 'Idea of a museum', pp. 46–50.

51 Morris, 'William Morris'; Norman Kelvin (ed.) and William Morris, *The Collected Letters of William Morris*, vol. 3 (Princeton, NJ: Princeton University Press 1996), p. 474.

52 Dinah Birch and Francis O'Gorman, 'Introduction', in D. Birch and F. O'Gorman (eds), *Ruskin and Gender*, p. 1.

53 Woodson-Boulton, *Transformative Beauty*.

54 Ruskin, Letter 88 (8 February 1880), *Fors Clavigera: Letters to the Workmen and Labourers of Great Britain*, vol. 8 (Orpington: George Allen 1884), p. 106.

55 Woodson-Boulton, *Transformative Beauty*, p. 49.

56 Woodson-Boulton demonstrates this but also importantly details the debates over which of a wide range of types of art should be displayed. *Transformative Beauty*, chapter 3.

57 Woodson-Boulton, *Transformative Beauty*, pp. 32–40 (on the Walker Art Gallery); see also Hill, *Culture and Class*, for more consideration of how museums might

serve middle-class rather than working-class interests, and what consequences this might have.

58 For Horsfall's involvement in Manchester City Art Gallery, see Woodson-Boulton, *Transformative Beauty*, pp. 42–52; on disillusion with the City Art Gallery, pp. 102–103 of the same.

59 Michael Harrison, 'Art and philanthropy: T. C. Horsfall and The Manchester Art Museum', in A. Kidd (ed.), *City, Class and Culture: Studies of Cultural Production and Social Policy in Victorian Manchester* (Manchester: Manchester University Press 1985), p. 121.

60 Gavin Budge, in 'Poverty and the picture gallery: the Whitechapel exhibitions and the social project of Ruskinian aesthetics', *Visual Culture in Britain* 1: 2 (2000), pp. 43–56, discusses the complex view of both Ruskin himself and the Barnetts on the relationship between beauty and social reform.

61 Barnett quoted in Lucinda Matthews-Jones, 'Lessons in seeing: art, religion and class in the East End of London, 1881–1898', *Journal of Victorian Culture* 16: 3 (2011), pp. 385–403.

62 Giles Waterfield and Nicola Smith, 'Art for the people', *History Today* 44: 6 (June 1994), pp. 55–60.

63 The fact that the public realm was envisaged as exclusively masculine is clear throughout Woodson-Boulton, *Transformative Beauty*; the benefits were felt to accrue to children and families, but also young single men of the working class, who were not, by many measures of Victorian middle-class manhood, fully masculine.

64 See also Lucinda Matthews-Jones, 'St Francis of Assissi and the making of settlement masculinity', in John H. Arnold and Sean Brady (eds), *What Is Masculinity? Historical Dynamics from Antiquity to the Contemporary World* (London: Palgrave Macmillan 2011), pp. 285–302; and Seth Koven, *Slumming: Sexual and Social Politics in Victorian London* (Princeton, NJ: Princeton University Press 2004), chapter 5.

65 See Hill, *Culture and Class*, chapter 8, for a discussion of how museum reformers targeted women; see also Daniel Bivona and Roger B. Henckle, *The Imagination of Class: Masculinity and the Urban Poor* (Columbus: Ohio State University Press 2006), p. 23 for the feminisation of the slums.

66 F. Prochaska, *Women and Philanthropy in Nineteenth-Century England* (Oxford: Clarendon Press 1980), p. 7; Koven, *Slumming*, chapter 4.

67 Leonore Davidoff and Catherine Hall, *Family Fortunes: Men and Women of the English Middle Class, 1780–1850*, rev. edn (London: Routledge 2002), chapter 10; Prochaska, *Women and Philanthropy*, chapter 4.

68 Prochaska, *Women and Philanthropy*, p. 130; Gillian Darley, 'Hill, Octavia (1838–1912)', *Oxford Dictionary of National Biography* (Oxford: Oxford University Press 2004; online edn, May 2012) available at www.oxforddnb.com.proxy.library.lincoln.ac.uk/view/article/33873, accessed 25 June 2014. Hill and Ruskin later fell out over the relationship between his Guild of St George and her housing schemes in which he had invested. Hill also exemplified other aspects of women's involvement in museums, being, for example, a keen picture copyist working in Dulwich Art Gallery and the National Gallery, and shared with her sister Miranda a sense of the importance of bringing beauty into the lives of the poor.

69 Darley, 'Hill, Octavia'.

70 John Tosh, *A Man's Place: Masculinity and the Middle-Class Home in Victorian England* (New Haven, CT: Yale University Press 1999), p. 170; Matthews-Jones, 'St Francis of Assissi'.

71 Darley, 'Hill, Octavia'; Mary Danvers Stocks, *Fifty Years in Every Street: The Story of the Manchester University Settlement* (Manchester: Manchester University Press 1945); Katherine Bentley Beauman, *Women and the Settlement Movement* (London: Radcliffe Press 1996), esp. Part 1 and chapter 5.

72 For example, setting up the Children's Holiday Committee in 1876, and the Art for Schools Association, as well as the more obviously museological interventions discussed later in the chapter. Beauman, *Women*, p. 16.

73 Beauman, *Women*, p. 29.

74 Eagles, *After Ruskin*, p. 53.

75 Eagles, *After Ruskin*, p. 74.

76 Bailkin notes the link between women's philanthropic orientation and museums, and sees this as one basis of a distinctively feminine vision of museums' roles. *Culture of Property*, pp. 128–131.

77 Harrison, 'Art and philanthropy', p. 138.

78 Leonee Ormond, 'A Leighton memorial: Frederic Leighton and the South London Art Gallery', in Giles Waterfield (ed.), *Art for the People: Culture in the Slums of Late Victorian Britain* (London: Dulwich Picture Gallery 1994), p. 20.

79 Ormond, 'A Leighton memorial', p. 21.

80 Ormond, 'A Leighton memorial', pp. 23, 28.

81 Harrison, 'Art and philanthropy', p. 124.

82 *British Architect*, 27 December 1907: account of speech by Horsfall.

83 *University Settlement Manchester First Annual Report* (Manchester: Cuthbertson & Black 1987); *University Settlement Manchester Second to Fifth Annual Reports* (Manchester: William Hough & Sons 1898–1901); *Manchester Art Museum and University Settlement Annual Reports* (Manchester: William Hough & Sons 1902–1903); *Manchester Art Museum and University Settlement Annual Reports* (Manchester: The William Morris Press 1904–1914).

84 *University Settlement Manchester Fourth Annual Report* (Manchester: William Hough & Sons 1900).

85 *Manchester Art Museum and University Settlement Annual Report* (Manchester: The William Morris Press 1907); census returns for 1901, online, available at ancestry. co.uk, accessed 14 July 2014.

86 *Manchester University Settlement and Art Museum Annual Report* (Manchester: The William Morris Press 1914).

87 Harrison, 'Art and philanthropy', p. 140.

88 Asa Briggs and Anne Macartney, *Toynbee Hall: The First Hundred Years* (London: Routledge 2013 [1984]) p. 58; Seth Koven, 'Henrietta Barnett, 1851–1936: the (auto)biography of a late Victorian marriage' in Peter Mandler and Susan Pederson (eds), *After the Victorians: Private Conscience and Public Duty In Modern Britain* (London: Routledge 1994), p. 41. See also Shelagh Wilson, '"The highest art for the lowest people": the Whitechapel and other philanthropic art galleries, 1877–1901', in

Paul Barlow and Colin Trodd (eds), *Governing Cultures: Art Institutions in Victorian London* (Aldershot: Ashgate 2000).

89 Juliet Steyn, 'Inside-out: assumptions of "English" modernism in the Whitechapel Art Gallery, London, 1914', in Marcia Pointon (ed.), *Art Apart: Art Institutions and Ideology Across England and North America* (Manchester: Manchester University Press 1994).

90 On Jonathan Hutchinson's museum, see E. W. Swanton, *A Country Museum* (Haslemere: Education Museum 1947); Hutchinson also produced a periodical, *The Haslemere Museum Gazette, A Journal of Objective Education and Field Study*, from 1906. On Jekyll's collection or proto-museum, see Bridget Yates, 'Volunteer-run museums in English market towns and villages' (unpublished PhD thesis, University of Gloucester 2010), pp. 179–184.

91 Giles Waterfield, *Palaces of Art: Art Galleries in Britain 1790–1990* (London: Dulwich Picture Gallery 1991), p. 98.

92 Indeed the existence of a small museum largely filled from the South Kensington Museum's Circulating Department at Ashbee's Guild has only recently been explored, by Aurelie Petiot in her thesis, ' "Should we stop teaching art?" Charles Robert Ashbee's educational theories and practices, 1886–1940' (unpublished PhD thesis, University of Cambridge 2013).

93 Emma Shepley, 'The Haslemere context', in David Crowley and Lou Taylor (eds), *The Lost Arts of Europe: The Haslemere Museum Collection of European Peasant Art* (Haslemere: Haslemere Educational Museum 2000), p. 8.

94 Shepley, 'The Haslemere context), p. 8.

95 A. Myzelev, 'Collecting peasant Europe: peasant utilitarian objects as museum artifacts', in J. Potvin and A. Myzelev (eds), *Material Cultures 1740–1920: The Meanings and Pleasures of Collecting* (Aldershot: Ashgate 2009).

96 Myzelev, 'Collecting peasant Europe', p. 176.

97 Harrison, 'Art and philanthropy', p. 131.

98 Manchester University Special Collections MUS/4/1/2, *Manchester Art Museum and University Settlement Winter Programme 1909–10* (Manchester: The William Morris Press 1909).

99 Myzelev, 'Collecting peasant Europe', pp. 185–186.

100 Gertrude Jekyll, *Old West Surrey: Some Notes and Memories* (London: Longman, Green and Co. 1904).

101 Gertrude Jekyll, *Old English Household Life: Some Account of Cottage Objects and Country Folk*, [1925] (JM Classic Editions 2007), p. 5.

102 'Flowers in Whitechapel', *The Times*, 3 July 1908.

103 Lou Taylor, in *Establishing Dress History* (Manchester: Manchester University Press 2004) points out the dissemination of this idea throughout the Scandinavian countries and the Netherlands; she also shows that even such a seeker of authentic tradition as Arthur Hazelius was also interested in urban and non-peasant artefacts: pp. 210–214.

104 Sandberg, *Living Pictures*, p. 159.

105 Elizabeth Edwards, *The Camera as Historian: Amateur Photographers and Historical Imagination, 1885–1918* (Durham, NC and London: Duke University Press 2012), chapter 5.

106 Jekyll, *Old English Household Life*, p. 6.

107 This was not an isolated incident either, the V&A were persistently denigratory about toys. Anthony Burton, 'Design history and the history of toys', *Journal of Design History* 10: 1 (1997).

108 Letter from Mrs Mary Greg to Mr Batho, 22 May 1923, Greg Correspondence, Manchester City Art Gallery.

109 Geoffrey Lewis, *For Instruction and Recreation: A Centenary History of the Museums Assocation* (London: Quiller Press 1989), p. 9.

110 Letters from Edward Lovett to the London County Council's Local Government, Records and Museums Committee, 15 July 1909, 21 July 1909, London Metropolitan Archives LCC/MIN/08132-3.

111 Harrison, 'Art and philanthropy', p. 136.

112 Harrison, 'Art and philanthropy', pp. 141–142.

113 Burton, 'Design history', pp. 1–2. Miss Spiller was given an OBE for her museum work with children in 1926.

114 Nicola Smith, 'A brief account of the origins of the South London Art Gallery', in G. Waterfield (ed.), *Art for the People*, p. 13.

115 Gary Cross, *Kids' Stuff: Toys and the Changing World of American Childhood* (Cambridge, Mass.: Harvard University Press 2009), pp. 137–138; the increasing attention paid to the material culture of children is noted by Jane Hamlett, *Material Relations: Domestic Interiors and Middle-Class Families in England, 1850–1910* (Manchester: Manchester University Press 2010), chapter 3.

116 Burton, 'Design history', p. 8.

117 See Chapter 1.

118 See essays in K. Hanley and B. Maidment (eds), *Persistent Ruskin*, and Eagles, *After Ruskin*.

119 Discussed in relation to art in the inter-war period in A. Stephenson, ' "Telling decoratively": Ben Nicholson's *white reliefs* and debates around abstraction and modernism in the home in the late 20s and 30s', *Visual Culture in Britain* 9: 2 (2008), pp. 43–60; and in Andreas Huyssen, *After the Great Divide: Modernism, Mass Culture, Postmodernism* (Bloomington: Indiana University Press 1986), chapter 3.

120 Outka, *Consuming Traditions*, chapter 4.

121 Outka, *Consuming Traditions*; Sandberg, *Living Pictures*.

Conclusion

In 1914, as the First World War began, museums started to find their staff leaving 'to join the colours'. By 1918, a substantial number of male museum staff had enlisted, although in some places many were too old to do so.[1] Women were, on occasion, employed to replace these absent men, as they did in other occupational areas. However, this was not in itself a turning point in the gendering of museums; the men who had gone were mostly young and junior, and women continued to be employed in assistant roles as they had before the war, merely in slightly higher numbers. Any difficulty in filling museum vacancies was attributed, not to the loss of male staff during the war, but to the low salaries such positions commanded, and this lent itself to a gradual feminisation of the workforce.[2] Museums, though they did not purge women employees after 1918, did not significantly change their hiring practices; rather, the number of women drifted up slowly. By the 1930s, there were more signs of significant feminisation of the museum workforce, and of the museum as a concept and institution. Women as a proportion of donors to the Pitt Rivers Museum peaked, while Mary Greg and Queen Mary made sufficient donations to create a Museum of Childhood in Bethnal Green.[3] Quantitatively, women were much more fully involved in museums by 1939 than they were before the First World War.

The nature of women's involvement, however, was ambiguous in this later period; Hoberman suggests that by the interwar period, women had rejected the idea of partnership with men and sought instead a segregated, exclusively feminine space in some museums and libraries.[4] Such a characterisation seems overly schematic, not least because some women show signs of wanting such separation before 1914 as well; I would suggest rather that the acceptable contours of women's involvement with museums were clearer, in a way they had not been in the previous period. It now seemed axiomatic that women would be involved in promoting social history objects and other artefacts which highlighted relational and affective forms of knowledge, in education and community engagement activities, and in assisting male scientists, archaeologists and others with the mundane material practices of museum work; while their dominant position among museum visitors was further reinforced.[5] Leading curatorial roles, however, remained male. While professionalisation progressed, and women accessed specific professional activities, Mary Greg and her collections show that women's 'amateur' and philanthropic expertise, arising from their domestic, gendered skills in understanding children and the poor, and appreciating objects on an emotional level, was still, or even increasingly, acknowledged in museums.[6] Women and women's things, then, were more firmly present in museums than before the First World War, but along the lines and in the activities made feminine before that period.

This suggests, then, that the period between 1850 and 1914 was a window of opportunity, of fluidity, for both women and museums, which offered progress up to a point for women and resulted in new norms for them both. After 1918, it has been noted that museums were far less dynamic places than they had been before that period (though broadly defined 'heritage' was certainly not).[7] The fact that between 1850 and 1914 museums were themselves in flux, trying to develop a nascent professionalisation, negotiating the meaning and purpose of public museums, torn between embodying the nation, advancing knowledge and serving the community, meant that the agency of dispersed networks of objects and people was more potent than possibly at any time during the twentieth century. At the same time, changes in women's roles in the nineteenth and early twentieth centuries, combining more public presences with domestic rhetoric, offered compelling new, flexible but coherent versions of modern femininity. After 1918, while changes in women's roles, representations and opportunities were equally notable, the picture of change and continuity in gender identities was much more complex.[8]

It is this that explains women's activities as museum makers in a number of ways, but ultimately within limits. Women were seeking job opportunities, professional identities and the chance to contribute to public life in the way men did, but they were also seeking to revalue and expand the things women already did: clean rooms, work with children and interpret ideas to the general public. Many aspects of the nineteenth-century women's movement were underpinned by a sense of the moral contribution women could make by virtue of their domestic femininity, and this can be seen across women's involvement in museums. By and large, women sought to domesticate museum knowledge, museum objects and museum visitors during this period, as well as to bring the domestic into public view; to make the museum more home-like; and to give public prominence to the values, practices and emotional economy of the home.

This can be seen particularly in women's material practices. Work on feminine engagement with materiality has stressed the extent to which women could use things to develop subjectivities and identities which distinguished them from men and empowered them to show the value of domestic practices and spaces, and of emotional, embodied and aesthetic responses to materiality.[9] This study strongly supports such conclusions; it is clear that women used museums as a way of reproducing and accruing public value for assertively feminine things and arrangements of things, and to explore the subjective aspects of distinct feminine identities. However, there is also evidence that the relationship between gender and materiality is more complex than this would suggest. 'Masculine' and 'feminine' were constructions produced both discursively, and through material practices, as we have seen; women and men generally understood that male collecting was more serious, objective and scientific than women's, which was viewed instead as intentionally subjective, and as instantiating a different value system. This distinction was also produced materially, for example by the restrictions women faced in accessing particular things, spaces and equipment, and was powerfully cut across by class identities in particular. 'Masculine' collecting is better understood as the exclusive practice of an educated, professional group who were men; but not all men could achieve or emulate this. New forms of fieldwork and new material research practices, though partly developed to produce the male professional scientist, created new roles and possibilities for women, though these were positioned as subordinate to men. Women's collecting and work with objects responded to their exclusion from 'masculine' practices not just by developing distinct feminine practices which revalued the emotional and the domestic, but also by seeking to contest their exclusion from the objective, scientific and public world of the 'masculine' collection. In other words, they were poised between asserting and denying gendered competences in the material world.

This is merely one of several ways in which women's involvement in museums blurred and undermined dichotomising categories of modernity, and may be understood as working in important ways on the borders of such categories. One of the most important sets of these categories is public/scholarly and private/domestic. Historians have shown how profoundly understandings of private and public were changing around the *fin de siècle*, and how closely the changing categories were linked to gender; museums allowed women to bring public and domestic into conjunction with each other in new and distinctive ways. Women's multifarious championing of the domestic and familial, their 'militant domesticity' in Cohen's words, supported their emergence into the public and allowed specifically feminine skills, values and objects to become public.[10] Women's objects were domestic: products of domestic craft, belonging to children and relatives, and echoing the memory practices of individual parlours and rooms where the dead were remembered through the objects which they had used. Thus categories of public and private were both confirmed and blurred.

One of the main aims of this study has been to examine what an understanding of the museum as a distributed entity means for women's agency as museum makers. It is undoubtedly true that women's agency, as actors outside the museum proper, has been hidden and that when we look at their donations, fundraising, volunteering, lecturing and other activities as part of the distributed museum, their substantial role in producing the modern museum, alongside the men who were curators, major benefactors and governors, becomes clear. Any analysis of a museum which ignores such feminine activity cannot account for the way museums changed between 1850 and 1914; although any single woman may not have changed museums much, cumulatively their effect was significant.[11] Although analysis of the distributed museum starts from the presupposition of a flat network, in order to recover all traces of agency, sooner or later we need to acknowledge that the network was not, in fact, flat; hierarchy and power were enacted through the distributed museum and some people had more agency than others.[12] Women's contribution, though real, was structured by wealth and intellectual capital, and tended to be corralled in certain areas; and their agency was limited by the difficulty in leading that contemporary gender norms imposed, even on 'modern' women.

Women made modern museums, and museums made modern women. The modern museum was not just a place where national identities and scientific objectivity were produced and disseminated, it was also a place where modern subjectivities were forged, and ideas of local belonging and community were explored, and women led this development. Women's fascination with 'authenticity' as a material quality relating to oldness, personal associations and 'aura' enabled a significant change in the idea of the museum object, which since at least the middle of the nineteenth century had been dominantly understood more and more as a specimen, and less and less as a relic; women were substantially responsible for the rehabilitation of the authentic souvenir.[13] Moreover, modern female identities were strongly shaped by the experience of involvement with museums; women as visitors and consumers, or as donors, workers and patrons, wrestled with the issues of what a modern, particularly middle-class woman was like, and how she could contribute to and engage with modern life. New ways of building a career, of using the experience of higher education, of interacting with those from other classes, of being a wife or widow, and of dealing with family loss, were all explored through museums.

In fact, as this suggests, both museums and women made modernity. Of course, modernity is a contradictory and multifaceted condition, but the way in which women in museums both highlighted and undermined key opposing categories, the way in which they juxtaposed tradition and modernity, public and domestic, and proposed new understandings of authenticity, memory and service, all contributed to a modern culture which contrasted technology, progress and science with authentic traditions guaranteed by domestic, family memories. Although, as McTavish asserts, there may be no such thing as the modern museum, museums have certainly been key cultural institutions in the creation and assertion of a multiplicity of modernities, from the hyper-mobile traveller through time and space of Sandberg's wax museums, to the national citizen of Prior's art museums, to the colonial desires of ethnographic museums.[14] The modernities which were produced by women in museums were as diverse as any assemblage of modernities, but they were significant for our understandings of gender, and the museum, in the nineteenth century and since.

Notes

1 Patrick N. Wyse Jackson and Mary E. Spencer Jones, 'The quiet workforce: the various roles of women in geological and natural history museums during the early to mid-1900s', in C. V. Burek and B. Higgs (eds), *The Role of Women in the History of Geology*, Geological Society, London, Special Publications 281 (2007), p. 105.

2 Geoffrey Lewis, *For Instruction and Recreation: A Centenary History of the Museums Association* (London: Quiller Press 1989), p. 32.

3 Anthony Burton, 'Design history and the history of toys', *Journal of Design History* 10: 1 (1997).

4 Ruth Hoberman, *Museum Trouble: Edwardian Fiction and the Emergence of Modernism* (Charlottesville, VA: University of Virginia Press 2011).

5 See, for example, Noel Streatfeild's 1936 children's book *Ballet Shoes* (London: Penguin 1949 [1936]), p. 52: 'Nana thought nicely brought-up children ought to be out of the house between twelve and one, even on wet days, and she took them to see the dolls' houses at the Victoria and Albert'.

6 Laura Carter also suggests women made more progress outside the world of professional curation than inside it. 'Women as "history makers" in mid-twentieth-century Britain', unpublished conference paper, 2014.

7 Lewis, *For Instruction*, pp. 32–33; Kate Hill, *Culture and Class in English Public Museums, 1850–1914* (Aldershot: Ashgate 2005), p. 149.

8 Adrian Bingham, '"An era of domesticity?" Histories of women and gender in inter-war Britain', *Cultural and Social History* 1: 2 (2004).

9 See particularly Dianne Sachko Macleod, *Enchanted Lives, Enchanted Objects: American Women Collectors and the Making of Culture 1800–1940* (Berkeley, CA: University of California Press 2008) and Beverley Gordon, *The Saturated World: Aesthetic Meaning, Intimate Objects, Women's Lives 1890–1940* (Knoxville, TN: University of Tennessee Press 2006).

10 Deborah Cohen, *Household Gods: The British and Their Possessions* (New Haven, CT and London: Yale University Press 2006), p. 105.

11 Cf Ann Whitelaw, 'Women, museums and the problem of biography', in K. Hill (ed.), *Museums and Biographies: Stories, Objects, Identities* (Woodbridge: Boydell and Brewer 2012).

12 Rodney Harrison, 'Consuming colonialism: curio dealers' catalogues, souvenir objects, and indigenous agency in Oceania', in S. Byrne, A. Clarke, R. Harrison and R. Torrence (eds), *Unpacking the Collection: Networks of Material and Social Agency in the Museum* (New York: Springer 2011).

13 Susan Stewart, *On Longing: Narratives of the Miniature, the Gigantic, the Souvenir, the Collection* (Durham, NC: Duke University Press 1993).

14 Lianne McTavish, *Defining the Modern Museum* (Toronto: University of Toronto Press 2013); Mark B. Sandberg, *Living Pictures, Missing Persons: Mannequins, Museums and Modernity* (Princeton, NJ and Oxford: Princeton University Press 2003); Nick Prior, *Museums and Modernity: Art Galleries and the Making of Modern Culture* (Oxford: Berg 2002); Sarah Longair and John McAleer (eds), *Curating Empire: Museums and the British Imperial Experience* (Manchester: Manchester University Press 2012).

Bibliography

Archival sources

Birmingham Museum and Art Gallery

Birmingham Museum and Art Gallery Inventory vol. 1, 1885–1905
Birmingham Museum and Art Gallery Master Inventory, 1906–1915

Brighton Museum and Art Gallery

Brighton Museum Accession Register, 1880–1914
Brighton Free Library, Museum and Picture Gallery, Royal Pavilion,
   Annual Report 1884–1886 (1885–1887)
Brighton Corporation, *Public Library, Museums and Art Galleries
   Annual Report of the Director for 1905–1912* (1906–1913)

Bristol Museum

Bristol Museum Accession Register, 1889–1898

Bristol Record Office

Bristol Museum and Library, *Report of Proceedings at the Annual
   Meeting 1880–1893* (Bristol 1881–1894)
City and County of Bristol, *Report of the Museum Committee 1894–1914*
   (Bristol 1895–1915)

British Museum

British Museum Book of Presents (microfilm), 1881–1914
British Museum Book of Presents Supplement, vol. 2 (microfilm),
   1890–1896

Cheltenham Museum and Art Gallery

Cheltenham Museum and Art Gallery Accession Register, vol. 1,
   1889–1914
Hallett, Samantha, 'Report on Cheltenham Art Gallery and Museum
   Herbarium', October 2000–March 2001

Egypt Exploration Society, Lucy Gura Archive

Egypt Exploration Fund, Report of the Fifth Annual General Meeting (London 1887)

Egypt Exploration Fund, Report of Second Ordinary General Meeting (London 1888)

Egypt Exploration Fund, Report of the Fourth Ordinary General Meeting (London 1890)

Egypt Exploration Fund distribution lists, 1890–1896

Egypt Exploration Fund, Report of the Sixth Ordinary General Meeting (London 1892)

Egypt Exploration Fund, Report of Tenth Ordinary General Meeting (London 1896)

Horniman Museum and Gardens

Horniman Free Museum Annual Reports, 1891–1898 (London 1892–1899)

Horniman Museum Accession Registers, 1897–1914

London County Council, Annual Report of Horniman Museum 1901–1914 (London 1902–1915)

Ipswich Museum

Ipswich Corporation Museum Minute Book, 1880–1893

Ipswich Corporation Museum Accession Register, 1894–1911

S. J. Plunkett, 'Correspondence of Nina Frances Layard (1853–1935), transcribed and collected by Steven J. Plunkett', 1992–1993

Lancashire Archives

Preston Council Free Public Library Committee, minutes 17 October and 20 October 1893, CBP 29/2

Leicester Museum Service

Leicester Museum Accession Books, 1880–1914

Liverpool Museums Archives

Annual Reports of the Committee of the Free Public Libraries and Museums of the Borough of Liverpool, Liverpool, 1857–1914

Minutes of the Museum Sub-Committee, 1868–1914

'Cast metal work from Benin', *Bulletin of the Liverpool Museums*, 2 (1900), MM/15/2

A General Guide to the Collections contained in the Free Public Museums (William Brown Street) Liverpool (Liverpool 1906), MM/14/4

London Metropolitan Archives

London County Council, Historical Records and Buildings Committee Minutes 1901–1903, LCC/MIN/07225-7235

London County Council, Local Government, Records and Museum Committee Minutes 1904–1909, LCC/MIN/08129-34

Letters from Edward Lovett to the London County Council's Local Government, Records and Museums Committee, 15 July 1909, 21 July 1909, LCC/MIN/08132-3

Ironmongers' Almshouses/Geffrye Museum file, GLC/AR/ HB/01/0229: Petition to LCC, 1911; Lawrence Gomme, 'Preliminary report, proposed museum for craftsmen', 1911; Letter from Ernest Gray to Lawrence Gomme, 3 April 1911; note by Gomme to Records and Museums Sub-Committee, 10 November 1911

Minutes of Proceedings at a Meeting of the Council of the Administrative County of London: Report of Local Government, Records and Museums Committee, 17 December 1912

Manchester Art Gallery

Greg Correspondence, letters from 1920 to 1922, 2009.12

Manchester Museum

Manchester Museum, *Annual Reports 1889–1913* (Manchester: Cornish 1890–1914)

Manchester University Special Collections

MUS/4/1/2, *Manchester Art Museum and University Settlement Winter Programme 1909–10* (Manchester: The William Morris Press 1909)

Museum of Archaeology and Anthropology, University of Cambridge

Note from Durham to Ridgeway, 17 March 1908, W10/3/4

Letter from Durham to Ridgeway, 17 October 1910, W10/3/4
Letter from Durham to Ridgeway, 15th (no month given), 1911, W10/3/4
Letter from T. A. Stewart to Mrs Charlotte Wheeler Cuffe, 31 July 1914, W10/3/26

National Portrait Gallery Heinz Archive and Library

NPG82/2/2 Warding and Security Staff Duty Reports, Report 18 November 1909
NPG82/2/2, Warding and Security Staff Duty Reports, letter from George Zabriskie, 12 August 1912
Press Cuttings vol. 49, 1914

Norwich Castle Museum

Norwich Museum Accession Registers 1880–1914
Norwich Castle Museum and Art Gallery public catalogue
Norwich Museum donor index

Petrie Museum, University College London

Letter from Flinders Petrie to F. Spurrell, 22 September 1897, PMA/WFP1 16/2/1
Letter from Hilda Petrie to William Flinders Petrie, n.d., annotated in pencil 'Jan? 1910', PMA/WFP1 16/2/2

Sheffield Museums Trust

Visitors' Book, St George's Museum, September 1880–September 1881
Minutes of the Museums Sub-Committee 1881–1914
Card catalogues: mammals, birds, reptiles, fishes, mollusc, arthropods, other invertebrates
Gatty/Eden correspondence

Sunderland Museum and Art Gallery

Sunderland Borough Museum Stock Book 1880–1914

Thomas Cook Archives

Miss Riggs, 'Diary of a Grand Tour to the Nile and Palestine' (photo-copy of manuscript, 1869)

William Bemrose, 'Recollections of Egypt and Palestine' (photocopy of manuscript, 1882)

Miss Emmeline Barnsley, 'Diary' (photocopy of manuscript, 1888)

Victoria and Albert Museum Archives

Circulating Collection file ED84/119: memo, no author, 'Memorandum on letters from Mr Dixon and Mr Aitken', n.d.; no author, '1875–1879', n.d.; letter from Bradford Town Clerk, 14 June 1880

Circulating Collection files ED84/105: memo by J. Bailey, 'Memorandum and notes upon the Circulation Division of the Victoria and Albert Museum', 1909; memo by J. Bailey, 'Memorandum upon the Circulation Department of the Victoria and Albert Museum', 1913; letter from Whitworth Wallis to Secretary of Board of Education, 26 June 1914; memo by F. Burridge, 'Memorandum on the Circulation Department', 1919

Warrington Museum

Warrington Museum Receiving Book 1880–1914

Whitby Museum

Whitby Literary and Philosophical Society, *Reports of the Whitby Literary and Philosophical Society, 1880–1914* (Whitby 1881–1915)

Census for England and Wales, 1881, 1891, 1901, online, available at www.ancestry.co.uk, accessed 9 September 2011

Parliamentary papers

Report from the Select Committee on Arts and Manufactures (1835)

Report from the Select Committee on Arts and Their Connexion with Manufactures (1836)

Report from the Select Committee on National Monuments and Works of Art (1841)

Report from the Select Committee on the National Gallery (1850)
Report of the Select Committee on the South Kensington Museum (1860)
Second Report from the Select Committee on Museums of the Science
and Art Department (1898)

Published sources

'A Lady' (H. M. L. S.), *Travelling and Its Requirements. Addressed to Ladies by a Lady* (London: Thomas Cook and Son/Simpkin, Marshall and Co. 1878)

Ajmar, Marta, 'Toys for girls: objects, women and memory in the Renaissance household', in M. Kwint, C. Breward and J. Aynsley, (eds), *Material Memories: Design and Evocation* (Oxford: Berg 1999)

Alberti, Samuel J. M. M., 'Field, lab and museum: the practice and the place of Life Science in Yorkshire, 1870–1904' (unpublished PhD thesis, University of Sheffield 2000)

——'Amateurs and professionals in one county: biology and natural history in later Victorian Yorkshire', *Journal of the History of Biology*, 34 (2001), pp. 115–147

——'Conversaziones and the experience of science in Victorian England', *Journal of Victorian Culture* 8: 2 (2003), pp. 208–230

——'Objects and the museum', *Isis* 96: 4 (2005), pp. 559–571

——'The museum affect: visiting collections of anatomy and natural history', in A. Fyfe and B. Lightman (eds), *Science in the Marketplace: Nineteenth-Century Sites and Experiences* (Chicago, IL: University of Chicago Press 2007)

——*Nature and Culture: Objects, Disciplines and the Manchester Museum* (Manchester and New York: Manchester University Press 2009)

Alexander, Edward, *Museum Masters: Their Museums and Their Influence* (Nashville, TN: American Association for State and Local History 1983)

Allen, D. E. 'The women members of the Botanical Society of London, 1836–1856', *British Journal for the History of Science* 13: 3 (1980), pp. 240–254

——*The Naturalist in Britain: A Social History* (New Haven, CT: Princeton University Press 1994)

——*Naturalists and Society: The Culture of Natural History in Britain 1700–1900* (Aldershot: Ashgate Variorum 2001)

Allott, Peter W., 'Hügel, Anatole Andreas Aloys von, Baron von Hügel in the nobility of the Holy Roman empire (1854–1928)', *Oxford Dictionary of National Biography* (Oxford: Oxford University Press 2012), online, available at www.oxforddnb.com. proxy.library.lincoln.ac.uk/view/article/103702, accessed 14 July 2015

Altick, Richard, *The Shows of London: A Panoramic History of Exhibitions 1600–1862* (Cambridge, MA., and London: Belknap Press 1978)

Anderson, A., '"Chinamania": collecting Old Blue for the House Beautiful, c. 1860–1900', in J. Potvin and A. Myzelev (eds), *Material Cultures 1740–1920: The Meanings and Pleasures of Collecting* (Aldershot: Ashgate 2009)

Anon., 'News: Miss Grace Wigglesworth', *Nature* 154 (August 1944), p. 234

Appadurai, Arjun (ed.), *The Social Life of Things: Commodities in Cultural Perspective* (Cambridge: Cambridge University Press 1986)

Archaeologica Cantiana 1 (1858)

Arnold, Ken, *Cabinets for the Curious: Looking Back at Early English Museums* (Aldershot: Ashgate 2006)

Ashmore, Sonia, 'Liberty and lifestyle: shopping for art and luxury in nineteenth-century London', in D. E. Hussey and M. Ponsonby (eds), *Buying for the Home: Shopping for the Domestic from the Seventeenth Century to the Present* (Aldershot: Ashgate 2008)

BAAS, *Report of the 57th Meeting of the British Association for the Advancement of Science (1887)* (London 1888)

Bailkin, Jordanna, 'Picturing feminism, selling Liberalism: the case of the disappearing Holbein', *Gender and History* 11: 1 (1999), pp. 145–163

——*The Culture of Property: The Crisis of Liberalism in Modern Britain* (Chicago, IL: University of Chicago Press 2004)

Baker, Anne P., 'Edwards, Edwin (1823–1879)', *Oxford Dictionary of National Biography* (Oxford: Oxford University Press 2004), online, available at www.oxforddnb.com/view/article/8536, accessed 4 March 2011

Beauman, Katherine Bentley, *Women and the Settlement Movement* (London: Radcliffe Press 1996)

Beidelman, T. O., 'Altruism and domesticity: images of missionizing women among the Church Missionary Society in nineteenth-century East Africa', in Mary Taylor Huber and Nancy C. Lutkehaus (eds), *Gendered Missions: Men and Women in Missionary Discourse and Practice* (Ann Arbor, MI: University of Michigan Press 1999)

Bennett, Tony, *The Birth of the Museum* (London and New York: Routledge 1995)

Bernstein, S. D. '"Supposed differences": Lydia Becker and Victorian women's participation in the BAAS', in D. Clifford, E. Wadge, A. Warwick and M. Willis (eds), *Repositioning Victorian Sciences: Shifting Centres in Nineteenth-Century Scientific Thinking* (London: Anthem 2006)

Bessborough, Earl of (ed.), *Lady Charlotte Schreiber: Extracts from her Journal 1853–1891* (London: John Murray 1952)

Betham-Edwards, Matilda B., *Holiday Letters from Athens, Cairo and Weimar* (London: Strahan & Co. 1873)

Bingham, Adrian, '"An era of domesticity?" Histories of women and gender in interwar Britain', *Cultural and Social History* 1: 2 (2004), pp. 225–233

Birch, Dinah, 'Introduction', in D. Birch (ed.), *Ruskin and the Dawn of the Modern* (Oxford: Clarendon Press 1999)

——'Ruskin's "womanly mind"', in D. Birch and F. O'Gorman (eds), *Ruskin and Gender* (Basingstoke: Palgrave 2002)

——'"What teachers do you give your girls?" Ruskin and women's education', in D. Birch and F. O'Gorman (eds), *Ruskin and Gender* (Baskingstoke: Palgrave 2002)

——and Francis O'Gorman, 'Introduction', in D. Birch and F. O'Gorman (eds), *Ruskin and Gender* (Basingstoke: Palgrave 2002)

Birkett, Dea, *Spinsters Abroad: Victorian Lady Explorers* (Oxford: Basil Blackwell 1989)

Birmingham Museum and Art Gallery, *John and Christina Feeney* (Birmingham 1985)

Bivona, Daniel and Roger B. Henckle, *The Imagination of Class: Masculinity and the Urban Poor* (Columbus, OH: Ohio State University Press 2006)

Black, Graham, *The Engaging Museum: Developing Museums for Audience Involvement* (Abingdon: Routledge 2005)

Blair, Mary E., *A Life Well Led: The Biography of Barbara Freire-Marreco Aitken, British Anthropologist* (Santa Fe, NM: Sunstone Press 2008)

Bland, Lucy, *Banishing the Beast: Feminism, Sex and Morality* (Harmondsworth: Penguin 1995)

Bolton Museum and Archive Service, 'Caroline Birley', online, available at www.bolton-museums.org.uk/collections/geology/collectorscollections/caroline-francis-birley/, accessed 28 November 2007

——'Egyptology: Provenance', online, available at www.boltonmuseums.org.uk/collections/egyptology/egyptology-collection/for-researchers/provenance/, accessed 7 August 2013

Bourdieu, Pierre, *Distinction: A Social Critique of the Judgement of Taste*, trans. R. Nice (London: Routledge 1989)

Bowley, Arthur L., *Wages in the United Kingdom in the Nineteenth Century* (Cambridge: Cambridge University Press 1900)

Brassey, Annie, *The Last Voyage* (London: Longman, Green and Co. 1889)

Briggs, Asa and Anne Macartney, *Toynbee Hall: The First Hundred Years* (London: Routledge 2013 [1984])

Briggs, Louisa, 'An "all-consuming drive": Margaret's later collecting', in O. Fairclough (ed.), *'Things of Beauty': What Two Sisters Did for Wales* (Cardiff: National Museum Wales Books 2007)

Budge, Gavin, 'Poverty and the picture gallery: the Whitechapel exhibitions and the social project of Ruskinian aesthetics', *Visual Culture in Britain* 1: 2 (2000), pp. 43–56

Burstyn, J., *Victorian Education and the Ideal of Womanhood* (London: Croom Helm 1980)

Burton, Anthony, 'Design history and the history of toys', *Journal of Design History* 10: 1 (1997), pp. 1–21

——*Vision and Accident: The Story of the Victoria and Albert Museum* (London: V&A Publications 1999)

——'The uses of the South Kensington art collections', *Journal of the History of Collections* 14: 1 (2002), pp. 79–95

Buxton, Cara, *Adventurous Norfolk Lady: Miss Cara Buxton's Sport in Africa* (St. Albans: Fisher Knight & Co. n.d.)

Byrne, Sarah, Anne Clarke, Rodney Harrison and Robin Torrence, 'Networks, agents and objects: frameworks for unpacking museum collections', in S. Byrne, A. Clarke, R. Harrison and R. Torrence (eds), *Unpacking the Collection: Networks of Material and Social Agency in the Museum* (New York: Springer 2011)

——(eds), *Unpacking the Collection: Networks of Material and Social Agency in the Museum* (New York: Springer 2011)

Calhoun, Craig (ed.), *Habermas and the Public Sphere* (Cambridge, MA: MIT Press 1992)

Callen, Anthea, *Angel in the Studio: Women in the Arts and Crafts Movement 1870–1914* (London: Astragal Books 1979)

Cannizzo, J., 'Gathering souls and objects: missionary collections', in T. Barringer and T. Flynn (eds), *Colonialism and the Object* (London: Routledge 1998)

Carr, L. C., *Tessa Verney Wheeler: Women and Archaeology before World War Two* (Oxford: Oxford University Press 2012)

Carreau, Lucie, 'Individual, collective and institutional biographies: the Beasley collection of Pacific artefacts', in K. Hill (ed.), *Museums and Biographies: Stories, Objects, Identities* (Woodbridge: Boydell & Brewer 2012)

Catalani, Anna and Susan Pearce, '"Particular thanks and obligations": the communications made by women to the Society of Antiquaries between 1776 and 1837 and their significance', *The Antiquaries Journal* 86 (2006), pp. 254–278

Caygill, M. and J. Cherry (eds), *A. W. Franks: Nineteenth-Century Collecting and the British Museum* (London: British Museum Press 1997)

Cesare, Carla, 'Sewing the self: needlework, femininity and domesticity in interwar Britain' (unpublished doctoral thesis, Northumbria University 2012)

Challis, Debbie, *The Archaeology of Race: The Eugenic Ideas of Francis Galton and Flinders Petrie* (London: Bloomsbury 2013)

Cherry, Deborah, *Painting Women: Victorian Women Artists* (London: Routledge 1993)

——'Women artists and the politics of feminism 1850–1900', in Clarissa Campbell Orr (ed.), *Women in the Victorian Art World* (Manchester: Manchester University Press 1995)

Christenson, Andrew L. (ed.), *Tracing Archaeology's Past: The Historiography of Archaeology* (Carbondale, IL: Southern Illinois University Press 1989)

Cohen, Deborah, *Household Gods: The British and Their Possessions* (New Haven, CT and London: Yale University Press 2006)

Combs, Mary Beth, '"A measure of legal independence": the 1870 Married Women's Property Act and the portfolio allocations of British wives', *Journal of Economic History* 65: 4 (2005), pp. 1028–1057

Coombes, Annie E., *Reinventing Africa: Museums, Material Culture and Popular Imagination in Late Victorian and Edwardian England* (New Haven, CT and London: Yale University Press 1994)

Coote, Jeremy, 'Archaeology, anthropology and museums, 1851–2014: rethinking Pitt Rivers and his legacy – an introduction', *Museum History Journal* 7: 2 (2014), pp. 126–134

Cowman, Krista, 'Collective biography', in S. Gunn and L. Faire (eds), *Research Methods for History* (Edinburgh: Edinburgh University Press 2011)

Crane, Susan, 'Story, history and the passionate collector', in M. Myrone and L. Pelz (eds), *Producing the Past: Aspects of Antiquarian Culture and Practice 1700–1850* (Aldershot: Ashgate 1999)

Crooke, Elizabeth, 'The "world of objects at rest": memories, material culture and the museum' (2014) online, available at https://www.academia.edu/7030338/The_world_of_objects_at_rest_memories_material_culture_and_the_museum, accessed 1 October 2014

Cross, Gary, *Kids' Stuff: Toys and the Changing World of American Childhood* (Cambridge, Mass.: Harvard University Press 2009)

Daly, Nick, 'That obscure object of desire: Victorian commodity culture and fictions of the mummy', *Novel: A Forum on Fiction*, 28 (1994), pp. 24–51

Darley, Gillian, 'Hill, Octavia (1838–1912)', *Oxford Dictionary of National Biography* (Oxford: Oxford University Press 2004; online edn, May 2012) available at www.oxforddnb.com.proxy.library.lincoln.ac.uk/view/article/33873, accessed 25 June 2014

Daunton, M. J., and Rieger, B. (eds), *Meanings of Modernity: Britain from the late-Victorian Era to World War II* (Oxford: Berg 2001)

Davenport-Hines, Richard, 'Groom, Charles Ottley (1839–1894)', *Oxford Dictionary of National Biography* (Oxford: Oxford University Press 2004), online, available at www.oxforddnb.com/view/article/54058, accessed 1 April 2011

Davidoff, L., and Hall, C., *Family Fortunes: Men and Women of the English Middle Class 1780–1850*, rev. edn (London: Routledge 2002)

Davies, Stuart, *By the Gains of Industry: Birmingham Museums and Art Gallery 1885–1985* (Birmingham: Birmingham Museums and Art Gallery 1985)

Davin, Delia, 'British women missionaries in nineteenth-century China', *Women's History Review* 1: 2 (1992), pp. 257–271

Dawkes, Bryony, 'A taste for modernity: the Davies sisters as art collectors', *Becoming Modern* (Oriel Davies 2008), online, available at www.orieldavies.org/en/resources/taste-modernity-davies-sisters-art-collectors, accessed 2 June 2012

De Selincourt, E., A. G. Hill and M. Moorman (eds), *The Letters of William and Dorothy Wordsworth*, vol. 3: *The Middle Years, Part 2, 1812–1820*, 2nd edn (Oxford: Clarendon Press 1970)

Desmond, R. (ed.), *Dictionary of British and Irish Botanists and Horticulturalists* (London: Taylor and Francis/The Natural History Museum 1994)

Dickinson, Rachel, 'Of Ruskin, women and power', in Keith Hanley and Brian Maidment (eds), *Persistent Ruskin: Studies in Influence, Assimilation and Effect* (Aldershot: Ashgate 2013)

Digby, Anne, 'New schools for the middle-class girl', in P. Searby (ed.), *Educating the Victorian Middle Class* (Proceedings of the 1981 Annual Conference of the History of Education Society) (Leicester: Leicester University Press 1982)

Dixon, Diana, 'Children's magazines and science in the nineteenth century', *Victorian Periodicals Review* 34: 3 (2001), pp. 147–199

Dodd, Sara M., 'Art education for women in the 1860s: a decade of debate', in Clarissa Campbell Orr (ed.), *Women in the Victorian Art World* (Manchester: Manchester University Press 1995)

Douglas, Oliver, 'Upstairs, downstairs: the materialisation of Victorian folklore studies', 2009, online, available at http://england.prm.ox.ac.uk/englishness-Douglas-paper.html, accessed 2 November 2010

Drower, Margaret S., *Flinders Petrie: A Life in Archaeology* (Madison, WI: University of Wisconsin Press 1995)

—— (ed.), *Letters from the Desert: The Correspondence of Flinders and Hilda Petrie* (Oxford: Oxbow Books 2004)

——'Margaret Alice Murray (1863–1963)', in Getzel M. Cohen and Martha Sharp Jonkowsky (eds), *Breaking Ground: Pioneering Women Archaeologists* (Ann Arbor, MI: University of Michigan Press 2004)

——'Hilda Petrie', Brown University Women in Old World Archaeology project, online, available at www.brown.edu/Research/Breaking_Ground/results.php?d=1&first=Hilda&last=Petrie, accessed 7 August 2013

Duncan, Carol, *Civilising Rituals: Inside Public Art Museums* (London: Routledge 1995)

Duncan, Carol, and Wallach, A., 'The universal survey museum', *Art History* 3: 4 (1980)

Dyhouse, Carol, *No Distinction of Sex? Women in British Universities 1870–1939* (London: UCL Press 1995)

Eagles, Stuart, *After Ruskin: The Social and Political Legacies of a Victorian Prophet, 1870–1920* (Oxford: Oxford University Press 2011)

East Riding Antiquarian Society, 'Third Annual Report', *Transactions of the East Riding Antiquarian Society*, vol. 3 (Hull: William Andrews and Co. 1895), pp. xv–xviii

Eastlake, Elizabeth and Harriet Grote, 'The British Museum', *Quarterly Review* 124 (1868), pp. 147–179

Eatwell, Ann, 'Private pleasure, public beneficence: Lady Charlotte Schreiber and ceramic collecting', in C. C. Orr (ed.), *Women in the Victorian Art World* (Manchester: Manchester University Press 1995)

Edwards, Clive, 'Women's home-crafted objects as collections of culture and comfort, 1750–1900', in J. Potvin and A. Myzelev (eds), *Material Cultures 1740–1920: The Meanings and Pleasures of Collecting* (Aldershot: Ashgate 2009)

Edwards, Clive, and Margaret Ponsonby, 'A desirable commodity or practical necessity? The sale and consumption of secondhand furniture 1750–1900', in M. Ponsonby and D. Hussey (eds), *Buying for the Home: Shopping for the Domestic from the Seventeenth Century to the Present* (Aldershot: Ashgate 2008)

Edwards, Elizabeth, *The Camera as Historian: Amateur Photographers and Historical Imagination, 1885–1918* (Durham, NC and London: Duke University Press 2012)

Edwards, Hilary, 'Protecting life from language: John Ruskin's museum as autobiography', *Biography* 32: 2 (2009), pp. 297–315

Eley, Geoff, 'Nations, publics and political cultures: placing Habermas in the nineteenth century', in N. Dirks, G. Eley and S. Ortner (eds), *Culture/Power/History: A Reader in Contemporary Social Theory* (Princeton, NJ: Princeton University Press 1994)

'Elizabeth Ruth Edwards, ca 1833–1907', in Margaret F. MacDonald, Patricia de Montfort, and Nigel Thorp (eds), *The Correspondence of James McNeill Whistler, 1855–1903*, online, University of Glasgow, available at www.whistler.arts.gla.ac.uk/correspond-ence/biog/display/?bid=Edwa_Mrs, accessed 4 March 2011

Elliott, Mark, 'Sculptural biographies in an anthropological collection: Mrs Millward's Indian "types"', in K. Hill (ed.), *Museums and Biographies: Stories, Objects, Identities* (Woodbridge: Boydell and Brewer 2012)

Ellis, A. R. (ed.), *The Early Diary of Frances Burney 1768–1778*, 2 vols, vol. 2 (London: George Bell and Sons, 1889)

Ellis, Heather, 'Knowledge, character and professionalization in nineteenth-century British science', *History of Education* 43: 6 (2014), pp. 777–792

Evans, Mark, 'The Davies sisters of Llandinam and Impressionism for Wales, 1908–1923', *Journal of the History of Collections*, 16: 2 (2004), pp. 219–263

Fairclough, Oliver, '"Knocked to pieces": the impact of the Great War', in Oliver Fairclough (ed.), *'Things of Beauty': What Two Sisters Did for Wales* (Cardiff: National Museum Wales Books 2007)

Felski, Rita, *The Gender of Modernity* (Cambridge, MA: Harvard University Press 1995)

Finn, Margot, 'Women, consumption and coverture in England, c. 1760–1860', *Historical Journal* 39: 3 (1996), pp. 703–722

——'Men's things: masculine possessions in the consumer revolution', *Social History* 25: 2 (2000), pp. 133–155

Fletcher, Sheila, *Feminists and Bureaucrats: A Study in the Development of Girls' Education in the Nineteenth Century* (Cambridge: Cambridge University Press 1980)

Frawley, Maria H., *A Widening Sphere: Travel Writing by Women in Victorian England* (Rutherford, NJ: Fairleigh Dickinson University Press 1994)

Frederickson, Kristen, 'Introduction', in K. Frederickson and S. Webb (eds), *Singular Women: Writing the Artist* (Berkeley, CA: University of California Press 2003)

Frost, Mark, *Curator and Curatress: The Swans and St George's Museum, Sheffield* (York: Guild of St George Publications 2013)

Froude, J. A. (ed.), *Letters and Memorials of Jane Welsh Carlyle*, vol. 1 (New York: Charles Scribner and Sons 1883)

Fyfe, Gordon, 'Auditing the RA: official discourse and the nineteenth-century Royal Academy', in Rafael Cardoso Denis and Colin Trodd (eds), *Art and the Academy in the Nineteenth Century* (Manchester: Manchester University Press 2000)

Gardner, Helen, 'Gathering for God: George Brown and the Christian economy in the collection of artefacts', in M. O'Hanlon and R. L. Welsch (eds), *Hunting the Gatherers: Ethnographic Collectors, Agents and Agency in Melanesia 1870s–1930s* (Oxford: Berghahn 2000)

Garner, Shaun, 'Sir Merton Russell-Cotes and his Japanese collection: the importance and impact of an unplanned trip to Japan in 1885', in A. Shelton (ed.), *Collectors: Individuals and Institutions* (London: Horniman Museum and Gardens/Museu Antropologico da Universidade de Coimbra 2001)

Gates, B. T., 'Those who drew and those who wrote: women and Victorian popular science illustration', in A. B. Shteir and B. Lightman (eds), *Figuring It Out: Science, Gender and Visual Culture* (Hanover, NH: Dartmouth College Press 2006)

Gates, B. T. and A. B. Shteir (eds), *Natural Eloquence: Women Reinscribe Science* (Madison, WI: University of Wisconsin Press 1997)

Gere, Charlotte, *The House Beautiful: Oscar Wilde and the Aesthetic Interior* (Aldershot: Lund Humphries/The Geffrye Museum 2000)

Giles, M., 'Collecting the past, constructing identity: the antiquarian John Mortimer and the Driffield Museum of Antiquities and Geological Specimens', *The Antiquaries Journal* 86 (2006), pp. 279–316

Gill, David, '"The passion of hazard": women at the British School at Athens before the First World War', *Annual of the British School at Athens*, 97 (2002), pp. 491–510

Goggin, Maureen D. and Tobin, Beth F. (eds), *Material Women, 1750–1950: Consuming Desires and Collecting Practices* (Aldershot: Ashgate 2009)

—— (eds), *Women and Things, 1750–1950: Gendered Material Strategies* (Aldershot: Ashgate 2009)

Gooday, Graeme, '"Nature" in the laboratory: domestication and discipline with the microscope in Victorian life science', *British Journal for the History of Science* 24 (1991), pp. 307–341

Gordon, Beverley, *The Saturated World: Aesthetic Meaning, Intimate Objects, Women's Lives 1890–1940* (Knoxville, TN: University of Tennessee Press 2006)

Gosden, Chris, and Knowles, Chantal (eds), *Collecting Colonialism: Material Culture and Colonial Change* (Oxford: Berg 2001)

Gosden, Chris and Frances Larson, *Knowing Things: Exploring the Collections at the Pitt Rivers Museum* (Oxford: Oxford University Press 2007)

Gosden, Chris, and Yvonne Marshall, 'The cultural biography of objects', *World Archaeology* 31: 2 (1999), pp. 169–178

Green, David, 'Independent women, wealth and wills in nineteenth-century London', in Jon Stobart and Alastair Owens (eds), *Urban Fortunes: Property and Inheritance in the Town, 1700–1900* (Aldershot: Ashgate 2000)

Greenwood, Thomas, *Museums and Art Galleries* (London: Simpkin, Marshall & Co. 1888)

Griffin, Delia, 'The Children's Museum of Boston, USA', *Museums Journal* 14: 6 (1914), pp. 201–204

Grimsditch, H. B., 'MacColl, Dugald Sutherland (1859–1948)', rev. Robert Upstone, *Oxford Dictionary of National Biography* (Oxford: Oxford University Press 2004), online, available at www.oxforddnb.com/view/article/34687, accessed 6 April 2011

Guest, Montague (ed.), *Lady Charlotte Schreiber's Journals; Confidences of a Collector of Ceramics and Antiquities Throughout Britain, France, Holland, Belgium, Spain, Portugal, Turkey, Austria and Germany from the year 1869 to 1885*, vol. 1 (London: John Lane 1911)

Habermas, Jürgen, *The Structural Transformation of the Public Sphere*, trans. T. Burger (Cambridge, MA: MIT Press 1989)

Hall, Catherine, Keith McClelland and Jane Rendall, *Defining the Victorian Nation: Class, Race, Gender and the Reform Act of 1867* (Cambridge: Cambridge University Press 2000)

Hall, Catherine and Sonia Rose, 'Introduction: being at home with the Empire', in C. Hall and S. Rose (eds), *At Home with the Empire: Metropolitan Culture and the Imperial World* (Cambridge: Cambridge University Press 2006)

Hall, Edward (ed.), *Miss Weeton's Journal of a Governess*, 2 vols, vol. 2: *1811–1825* (New York: Augustus M. Kelly 1969)

Hall, Kate M., 'The smallest museum', *Museums Journal* 1: 2 (1901), pp. 38–45

Hall, L. A., 'Stopes, Marie Charlotte Carmichael (1880–1958)', *Oxford Dictionary of National Biography* (Oxford: Oxford University Press 2004), online, available at www.oxforddnb. com/view/article/36323, accessed 9 September 2011

Hamam, Iman, '"A race for incorporation": Ancient Egypt and its mummies in science and popular culture', in Richard Pearson (ed.), *The Victorians and the Ancient World: Archaeology and Classicism in Nineteenth-Century Culture* (Newcastle: Cambridge Scholars Press, 2006)

Hamlett, Jane, *Material Relations: Domestic Interiors and Middle-Class Families in England, 1850–1910* (Manchester: Manchester University Press 2010)

Hammerton, A. James, 'The English weakness? Gender, satire, and "moral manliness" in the lower middle class, 1870–1920', in A. Kidd and D. Nicholls (eds) *Gender, Civic Culture and Consumerism: Middle-Class Identity in Britain 1800–1940* (Manchester: Manchester University Press 1999)

Harding, Sandra, *Whose Science? Whose Knowledge? Thinking from Women's Lives* (Ithaca, NY: Cornell University Press 1991)

Hardy, Charles E., *John Bowes and the Bowes Museum* (Bishop Auckland: The Friends of Bowes Museum 1989)

Harraden, Beatrice, 'Obituary: Kate Marion Hall', *Proceedings of the Linnaean Society of London*, 130th Session 1917–1918, 1918, 61–63

Harrison, Michael, 'Art and philanthropy: T. C. Horsfall and the Manchester Art Museum' in A. Kidd (ed.), *City, Class and Culture: Studies of Cultural Production and Social Policy in Victorian Manchester* (Manchester: Manchester University Press 1985)

Harrison, Rodney, 'Consuming colonialism: curio dealers' catalogues, souvenir objects, and indigenous agency in Oceania', in S. Byrne, A. Clarke, R. Harrison and R. Torrence (eds), *Unpacking the Collection: Networks of Material and Social Agency in the Museum* (New York: Springer, 2011)

Harrison, S., 'A local hero: John Robert Mortimer and the birth of archaeology in east Yorkshire', *Bulletin of the History of Archaeology* 19 (2009), online, available at www.archaeologybulletin.org/article/view/47, accessed 19 May 2014

——'John Robert Mortimer: a founding father of modern British archaeology', *Antiquity* Project Gallery 84: 325 (2010), online, available at www.antiquity.ac.uk/projgall/harrison325/, accessed 9 September 2011

Harrison, S. J., 'Skulls and scientific collecting in the Victorian military: keeping the enemy dead in British frontier warfare', *Comparative Studies in Society and History* 50: 1 (2008), pp. 285–303

Haslemere Museum, 'Natural history – taxidermy trade labels', online, available at www.haslemeremuseum.co.uk/birdtaxidermy.html#TL3, accessed 9 September 2011

Hazbun, Waleed, 'The East as exhibit: Thomas Cook & Son and the origins of the international tourism industry in Egypt', in Philip Scranton and Janet F. Davidson (eds), *The Business of Tourism: Place, Faith and History* (Philadelphia, PA: University of Pennsylvania Press 2007)

Hicks, Dan, 'Excavating Pitt-Rivers: studying the archaeological collections made by Augustus Henry Lane Fox Pitt-Rivers', online, available at http://excavatingpittrivers.blogspot.co.uk/, accessed 19 May 2014

Hill, Kate, '"Civic pride" or "far-reaching utility"? Liverpool Museum c. 1860–1914', *Journal of Regional and Local Studies* 20: 1 (2000), pp. 3–28

——*Culture and Class in English Public Museums 1850–1914* (Aldershot: Ashgate 2005)

——'Collecting authenticity: domestic, familial and everyday "old things" in English museums, 1850–1939', *Museum History Journal* 4: 2 (2011), pp. 203–222

——'"He knows me … but not at the museum": women, natural history curating and museums, 1880–1914', in S. Dudley, A. Barnes, J. Binnie, J. Petrov and J. Walklate (eds), *Narrating Objects, Collecting Stories* (Abingdon: Routledge 2012)

——'Manufactures, archaeology and bygones: making a sense of place in civic museums, 1850–1914', *International Journal of Regional and Local History* 8: 1 (2013), pp. 54–74

Hoberman, Ruth, 'Women in the British Museum Reading Room during the late-nineteenth and early-twentieth centuries: from quasi- to counterpublic', *Feminist Studies* 28: 3 (2002), pp. 489–512

——*Museum Trouble: Edwardian Fiction and the Emergence of Modernism* (Charlottesville, VA and London: University of Virginia Press 2011)

Hodgkinson, Harry, 'Durham, (Mary) Edith (1863–1944)', *Oxford Dictionary of National Biography* (Oxford: Oxford University Press 2004), online, available at www.oxforddnb.com/view/article/37379, accessed 18 March 2011

Hollis, Patricia, *Ladies Elect: Women in English Local Government 1865–1914* (Oxford: Oxford University Press 1987)

Hooper-Greenhill, Eilean, *Museums and the Shaping of Knowledge* (London: Routledge 1992)

Hudson, Kenneth, *A Social History of Museums: What the Visitors Thought* (London: Macmillan 1975)

Hughes, Kathryn, *The Victorian Governess* (Rio Grande, OH: Hambledon Press 1993)

Huyssen, Andreas, *After the Great Divide: Modernism, Mass Culture, Postmodernism* (Bloomington, IN: Indiana University Press 1986)

James, Henry, *The Wings of the Dove* (London: Bodley Head 1969 [orig. pub. 1902])

Jameson, Anna, *A Handbook to the Public Galleries of Art in and near London* (London: John Murray 1842)

Jay, E., A. S. Hobbs, M. Noble (eds), *A Victorian Naturalist: Beatrix Potter's Drawings from the Armitt Collection* (London: Warne 1992)

Jekyll, Gertrude, *Old West Surrey: Some Notes and Memories* (London: Longmans and Green 1904)

——*Old English Household Life: Some Account of Cottage Objects and Country Folk*, [1925] (JM Classic Editions 2007)

Jenkins, Ian, *Archaeologists and Aesthetes in the Sculpture Galleries of the British Museum, 1800–1939* (London: British Museum Press 1992)

Joannou, Maroula and June Purvis (eds), *The Women's Suffrage Movement: New Feminist Perspectives* (Manchester: Manchester University Press 1998)

John, Angela V., 'Schreiber, Lady Charlotte Elizabeth (1812–1895)', *Oxford Dictionary of National Biography* (Oxford: Oxford University Press, 2004) online, available at www.oxforddnb.com.proxy.library.lincoln.ac.uk/view/article/24832, accessed 8 July 2014

Johnston, Judith, *Anna Jameson: Victorian, Feminist, Woman of Letters* (Aldershot: Scolar 1997)

Jones, Claire G., *Femininity, Mathematics and Science, c.1880–1914* (Basingstoke: Palgrave Macmillan 2009)

Jones, Sian, 'Negotiating authentic objects and authentic selves: beyond the deconstruction of authenticity', *Journal of Material Culture* 15: 2 (2010), pp. 181–203

Kane, Sarah, 'Turning bibelots into museum pieces: Josephine Coffin-Chevallier and the creation of the Bowes Museum, Barnard Castle', *Journal of Design History* 9, 1 (1996), pp. 1–21

Kavanagh, Gaynor, *History Curatorship* (Leicester: Leicester University Press 1990)

——*Dream Spaces: Memory and the Museum* (London: Leicester University Press 2000)

Kellner, Douglas, 'Habermas, the public sphere and democracy: a critical intervention', online, available at http://pages.gseis.ucla.edu/faculty/kellner/papers/habermas.htm, accessed 22 June 2014

Kelvin, Norman (ed.) and William Morris, *The Collected Letters of William Morris*, vol. 3 (Princeton, NJ: Princeton University Press 1996)

Kemble, Fanny, *Records of Later Life* (London: Richard Bentley and Son 1882)

Kemp, L. W., 'Biography and the museum', in M. S. Shapiro (ed.), *The Museum: A Reference Guide* (New York and Westport, CT: Greenwood Press 1990)

Knell, Simon, *The Culture of English Geology 1815–1851: A Science Revealed Through Its Collecting* (Aldershot: Ashgate 2000)

Kohlstedt, Sally Gregory, 'Innovative niche scientists: women's role in reframing North American museums, 1880–1930', *Centaurus* 55: 2 (2013), pp. 153–174

Kopytoff, Igor, 'The cultural biography of things: commoditisation as process', in A. Appadurai (ed.), *The Social Life of Things: Commodities in Cultural Perspective* (Cambridge: Cambridge University Press 1986)

Korn, Madeleine, 'Exhibitions of modern French art and their influence on collectors in Britain 1870–1918: the Davies sisters in context', *Journal of the History of Collections* 16: 2 (2004), pp. 191–218

Koven, Seth, 'Henrietta Barnett, 1851–1936: the (auto)biography of a late Victorian marriage' in Peter Mandler and Susan Pederson (eds), *After the Victorians: Private Conscience and Public Duty In Modern Britain* (London: Routledge 1994)

——'Barnett, Dame Henrietta Octavia Weston (1851–1936)', *Oxford Dictionary of National Biography* (Oxford: Oxford University Press 2004), online, available at www.oxford-ddnb.com/view/article/30610, accessed 23 September 2011

——'Barnett, Samuel Augustus (1844–1913)', *Oxford Dictionary of National Biography* (Oxford: Oxford University Press 2004), online, available at www.oxforddnb.com/view/article/30612, accessed 23 September 2011

——*Slumming: Sexual and Social Politics in Victorian London* (Princeton, NJ: Princeton University Press 2004)

Kriegel, Lara, *Grand Designs: Labor, Empire and the Museum in Victorian Culture* (Durham, NC and London: Duke University Press 2007)

Kucklick, Henrika, *The Savage Within: The Social History of British Anthropology, 1885–1945* (Cambridge: Cambridge University Press 1991)

Kwint, Marius, 'Introduction: The Physical Past' in Marius Kwint, Christopher Breward and Jeremy Aynsley (eds), *Material Memories: Design and Evocation* (Oxford: Berg 1999)

Lago, Mary, 'Christiana Herringham and the National Art Collections Fund', *The Burlington Magazine* 135: 1080 (1993), pp. 202–211

——'Herringham, Christiana Jane, Lady Herringham (1852–1929)', *Oxford Dictionary of National Biography* (Oxford: Oxford University Press 2004), online, available at www.oxforddnb.com/view/article/64758, accessed 5 March 2012

Landsberg, Alison, *Prosthetic Memory: The Transformation of American Remembrance in the Age of Mass Culture* (New York: Columbia University Press 2004)

Lankester, E. Ray, *The History of the Collections Contained in the Natural History Departments of the British Museum,* vol. 1 (London: British Museum 1904)

Larson, Frances, *An Infinity of Things: How Sir Henry Wellcome Collected the World* (Oxford: Oxford University Press 2009)

——'The curious and the glorious: science and the British past at the Wellcome Historical Medical Museum', *Museum History Journal* 4: 2 (2011), pp. 181–202

Lasic, Barbara, '"Splendid patriotism": Richard Wallace and the construction of the Wallace Collection', *Journal of the History of Collections* 21: 2 (2009), pp. 173–182

——'Going east: the Wallace Collection at Bethnal Green, 1872–1875', *Journal of the History of Collections* 26: 2 (2014), pp. 249–261

Ledger, Sally, *The New Woman: Fiction and Feminism at the Fin de Siècle* (Manchester: Manchester University Press 1997)

Leslie, Esther, 'Souvenirs and forgetting: Walter Benjamin's memory work', in M. Kwint, C. Breward and J. Aynsley (eds) *Material Memories: Design and Evocation* (Oxford: Berg 1999)

Levell, Nicky, *Oriental Visions: Exhibition, Travel and Collecting in the Victorian Age* (London: Horniman Museum and Gardens/Museu Antropologico da Universidade de Coimbra 2000)

——'Discontinuous histories: the Royal Albert Memorial Museum, Exeter, and its African collection, 1868–1996', in A. Shelton (ed.), *Collectors: Expressions of Self and Other* (London: Horniman Museum and Gardens/Museu Antropologico da Universidade de Coimbra 2001)

——'The translation of objects: R. and M. Davidson and the Friends' Foreign Mission Association, China, 1890–1894', in A. Shelton (ed.), *Collectors: Individuals and Institutions* (London: Horniman Museum and Gardens/Museu Antropologico da Universidade de Coimbra 2001)

Levine, Philippa, *The Amateur and the Professional: Antiquarians, Historians and Archaeologists in Victorian England 1838–1886* (Cambridge: Cambridge University Press 1986)

——*Victorian Feminism 1850–1900* (Tallahassee, FL: Florida State University Press 1989)

Lewis, Geoffrey, *For Instruction and Recreation: A Centenary History of the Museums Association* (London: Quiller Press 1989)

Lightman, Bernard, 'Depicting nature, defining roles: the gender politics of Victorian illustration', in A. B. Shteir and B. Lightman (eds) *Figuring It Out: Science, Gender and Visual Culture* (Hanover, NH: Dartmouth College Press 2006)

Linder, Leslie (ed. and transcr.) *The Journal of Beatrix Potter from 1881 to 1897* (London and New York: Frederick Warne & Co. 1966)

Livne, Inbal, 'The many purposes of missionary work: Annie Royle Taylor as missionary, travel writer, collector and empire builder', in H. Nielssen and I. M. Okkenhaug (eds), *Protestant Missions and Local Encounters in the Nineteenth and Twentieth Centuries: Unto the Ends of the World* (Leiden: Brill 2011)

Lloyd-Morgan, Ceridwen, 'Davies, Gwendoline Elizabeth (1882–1951)', *Oxford Dictionary of National Biography* (Oxford: Oxford University Press 2004), online, available at www.oxforddnb.com/view/article/39573, accessed 19 May 2012

Logan, Thad, *The Victorian Parlour: A Cultural Study* (Cambridge: Cambridge University Press 2001)

Longair, Sarah and John McAleer (eds), *Curating Empire: Museums and the British Imperial Experience* (Manchester: Manchester University Press 2012)

Loughney, Claire, 'Colonialism and the development of the English provincial museum 1823–1914', unpublished PhD thesis, University of Newcastle 2006

Lower, M. A., and Chapman, R., 'The antiquities preserved in the museum of Lewes Castle', *Sussex Archaeological Collections* 18 (1866), pp. 60–73

Macaulay, Thomas B., *The History of England from the Accession of James II* (London: Longman 1856)

MacGregor, Arthur (ed.), *Tradescent's Rarities: Essays on the Foundation of the Ashmolean Museum, 1683* (Oxford: Clarendon Press 1983)

MacGregor, Arthur, 'Collectors, connoisseurs and curators in the Victorian age', in M. Caygill and J. Cherry (eds), *A. W. Franks: Nineteenth-Century Collecting and the British Museum* (London: British Museum Press 1997)

Macleod, Dianne Sachko, 'Homosociality and middle-class identity in early Victorian patronage of the arts', in Alan Kidd and David Nicholls (eds), *Gender, Civic Culture and Consumerism* (Manchester: Manchester University Press 1999)

——*Enchanted Lives, Enchanted Objects: American Women Collectors and the Making of Culture 1800-1940* (Berkeley, CA: University of California Press 2008)

——'Art collecting as play: Lady Charlotte Schreiber (1812-1895)', *Visual Resources* 27: 1 (2011), pp. 18–31

MacLeod, Suzanne, 'Civil disobedience and political agitation: the art museum as a site of protest in the early twentieth century', *Museum and Society* 5: 1 (2007), online, available at www2.le.ac.uk/departments/museumstudies/museumsociety/documents/volumes/macleod.pdf, accessed 31 October 2011

——'Significant lives: telling stories of museum architecture', in Kate Hill (ed.), *Museums and Biographies* (Woodbridge: Boydell and Brewer 2012)

Macovicky, Nicolette, 'Lace maker's bobbins', The Other Within, online, available at http://england.prm.ox.ac.uk/englishness-lace-makers-bobbins.html, accessed 17 October 2011

Madsen-Brooks, Leslie, 'Challenging science as usual: women's participation in American natural history museum work, 1870–1950', *Journal of Women's History* 21: 2 (2009), pp. 11–38

Malley, Shaun, *From Archaeology to Spectacle in Victorian Britain: The Case of Assyria, 1845-1854* (Aldershot: Ashgate 2013)

Mallowan, Max, 'Murray, Margaret Alice (1863-1963), Egyptologist and folklorist', rev. R. S. Simpson, *Oxford Dictionary of National Biography* (Oxford: Oxford University Press 2004), online, available at http://oxforddnb.com/view/article/35169, accessed 14 October 2011

Manchester Art Gallery, 'Mary, Mary, quite contrary', blog, available at www.marymaryquitecontrary.org.uk, accessed 17 October 2011

Manchester Art Museum and University Settlement Annual Reports (Manchester: William Hough & Sons 1902-1903)

Manchester Art Museum and University Settlement Annual Reports (Manchester: The William Morris Press 1904-1914)

Mandler, Peter, *The Fall and Rise of the Stately Home* (New Haven, CT: Yale University Press 1997)

——'"The wand of fancy": the historical imagination of the Victorian tourist', in M. Kwint, C. Breward and J. Aynsley (eds) *Material Memories: Design and Evocation* (Oxford: Berg 1999)

Manley, Deborah, 'Edwards, Amelia Ann Blanford (1831-1892)', *Oxford Dictionary of National Biography* (Oxford: Oxford University Press 2004), online, available at www.oxforddnb.com.proxy.library.lincoln.ac.uk/view/article/8529, accessed 7 August 2013

Marchioness of Dufferin and Ava, *Our Viceregal Life in India: Selections from my Journal 1884-1888* (New York: Charles Scribner 1891)

Martin, Paul, *Popular Collecting and the Everyday Self: The Reinvention of Museums?* (London: Leicester University Press 1999)

Matthews-Jones, Lucinda, 'Lessons in seeing: art, religion and class in the East End of London, 1881–1898', *Journal of Victorian Culture* 16: 3 (2011), pp. 385–403

——'St Francis of Assisi and the making of settlement masculinity', in John H. Arnold and Sean Brady (eds), *What Is Masculinity? Historical Dynamics from Antiquity to the Contemporary World* (London: Palgrave Macmillan 2011)

Maurice, C. Edmund (ed.), *Life of Octavia Hill, As Told in Her Letters* (London: Macmillan 1913)

McCombe, Robert, 'Anglo-Saxon artefacts and nationalist discourse: acquisition, interpretation and display in the nineteenth century', *Museum History Journal* 4: 2 (2011), pp. 139–160

McNiven, Peter, 'Manchester University archive collections in the John Rylands University Library of Manchester', *Bulletin of the John Rylands Library* 71: 2 (1989), pp. 205–226

McTavish, Lianne, 'Strategic donations: Women and museums in New Brunswick 1862–1930', *Journal of Canadian Studies* 42: 2 (2008), pp. 93–116

——*Defining the Modern Museum* (Toronto: University of Toronto Press 2013)

Merrill, Lynn, *The Romance of Victorian Natural History* (Oxford: Oxford University Press 1989)

Merriman, Nick, *Beyond the Glass Case: The Past, Heritage and the Public* (Leicester: Leicester University Press 1991)

Miele, Chris, 'Conservation and the enemies of promise?' in Chris Miele (ed.), *From William Morris: Building Conservation and the Arts and Crafts Cult of Authenticity, 1877–1939* (New Haven, CT and London: Yale University Press 2005)

——'Morris and conservation', in Chris Miele (ed.), *From William Morris; Building Conservation and the Arts and Crafts Cult of Authenticity* (New Haven, CT: Yale University Press 2005)

—— 'Preface', in Chris Miele (ed.), *From William Morris: Building Conservation and the Arts and Crafts Cult of Authenticity, 1877–1939* (New Haven, CT and London: Yale University Press 2005

Miller, Edward, *That Noble Cabinet: A History of the British Museum* (London: Andre Deutsch 1973)

Mills, Sara, *Discourses of Difference: An Analysis of Women's Travel Writing and Colonialism* (London: Routledge 1991)

Mills, Victoria, 'Introduction: Victorian fiction and the material imagination', *19: Interdisciplinary Studies in the Long Nineteenth Century* 6 (2008), online, available at www.19.bbk.ac.uk, accessed 9 September 2011

——'The museum as "dream space": psychology and affective response in George Eliot's *Middlemarch*', *19: Interdisciplinary Studies in the Long Nineteenth Century* 12 (2011), online, available at http://19.bbk.ac.uk/index.php/19/article/view/596/713, accessed 5 September 2011

Minihan, Janet, *The Nationalisation of Culture: The Development of State Subsidies to the Arts in Great Britain* (London: Hamish Hamilton 1977)

Mitchell, Rosemary, *Picturing the Past: English History in Text and Image, 1830–1870* (Oxford: Clarendon Press 2000)

Moon, Brenda, *More Usefully Employed: Amelia B. Edwards, Writer, Traveller and Campaigner for Ancient Egypt* (London: Egypt Exploration Society 2004)

Morgan, Simon, *A Victorian Woman's Place: Public Culture in the Nineteenth Century* (London: Tauris Academic 2007)

Morris, Barbara, 'William Morris and the South Kensington Museum', *Victorian Poetry* 13: 3 (1975), pp. 159–175

Morris, R. J., 'Voluntary societies and British urban elites, 1780–1850: an analysis', *Historical Journal* 26: 1 (1983), pp. 95–118

——*Men, Women and Property in England, 1780–1870: A Social and Economic History of Family Strategies Amongst the Leeds Middle Classes* (Cambridge: Cambridge University Press 2005)

Morse, Elizabeth J., 'MacDonald sisters (act. 1837–1925)', *Oxford Dictionary of National Biography* (Oxford: Oxford University Press 2004), online, available at http://oxforddnb.com/view/article/76071, accessed 29 September 2009

Moseley, Charles, 'Inn-parlour museums', *Museums Journal* 27 (1927), pp. 280–281

Moser, Stephanie, *Wondrous Curiosities: Ancient Egypt at the British Museum* (Chicago, IL and London: University of Chicago Press 2006)

Mundus (gateway to missionary collections in the United Kingdom), 'Slessor and Calabar collection', n.d., online, available at www.mundus.ac.uk/cats/57/1043.htm, accessed 2 June 2012

Murray, Margaret, *My First Hundred Years* (London: William Kimber 1963)

Mussell, James, 'Private practices and public knowledge: science, professionalization and gender in the late nineteenth century', *Nineteenth-Century Gender Studies* 5: 2 (2009), online, available at www.ncgsjournal.com/issue52/mussell.htm, accessed 22 October 2012

Myzelev, Alla, 'Collecting peasant Europe: peasant utilitarian objects as museum artifacts', in J. Potvin and A. Myzelev (eds), *Material Cultures 1740–1920: The Meanings and Pleasures of Collecting* (Aldershot: Ashgate 2009)

Naylor, Gillian, 'Design, craft and industry', in B. Ford (ed.), *The Cambridge Cultural History of Britain*, vol. 7: *Victorian Britain* (Cambridge: Cambridge University Press 1989)

Naylor, Simon, 'The field, the museum and the lecture hall: the spaces of natural history in Victorian Cornwall' *Transactions of the Institute of British Geographers*, 27: 4 (2002), pp. 494–513

Nördlinger, Clara, 'Visit to Miss Mestorf, directress of Schleswig-Holstein Museum of National Antiquities', *Proceedings of the Museums Association* 7 (1896), pp. 132–138

North, Marianne, *Recollections of a Happy Life: Being the Autobiography of Marianne North*, vol. 1 (Charlottesville, VA.: University of Virginia Press 1993 [1892])

Nunn, Pamela Gerrish, 'Critically speaking', in C. C. Orr (ed.), *Women in the Victorian Art World* 'Obituary, Sir Whitworth Wallis', *The Times* 17 January 1927

Ogilvie, M. and J. Harvey (eds), *Biographical Dictionary of Women in Science* (London: Routledge 2000)

Ormond, Leonee, 'A Leighton memorial: Frederic Leighton and the South London Art Gallery', in Giles Waterfield (ed.), *Art for the People: Culture in the Slums of Late Victorian Britain* (London: Dulwich Picture Gallery 1994)

Outka, Elizabeth, *Consuming Traditions: Modernity, Modernism and the Commodified Authentic* (Oxford: Oxford University Press 2009)

Parker, Rozsika, *The Subversive Stitch: Embroidery and the Making of the Feminine* (London: Women's Library 1984)

Pascoe, Judith, *The Hummingbird Cabinet: A Rare and Curious History of Romantic Collectors* (Ithaca, NY and London: Cornell University Press 2006)

Patten, Robert L., 'Cruikshank, George (1792–1878)', *Oxford Dictionary of National Biography* (Oxford: Oxford University Press 2004), online, available at www.oxforddnb.com/view/article/6843, accessed 29 September 2009

Pearce, Susan, *Archaeological Curatorship* (Leicester: Leicester University Press 1990)

——'Objects as meaning, or narrating the past', in S. Pearce (ed.), *Objects of Knowledge* (London: Athlone Press 1990)

——'Making up is hard to do', *Museums Journal* 93: 12 (1993), pp. 25–27

——*On Collecting: An Investigation into Collecting in the European Tradition* (London: Routledge 1995)

Pease, Allison, *Modernism, Feminism and the Culture of Boredom* (Cambridge: Cambridge University Press 2012)

Perkin, Harold, *The Rise of Professional Society: England since 1880* (London: Routledge 1989)

Perry, Lara, *History's Beauties: Women in the National Portrait Gallery 1856–1900* (Aldershot: Ashgate 2006)

Petch, Alison, 'Counting and calculating: some reflections on using statistics to examine the history and shape of the collections at the Pitt Rivers Museum', *Journal of Museum Ethnography* 18 (2006), pp. 149–156

——'Herbert Toms', Rethinking Pitt Rivers (2011), online, available at http://web.prm.ox.ac.uk/rpr/index.php/article-index/12-articles/695-herbert-toms, accessed 16 October 2011

——'Barbara Freire-Marreco (Mrs Robert Aitken)', The Other Within, online, available at http://england.prm.ox.ac.uk/englishness-Barbara-Freire-Marreco.html, accessed 14 May 2010

——'Edward Burnett Tylor', The Relational Museum, online, available at http://history.prm.ox.ac.uk/collector_tylor.html, accessed 25 February 2011

——'Edward Lovett', The Other Within, online, available at http://england.prm.ox.ac.uk/englishness-Edward-Lovett.html, accessed 14 May 2010

——'English folklorists', The Other Within, online, available at http://england.prm.ox.ac.uk/englishness-English-folklorists.html, accessed 14 May 2010

——'Henry Balfour and the intentions of the founding collection', The Other Within, online, available at http://england.prm.ox.ac.uk/englishness-Balfour-and-founding-collection.html, accessed 14 May 2010

——'Margaret Murray', The Other Within, online, available at http://england.prm.ox.ac.uk/englishness-Margaret-Murray.html, accessed 14 October 2011

——'Members of the Folklore Society and the Pitt Rivers Museum', The Other Within, online, available at http://england.prm.ox.ac.uk/englishness-FLS-members-and-donors.html, accessed 14 May 2010

——'Sellers' relationships with the Pitt Rivers Museum, part 1: England', The Other Within, online, available at http://england.prm.ox.ac.uk/englishness-Sellers-relationships-with-PRM-Part-1.html, accessed 30 August 2011

——'When objects were acquired', The Other Within, online, available at http://england. prm.ox.ac.uk/analysis-category-8.html, accessed 14 May 2010

Petch, A., Wingfield, C., and Gosden, C., 'Individuals that contributed more than 100 objects to the PRM's English collections, by size of collection', The Other Within, online, available at http://england.prm.ox.ac.uk/analysis-6.html, 14 February 2011

Peterson, Linda H., 'The feminist origins of "Of Queens' Gardens"' in Dinah Birch and Francis O'Gorman (eds), Ruskin and Gender (Basingstoke: Palgrave 2002)

Petiot, Aurelie, ' "Should we stop teaching art?" Charles Robert Ashbee's educational theories and practices, 1886–1940' (unpublished PhD thesis, University of Cambridge 2013)

Petrie, William M. Flanders, Methods and Aims in Archaeology (London: Macmillan 1904)

Petrov, Julia, '"The habit of their age": English genre painters, dress collecting and museums, 1910–1914', Journal of the History of Collections 20: 2 (2008), pp. 237–251

Pettitt, Clare, 'Peggotty's work-box: Victorian souvenirs and material memory', Romanticism and Victorianism on the Net, 23 (2009), online, available at www.erudit.org/revue/ ravon/2009/v/n23/029896ar.html, accessed 30 July 2009

Pitt Rivers Museum, Relational Museum Project, 'Statistical information, all individuals associated with PRM collections', online, available at http://history.prm.ox.ac.uk/ page_72.html, accessed 1 April 2011

——'Statistical information: field collectors', online, available at http://history.prm.ox.ac.uk/ page_74.html, accessed 1 April 2011

Plunkett, Steven J., 'Layard, Nina Frances (1853–1935)', Oxford Dictionary of National Biography (Oxford: Oxford University Press 2004), online, available at www. oxforddnb.com/view/article/58931, accessed 30 July 2009

Pointon, Marcia, 'Materialising mourning: hair, jewellery and the body', in M. Kwint, C. Breward and J. Aynsley (eds), Material Memories: Design and Evocation (Oxford: Berg 1999)

Pomeroy, Jordana (ed.), Intrepid Women: Victorian Artists Travel (Aldershot: Ashgate 2005)

Pomian, Krzysztof, 'The collection: between the visible and the invisible', in Susan M. Pearce (ed.), Interpreting Objects and Collections (London: Routledge 1994)

Porter, Gaby, 'Gender bias: representations of work in history museums', Continuum: The Australian Journal of Media and Culture 3: 1 (1990), pp. 70–83

Prettejohn, Elizabeth, 'From aestheticism to modernism and back again', 19: Interdisciplinary Studies in the Long Nineteenth Century 2 (2006), online, available at www.19.bbk. ac.uk/index.php/19/issue/view/65, accessed 7 July 2014

Prior, Nick, Museums and Modernity: Art Galleries and the Making of Modern Culture (Oxford: Berg 2002)

Prochaska, F., Women and Philanthropy in Nineteenth-Century England (Oxford: Clarendon Press 1980)

Proctor, J. H., 'Serving God and the Empire: Mary Slessor in south-eastern Nigeria, 1876–1915', Journal of Religion in Africa 30: 1 (2000), pp. 45–61

Rappaport, Erika D., Shopping for Pleasure: Women in the Making of London's West End (Princeton, NJ and Oxford: Princeton University Press 2000)

Readman, Paul, 'The place of the past in English culture c. 1890–1914', Past and Present 186 (2005), pp. 147–199

Rees Leahy, Helen, *Museum Bodies: The Politics and Practices of Visiting and Viewing* (Farnham: Ashgate 2012)

Rendall, Jane, 'Women and the public sphere', *Gender and History* 11: 3 (1999), pp. 475–488

Rentzhog, Sten, *Open Air Museums: The History and Future of a Visionary Idea* (Stockholm: Carlssons/Jämtli 2007)

Report of the 57th Meeting of the British Association for the Advancement of Science (1887) (London 1888)

Richards, Thomas, *The Commodity Culture of Victorian England: Advertising and Spectacle 1851–1914* (Palo Alto, CA: Stanford University Press 1991)

Robertson, Bruce, 'The South Kensington Museum in context: an alternative history', *Museum and Society* 2: 1 (2004), online, available at www2.le.ac.uk/departments/ museumstudies/museumsociety/volumes/volume2, accessed 7 July 2014

Roesler, Mrs, 'The work of an instructor in the American Museum of Natural History', *Museums Journal* 8: 10 (1909), pp. 303–313

Royal Pavilion and Brighton Museums blog, 'The Booth Museum and Brighton taxidermy', online, available at http://rpmcollections.wordpress.com/2011/05/12/the-booth-mu seum-and-brighton-taxidermy/, accessed 9 September 2011

Ruskin, John, *Sesame and Lilies, Two Lectures* (London: Smith, Elder & Co. 1865)

——Letter 88 (8 February 1880), *Fors Clavigera: Letters to the Workmen and Labourers of Great Britain*, vol. 8 (Orpington: George Allen 1884)

Ryan, Mary, *Women in Public: Between Banners and Ballots, 1825–1880* (Baltimore, MD and London: Johns Hopkins University Press 1990)

Sandberg, Mark B., *Living Pictures, Missing Persons: Mannequins, Museums and Modernity* (Princeton, NJ and Oxford: Princeton University Press 2003)

Sandell, Richard, and Eithne Nightingale, *Museums, Equality and Social Justice* (London: Routledge 2012)

Saunders, Peter, '"The choicest, best arranged museums I have ever seen": the Pitt-Rivers Museum, Dorset, 1880s-1970s', *Museum History Journal* 7: 2 (2014), pp. 205–233

Schadla-Hall, Tim, *Tom Sheppard, Hull's Great Collector* (Beverley: Highgate Publications 1989)

Scott, Owen Stanley, *Handbook to the Bowes Museum, Barnard Castle* (Barnard Castle: W. R. Atkinson, 1893)

Secord, Ann, 'Science in the pub: artisan botanists in early nineteenth-century Lancashire', *History of Science* 32 (1994), pp. 269–315

Shales, Ezra, 'Toying with design reform: Henry Cole and instructive play for children', *Journal of Design History* 22: 1 (2009), pp. 3–26

——*Made in Newark: Cultivating Industrial Arts and Civic Identity in the Progressive Era* (New Brunswick, NJ and London: Rivergate Books 2010)

Sheffield, Suzanne Le-May, *Revealing New Worlds: Three Victorian Women Naturalists* (London: Routledge 2001)

Sheldon, Julie, '"His best successor": Lady Eastlake and the National Gallery', in Kate Hill (ed.), *Museums and Biographies: Stories, Objects, Identities* (Woodbridge: Boydell and Brewer 2012)

Shelley, Henry C., *The Art of the Wallace Collection* (Boston, MA: L. C. Page, 1913)

Shepley, Emma, 'The Haslemere context', in David Crowley and Lou Taylor (eds), *The Lost Arts of Europe: The Haslemere Museum Collection of European Peasant Art* (Haslemere: Haslemere Educational Museum 2000)

Sheppard, Kathleen, 'The lady and the looking glass: Margaret Murray's life in archaeology' (unpublished PhD thesis, University of Oklahoma 2010)

——'Margaret Alice Murray and archaeological training in the classroom', in William Carruthers (ed.), *Histories of Egyptology: Interdisciplinary Measures* (London: Routledge 2014)

Shindler, K., 'Bate, Dorothea Minola Alice (1878–1951), palaeontologist', *Oxford Dictionary of National Biography* (Oxford: Oxford University Press 2004), online, available at www.oxforddnb.com/view/article/67163, accessed 9 September 2011

Shortt, S. E. D., 'Physicians, science and status: issues in the professionalization of Anglo-American medicine in the nineteenth century', *Medical History*, 27: 1 (1983), pp. 51–56

Shteir, Ann B., *Cultivating Women, Cultivating Science: Flora's Daughters and Botany in England 1760–1860* (Baltimore, MD: Johns Hopkins University Press 1999)

——'Women and the natural world: expanding horizons at home', in J. Pomeroy (ed.), *Intrepid Women: Victorian Artists Travel* (Aldershot: Ashgate 2005)

——'"Fac-similes of nature": Victorian wax flower modelling', *Victorian Literature and Culture* 35 (2007), pp. 649–661

Siegel, Jonah, *The Emergence of the Modern Museum* (Oxford: Oxford University Press 2008)

Silverman, Lois H., *The Social Work of Museums* (Abingdon: Routledge 2010)

Sir John Evans Centenary Project, Ashmolean Museum, 'Learned societies and awards', online, available at http://johnevans.ashmolean.org/evans/societies.html, accessed 14 May 2010

Smith, Nicola, 'A brief account of the origins of the South London Art Gallery', in G. Waterfield (ed.), *Art for the People* (London: Dulwich Picture Gallery 1994)

Smitley, Megan, *The Feminine Public Sphere: Middle-Class Women in Civic Life in Scotland, c.1870–1914* (Manchester: Manchester University Press 2009)

Squirrell, M. E., *The Autobiography of Elizabeth Squirrell of Shottishaur and Selections from her Writings* (London: Simpkin, Marshall & Co. 1873)

St George in the East church, 'Nature study museum' (n.d.), online, available at www.stgite.org.uk/naturestudy.html, accessed 9 September 2011

Stearn, William, *The Natural History Museum at South Kensington* (London: Heinemann 1981)

Stephenson, Andrew, '"Feminine" anatomies of taste and cultures of collecting in early twentieth-century Britain: Gwendoline and Margaret Davies as women art patrons', *Aurora* 4 (2003), pp. 174–185

——'"Telling decoratively": Ben Nicholson's *white reliefs* and debates around abstraction and modernism in the home in the late 20s and 30s', *Visual Culture in Britain* 9: 2 (2008), pp. 43–60

Stevenson, Alice, 'Artefacts of excavation: the British collection and distribution of Egyptian finds to museums, 1880–1915', *Journal of the History of Collections*, 26: 1 (2014), pp. 89–102

——'Between the field and the museum: archaeological context and finds distribution', unpublished conference paper, online, available at www.academia.edu/3807596/ Between_the_Field_and_the_Museum_archaeological_context_and_finds_distribution, accessed 7 August 2013

Stewart, Susan, *On Longing: Narratives of the Miniature, the Gigantic, the Souvenir, the Collection* (Durham, NC and London: Duke University Press 1993)

Steyn, Juliet, 'Inside-out: assumptions of "English" modernism in the Whitechapel Art Gallery, London, 1914', in Marcia Pointon (ed.), *Art Apart: Art Institutions and Ideology Across England and North America* (Manchester: Manchester University Press 1994)

Stocking, George, 'The ethnographer's magic: fieldwork in British anthropology from Tyler to Malinowski', in G. Stocking (ed.), *Observers Observed: Essays on Ethnographic Fieldwork* (Madison, WI: University of Wisconsin Press 1983)

——'Essays on museums and material culture', in G. Stocking (ed.), *Objects and Others: Essays on Museums and Material Culture* (Madison, WI: University of Wisconsin Press 1985)

Stocks, Mary Danvers, *Fifty Years in Every Street: The Story of the Manchester University Settlement* (Manchester: Manchester University Press 1945)

Styles, John and Amanda Vickery (eds), *Gender, Taste and Material Culture in Britain and North America 1700–1830* (New Haven, CT and London: Yale Center for British Art/ Paul Mellon Centre for Studies in British Art 2006)

Sutherland, Gillian, *In Search of the New Woman* (Cambridge: Cambridge University Press 2015)

Sutton, Thomas, 'The library and museums', *Sussex Archaeological Collections* 85 (1946), pp. 77–92

Swanton, E. W., *A Country Museum* (Haslemere: Education Museum 1947)

Swenson, Astrid, *The Rise of Heritage: Preserving the Past in France, Germany and England, 1789–1914* (Cambridge: Cambridge University Press 2013)

Swinney, Geoffrey N., 'What do we know about what we know? The museum "register" as museum object', in S. Dudley, A. Barnes, J. Binnie, J. Petrov and J. Walklate (eds), *The Thing About Museums: Objects and Experience, Representation and Contestation* (London: Routledge 2012)

Tate Collection online, entry for 'Mr and Mrs Edwin Edwards' by Henri Fantin-Latour, ref NO1952, online, available at www.tate.org.uk/servlet/ViewWork?cgroupid=9999999 61&workid=4223&searchid=11948, accessed 4 March 2011

Taylor, Lou, *Establishing Dress History* (Manchester: Manchester University Press 2004)

Teather, J. Lynne, 'Museology and its traditions: the British experience 1845–1945' (unpublished PhD thesis, University of Leicester 1984)

The McManus, 'Dundee and the world', n.d., online, available at www.themcmanus-dundee.gov.uk/sites/default/files/dworldp1.pdf, accessed 2 June 2012

Thirsk, Joan, 'Edwards, Matilda Barbara Betham (1836–1919)', *Oxford Dictionary of National Biography* (Oxford: Oxford University Press, 2004), online, available at www.oxforddnb.com.proxy.library.lincoln.ac.uk/view/article/32983, accessed 21 June 2014

Thomas, Nicholas, *Entangled Objects: Exchange, Material Culture and Colonialism in the Pacific* (Cambridge, MA: Harvard University Press 1991)

Thornton, Amara, 'The allure of archaeology: Agnes Conway and Jane Harrison at Newnham College, 1903–1907', *Bulletin of the History of Archaeology*, 21: 1 (2011), online, available at www.archaeologybulletin.org/article/view/bha.2114/7, accessed 7 August 2013

Tilly, Louise A. and Joan W. Scott, *Women, Work and Family* (London: Routledge 1989, 2nd edn)

Toms, Herbert and Tony Christina, 'The Cissbury earthworks', *Sussex Archaeological Collections* 67 (1926), pp. 55–84

Torrens, Hugh, 'Presidential Address: Mary Anning (1799–1847) of Lyme; "the greatest fossilist the world ever knew"', *British Journal of the History of Science*, 28 (1995), pp. 257–284

——'Anning, Mary (1799–1847)', *Oxford Dictionary of National Biography* (Oxford: Oxford University Press 2004), online, available at www.oxforddnb.com/view/article/568, accessed 30 June 2011

Tosh, John, *A Man's Place: Masculinity and the Middle-Class Home in Victorian England* (New Haven, CT and London: Yale University Press 1999)

——*Manliness and Masculinities in Nineteenth-Century Britain* (Harlow: Pearson Longman 2005)

Trodd, Colin, 'Culture, class, city: the National Gallery, London, and the spaces of education, 1822–57', in M. Pointon (ed.), *Art Apart: Art Institutions and Ideology Across England and North America* (Manchester: Manchester University Press 1994)

Tubbs, Mrs, 'The relation of museums to elementary education', *Proceedings of the Museums Association* 8 (1897), pp. 69–74

Turner, V., 'The factors affecting women's success in museum careers', *Journal of Conservation and Museum Studies* 8 (2002), online, available at www.jcms-journal.com/article/view/jcms.8022/23, accessed 23 September 2011

Tylecote, Mabel, *The Education of Women at Manchester University 1883–1933* (Manchester: Manchester University Press 1941)

Tythacott, Louise, 'From the fetish to the specimen: the Ridyard African collection at the Liverpool Museum, 1895–1916', in A. Shelton (ed.), *Collectors: Expressions of Self and Other* (London: Horniman Museum and Gardens/Museu Antropologico da Universidade de Coimbra 2001)

——'Classifying China: shifting interpretations of Buddhist bronzes in Liverpool Museum 1867–1997', in K. Hill (ed.), *Museums and Biographies: Stories, Objects, Identities* (Woodbridge: Boydell and Brewer 2012)

University Settlement Manchester First Annual Report (Manchester: Cuthbertson & Black 1987)

University Settlement Manchester Second to Fifth Annual Reports (Manchester: William Hough & Sons 1898–1901)

Vickery, Amanda, 'Golden Age to Separate Spheres: a review of the categories and chronologies of English women's history', *Historical Journal* 36: 2 (1993), pp. 383–414

Wainwright, Clive, 'The making of the South Kensington Museum II: collecting modern manufactures, 1851 and the Great Exhibition', *Journal of the History of Collections*, 14: 1 (2002), pp. 25–43

——'The making of the South Kensington Museum III: collecting abroad', *Journal of the History of Collections* 14: 1 (2002), pp. 45–61

Waithe, Marcus, 'John Ruskin and the idea of a museum', in K. Hanley and B. Maidment (eds), *Persistent Ruskin: Studies in Influence, Assimilation and Effect* (Aldershot: Ashgate 2013)

——'Ruskin at Walkley: reconstructing the St George's museum', online, available at http://ruskinatwalkley.org, accessed 6 July 2014

Walkowitz, Judith, *City of Dreadful Delight: Narratives of Sexual Danger in Late Victorian London* (London: Virago 1992)

Wallace Collection, 'Lady Wallace', online, available at www.wallacecollection.org/thecollection/historyofthecollection/thecollectors/ladywallace, accessed 10 May 2012

Waterfield, Giles, 'Picture hanging and gallery decoration', in G. Waterfield (ed.), *Palaces of Art: Art Galleries in Britain 1790–1990* (London: Lund Humphries 1991)

——'Anticipating the Enlightenment: museums and galleries in Britain before the British Museum', in R. G. W. Anderson, M. Caygill, A. G. McGregor and L. Syson, *Enlightening the British: Knowledge, Discovery and the Museum in the Eighteenth Century* (London: British Museum Press 2003)

Waterfield, Giles and Nicola Smith, 'Art for the people', *History Today* 44: 6 (June 1994), pp. 55–60

Waterfield, H., and King, J. C. H., *Provenance: Twelve Collectors of Ethnographic Art in England 1760–1990* (Paris: Somogy 2006)

West, Jenny, 'Appendix 1: The Society for the Protection of Ancient Buildings 1877–1896: committee, membership and casework', in C. Miele, *From William Morris: Building Conservation and the Arts and Crafts Cult of Authenticity, 1877–1939* (New Haven, CT and London: Yale University Press 2005)

Westgarth, Mark, 'A biographical dictionary of nineteenth-century antique and curiosity dealers', *Regional Furniture* 22 (Glasgow: Regional Furniture Society 2009)

Whitehead, Christopher, *The Public Art Museum in Nineteenth-Century Britain: The Development of the National Gallery* (Aldershot: Ashgate 2005)

Whitelaw, Ann, 'Women, museums and the problem of biography', in K. Hill (ed.), *Museums and Biographies: Stories, Objects, Identities* (Woodbridge: Boydell and Brewer 2012)

Wilcox, Timothy, 'The aesthete expunged: the career and collection of T. Eustace Smith, MP', *Journal of the History of Collections* 5: 1 (1993), pp. 43–57

Willis, M., 'Unmasking immorality: popular opposition to laboratory science in late Victorian Britain', in D. Clifford, E. Wadge, A. Warwick and M. Willis (eds), *Repositioning Victorian Sciences: Shifting Centres in Nineteenth-Century Scientific Thinking* (London: Anthem 2006)

Wilson, S., '"The highest art for the lowest people": the Whitechapel and other philanthropic art galleries, 1877–1901', in Paul Barlow and Colin Trodd (eds), *Governing Cultures: Art Institutions in Victorian London* (Aldershot: Ashgate 2000)

Wingfield, Chris, 'Back to the future? Locating and re-locating England' (2009), online, available at http://england.prm.ox.ac.uk/englishness-Wingfield-paper.html, accessed 4 December 2010

——'Donors, loaners, dealers and swappers: the relationships behind the English collections at the Pitt Rivers Museum', in S. Byrne, A. Clarke, R. Harrison and R. Torrence (eds), *Unpacking the Collection: Networks of Material and Social Agency in the Museum* (New York: Springer 2011)

——'Acquisition events: another way of approaching collections statistics', The Other Within, online, available at http://england.prm.ox.ac.uk/englishness-acq.events1.html, accessed 2 September 2011

——'Gender and donation: change over time', The Other Within, online, available at http://england.prm.ox.ac.uk/englishness-gender-and-donations.html, accessed 17 October 2011

Wingfield, Chris and Alison Petch, 'Diploma students in anthropology, University of Oxford 1907–1945', *Relational Museum Project*, Pitt Rivers Museum, online, available at http://history.prm.ox.ac.uk/students.php?all, accessed 14 July 2014

Wintle, Claire, *Colonial Collecting and Display: Encounters with Material Culture from the Andaman and Nicobar Islands* (New York and Oxford: Berghahn 2013)

Witcomb, Andrea, 'Using souvenirs to rethink how we tell histories of migration', in S. Dudley, A. Barnes, J. Binnie, J. Petrov and J. Walklate (eds), *Narrating Objects, Collecting Stories* (London: Routledge 2012)

Woodson-Boulton, Amy, '"Industry without art is brutality": aesthetic ideology and social practice in Victorian art museums', *Journal of British Studies* 46 (2007), pp. 47–71

——*Transformative Beauty: Art Museums in Industrial Britain* (Stanford, CA: Stanford University Press 2012)

Wynne, Deborah, *Women and Personal Property in the Victorian Novel* (Farnham: Ashgate 2010)

Wyse Jackson, P. N., and Spencer Jones, M. E., 'The quiet workforce: the various roles of women in geological and natural history museums during the early to mid-1900s' in C. V. Burek and B. Higgs (eds), *The Role of Women in the History of Geology*, Geological Society, London, Special Publications 281 (2007)

Yates, Bridget, 'Volunteer-run museums in English market towns and villages' (unpublished PhD thesis, University of Gloucester 2010)

Yeo, Eileen (ed.), *Radical Femininity: Women's Self-Presentation in the Public Sphere* (Manchester: Manchester University Press 1998)

Index

Page numbers in **bold** refer to illustrations.
'n' after a page reference indicates the number of a note on that page.

EU authorised representative for GPSR:
Easy Access System Europe, Mustamäe tee 50,
10621 Tallinn, Estonia
gpsr.requests@easproject.com